GRANDMASTER
SECRETS
OPENINGS

BY

GM Andrew Soltis

Caricatures by Rob Long

THINKERS' PRESS — Thinkers' Press, Inc. • Davenport IA • u.s.a. • 2002

Grandmaster Secrets: Openings

Copyright © 2002 by Andrew Soltis

First Printing: May 2002

ISBN: 0-938650-68-8

• ♘ •

Requests for permissions and republication rights should be addressed in writing to:

Thinkers' Press, Inc.
Editor, Bob Long
P.O. Box 8
Davenport IA 52805-0008 USA

CONTENTS

Preface v

1 • White To Play And Lose 7

2 • Opening - Think 15

3 • Book 37

4 • Picking And Choosing 57

5 • Overruled 81

6 • Decisions 103

7 • De-Booked 127

8 • Give And Take 145

9 • Materialism 165

10 • Getting Late 185

11 • Taking Stock 211

12 • The Chess Club 229

Index 234

Games 239

A sample of "Informant–Speak"

Explanations of Files, Ranks, Symbols, and the Queening Square.

Black Side

White Side

Explanation of Symbols

x	=	captures
†	=	check
+−	=	White has a winning advantage
−+	=	Black has a winning advantage
±	=	White has a definite advantage
∓	=	Black has a definite advantage
±	=	White has the better game
∓	=	Black has the better game
∞	=	Unclear
△	=	with the idea
N/f3	=	Knight on f3 (for example) or ♘/ f3
#	=	mate

Only some of these symbols may have been used in the current book.

Preface

The opening phase is the easiest part of the game to play—if all you want to do is get to the middlegame.

It's easy because it's the one part of a game in which you can rely on someone else's ideas, if not their exact moves.

Secondly, it's the one phase that you can learn and immediately apply what you've studied.

If you spend a weekend on the rudiments of the French Defense, for example, you can put them to work the next time someone opens 1. e4.

In contrast, if you study the minority attack, or a tactic such as smothered mate, it may take dozens of games before you can use what you've learned.

(And the endgame is worse: I was already an International Master before I won a Bishops-of-opposite-color ending.)

But while the opening is easy to play—if all you want to do is start the middlegame—it's very hard to play well.

And that's not surprising when you look at the literature these days. I wonder how any amateur can make sense of the endless analysis, dumbed-down generalizations and just plain bad writing of opening books. Chess players love to learn—but they hate being taught, especially if it's done that way.

This book is based on the premise that there is another way—that good instructional books can be entertaining as well as educational.

Several years ago, Bob Long and I set to work on finding a new format, using dialogue, lots of diagrams, charts, humor, caricatures and whatever else does the job.

First we covered the endgame. Now, in the second of the "Grandmaster Secrets" series, we're tackling the opening.

And, I suspect, Grandmaster Noah Tall probably has something to say about the middlegame.

Andy Soltis
New York • 2002

Scene:

    A chess club, home base of the veteran grandmaster, Noah Tall.

       Tall has been watching a tournament game played by Pat Sayre, a promising but very young amateur.

Chapter One:

White To Play And Lose

Sayre, with White, lost this way:

1

2

3

1. d4 e6 2. c4 Nf6 3. Nf3 d5 4. Nc3 Bb4 5. e3 c5 (Diagram 1) 6. a3? White confuses this position with the very similar one that arises after 6. Bd3 0-0 7. 0-0 Nc6 when 8. a3! is best.

6... Bxc3† 7. bxc3 0-0 8. Bd3? Losing a tempo. Better was 8. cxd5. **8... dxc4 9. Bxc4 Qc7!** Black threatens 10... cxd4 and 11... Qxc4. **10. Ba2** A typical move in similar positions is 10. Bd3 but here it fails to 10... cxd4 11. cxd4 Qc3† (and 12. Bd2 Qxd3).

10...Nc6 (Diagram 2) 11. Bb2? Misplacing the ♗. Better was 11. 0-0, delaying a decision about the ♗ until Black reveals his intentions. **11... e5 12. d5?** Overlooking Black's reply. There was nothing better than 12. h3.

12... e4! After 13. Nd2 Ne5 Black's positional edge grows. **13. dxc6 exf3 14. Qxf3 Bg4 15. Qg3 Qb6! 16. Bc1 Qa5 (Diagram 3).** Here 17. Bd2 Rad8 18. f3 would be met strongly by 18... bxc6! because 19. fxg4? Rxd2! 19 Kxd2? Ne4†.

17. 0-0 Be2 18. cxb7 Rab8 19. Re1 Qxc3. 0-1.

Pat: I don't get it. One minute I had a good game, the next I'm busted. And I'm like – where did I go wrong?

Noah: It was more than one move. You can't lose that quickly as White unless you hang your ♕ – or make a lot of little mistakes.

Pat: A lot?

Noah: Sure. At move six you mixed up two variations.

Pat: They all look like. But that didn't lose me the game.

Noah: No, but it cost you a real chance at an advantage, and as White you deserve that.

Pat: I deserve an advantage?

Noah: No, you deserve a chance.

Then at move eight you lost a tempo. Again, it wasn't fatal, but by then you had nothing better than equality – at best.

Pat: And it got worse.

Noah: Much worse. You made premature decisions, such as Bb2, when a non-commital move was best.

But most of all you didn't react the way you should have when you found yourself in a position that was new to you.

And later you didn't assess the outcome of the opening: When you chose 12. d5 you were still playing as if you stood well – instead of fighting to hang on.

Pat: Did I do anything right?

Noah: Well, you were doing okay with 1. d4 and 2. c4.

Pat: Thanks a lot.

Noah: But I was watching you for most of the game and I think I know the main reason why you lost so quickly.

Pat: Which was?

Noah: You broke the first – and most often violated – rule of the opening:

LOOK AT THE BOARD

Pat: But I did!

Noah: Not until it was already too late. You played the first ten moves quickly and mechanically as if you wanted to show off your memory. Players, even good ones, do this all the time – with disastrous results, such as in Diagram 4.

Rudensky-Hodgson
Benidorm 1991

| 1. e4 | d6 |
| 2. d4 | Nf6 |

| 3. Nc3 | c6 |
| 4. f4 | Qa5 |

4

| 5. Nf3?? | Nxe4 |

And Black won.

Blackburne-Janowski
Ostend 1905

1. e4	e5
2. f4	Bc5
3. Nf3	d6
4. Nc3	Nf6

5

5. d3?

Ivanchuk-Hjartarson
Intel Grand Prix 1995

1. e4	e5
2. Nf3	Nc6
3. Bb5	a6
4. Ba4	Nf6
5. 0-0	Nxe4
6. d4	b5
7. Bb3	d5
8. dxe5	Be6
9. c3	Nc5
10. Bc2	Bg4
11. Nbd2	Be7
12. Re1	0-0

13. Nf1	Bh5

6

14. Be3??

The obvious 14... Bxf3! would give Black the edge.

14. ...	Bg6??
15. Ng3	Qd7

Pat: What happened there?

Noah: White, an International Master (IM), mind you, knew all about this opening's main line, which is 5. Bd3 e5 6. Nf3.

But he brought the ♘ out before he played Bd3, losing a ♟.

Pat: Ouch. That must be pretty rare.

Noah: Not as rare as you think. Diagram 5 shows how one of the world's then-elite players locked in

his B/f1 and gave up any hope of an opening advantage.

Pat: Why did he do it?

Noah: Because he thought he had already developed the ♗ when he played 5. d3.

Pat: He wasn't looking at the board.

Noah: You've got it. Even worse is Diagram 6 because neither player was looking at the board. White was trying to reach a position he knew, 14. Ng3 Bg6 15. Be3. But he got the move order wrong.

Pat: And Black?

Noah: He didn't notice the difference because he, too, was playing

quickly. The bottom line is they got to the book position they wanted at move 15, but both players missed something big en route.

And sometimes the result of not-looking-at-the-board is downright dumb, as in Diagram 7.

Pat: Totally.

Noah: You'd be surprise how often good players get awful positions within the first minutes because they haven't started to think. The opening is the one part of a chess game when players believe they can get away without thinking.

Pat: I know what you mean. When-

ever I play a game there's always some point when I realize the position doesn't look familiar at all – and I have to start concentrating like crazy.

Noah: Unless it's too late, as in Diagram 9.

Pat: What's the deal here?

Noah: In the first diagram it's your garden-variety Dragon Sicilian – or at least it looked like that to White. He began playing automatic-pilot moves, the kind that are supposed to beat the Dragon.

Pat: You mean like Bc4 and Be3 and Qd2 and...

Noah: And mate somewhere around h8. But by the time White began looking at the board he realized Black wasn't playing a Dragon at all.

1. e4	c5
2. Nf3	d6
3. d4	cxd4
4. Nxd4	Nf6
5. Nc3	g6

English GM Jim Plaskett said he once played an inebriated GM who as Black played 1. e4 Nc6 2. d4 b6 3. Nf3 e5 4. dxe5, studied the position...

7

... and exclaimed "All my life I played the Gruenfeld Defense yet I never realized it lost a pawn!"

6. Be3 a6

8

7. f3 Nbd7
8. Bc4

Now 8... Bg7 9. Qd2 0-0 is what White expected.

Then 10. h4 Qa5 11. h5, e.g. 11... Nc5 12. hxg6 hxg6 13. Bh6 or 11... Nxh5 12. g4 Ngf6 13. 0-0-0.

8. ... b5
9. Bb3 Bb7
10. Qd2 Qa5
11. 0-0-0 Nc5
12. Kb1

And White is waiting for ...Bg7 and ...0-0 so he can mate after h4-h5 and Bh6.

9

12. ... e6!

This crosses White up and threatens 13... b4 14. Nce2 e5.

Black stands well, e.g, 13. a3 Be7 followed by ...0-0-0 and ...Kb8.

Pat: Sounds like me – not even knowing the name of the opening I'm playing.

Noah: Knowing the name doesn't matter. Recognizing the special nature of the opening does.

One of the reasons GMs play like GMs is that they realize the opening is characterized by a few special qualities that set it apart from the middlegame.

Pat: Like what?

Noah: Well, first of all, in the opening you are taking pieces off a well-protected first rank and developing them on forward squares. Inevitably this means they are not going to protect one another and be vulnerable to tactics.

But if you're careful, by move 15, on the cusp of the middlegame, you usually have everything safely covered.

Pat: White didn't even make it that far without blundering in Diagram 10.

Noah: True. White, who was another IM, only developed one piece before he lost it.

Pat: Maybe there's an IM disease that's going around.

Noah: Not just IMs. The world's No. 2-ranked player, Anatoly Karpov, made the blunder in Diagram 11.

Pat: What could he have been thinking?

Noah: He had a really good positional idea in mind – to work on the dark squares and, in particular to control the diagonal from b8 to h2. The correct way of doing that was 11... Qb8 and then 12. 0-0-0 Bd6 13. g3 Be5.

But Karpov was tired and played 11... Bd6 without thinking – as he admitted afterward. The message

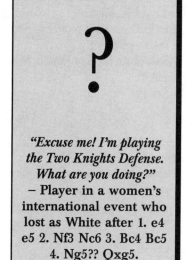

"Excuse me! I'm playing the Two Knights Defense. What are you doing?" – Player in a women's international event who lost as White after 1. e4 e5 2. Nf3 Nc6 3. Bc4 Bc5 4. Ng5?? Qxg5.

here is that positionally good moves often turn out to be tactically terrible.

Pat: And that's a special feature of the opening?

Noah: Not just of the opening. But because so much is unprotected in the opening, those positionally-good, tactically-bad moves occur more often. Another illustration of that is Diagram 12.

Pat: Black played some pretty weird stuff to get that far.

Noah: You mean 6... a5 and 7... Na6 and then retreating the ♘ to d7 ? Actually, those are perfectly sound moves. And since the center is closed Black can get away with the loss of time.

Pat: Up to a point, maybe.

Noah: And the point is reached by move 15. Black traded the dark-squared ♗s, a valid middlegame strategy because White might have been vulnerable on the long diagonal from g1 to b6. And Black wanted to play ...exf4 because then he can

occupy the best ♘ outpost on the board, at e5.

Pat: Makes sense.

Noah: It all made sense. But with his ♔ in the center it just wasn't safe.

P. Littlewood-Zeidler

Four Nations Chess League 1995

1.	d4	f5
2.	Bg5	h6
3.	Bh4	c5

An ancient trap goes 3... g5 4. Bg3 f4 5. e3 fxg3??? 6. Qh5#.

4.	e3	Qb6

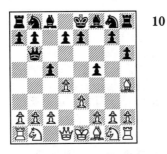

10

5.	d5??	Qb4†

And Black won after 6... Qxh4.

Christiansen-Karpov

Wijk aan Zee 1993

1.	d4	Nf6
2.	c4	e6
3.	Nf3	b6
4.	a3	Ba6
5.	Qc2	Bb7
6.	Nc3	c5
7.	e4	cxd4
8.	Nxd4	Nc6
9.	Nxc6	Bxc6
10.	Bf4	Nh5
11.	Be3	

11

11.	...	Bd6??
12.	Qd1!	1-0

"Paradoxically, what one often needs in these 'positional' lines is a sharp tactical eye."
—John Watson, on the English Opening.

Seirawan-Ivanchuk
FIDE World Championship 1997

1. d4	Nf6
2. c4	g6
3. Nc3	Bg7
4. e4	d6
5. Bd3	e5
6. d5	a5
7. Nge2	Na6
8. f3	Nd7
9. Be3	

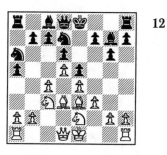

12

9. ...   Bh6?

Tactically sound in the short run (based on 10. Bxh6 Qh4† and 11... Qxh6) but risky in the long run.

10. Qd2	Bxe3

11. Qxe3	c6

Better was 11... 0-0.

12. Qh6	Ndc5
13. Rd1	Qb6?

The ♛ belongs on f6, guarding vulnerable squares.

14. Bb1	Ke7

Or 14... Qxb2 15. Qg7 Rf8 16. dxc6 bxc6 17. Rxd6! and White wins.

15. f4!	exf4?
16. Rf1	Rf8
17. Qxf4	

13

White has a winning attack, e.g 17... f6 18. dxc6 Qxc6 19. Nd4 Qe8 20. Nd5† Kd8 21. Qxd6† Bd7 22. Nb5! **1-0** (22... Qe6 23. Qxf8† or 22... Rc8 23. Qb6†).

Pat: What else makes the opening different?

Noah: An obvious feature is that the ♚s are not castled, so there are opportunies for checks and other forcing moves.

And that rachets up the tactical quotient. If you make a mistake in assumption you're more likely to pay a heavy price.

Pat: Assumption?

Noah: You know, when you make a move you think is forcing. "I go there and he has to go there."

But it often turns out that your forcing move doesn't force. One of the greatest players of the last fifty years lost in 11 moves that way, in Diagram 14.

Pat: I get it. He assumed Black had to retake the ♞ on d7.

Noah: But he assumed wrong. He lost at least a ♟ and the Exchange – and that was enough for him to call it quits.

Pat: All these positions look the same. I mean, I've had positions like that and they didn't end in 11 moves.

Noah: But they aren't the same. And that's why so many good players lose so quickly so often. They make routine moves because the position seems routine, as in Diagram 15.

Pat: I'd never guess 7... b6 was a blunder.

Noah: Yet it was. In similar positions, say with the white ♗ on d3 or e2, then ...b6 is a great way of developing the B/c8 and controlling e4. Here Black just wasn't thinking clearly.

Pat: Or maybe he wasn't looking at the board.

Kholmov-Sherbakov
Perm 1997

1. d4	d5
2. Nf3	c6
3. e3	Bf5
4. Nbd2	e6
5. c4	Nd7

6. b3	h6
7. Bb2	Ngf6
8. Be2	Bd6
9. Ne5	Ne4
10. Nxe4	Bxe4

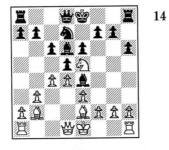

11. Nxd7??

White wanted to avoid 11. 0-0 Bxe5 12. dxe5 Qg5.

11. ...   Bxg2!

0-1

Because 12. Rg1 Bb4† costs the ♕.

Ye Rongguang-van Wely
Antwerp 1996

1. d4	Nf6

2. Nf3	g6
3. Bg5	Bg7
4. Nbd2	0-0
5. e3	d6
6. Bc4	c5
7. c3	

7. ...	b6??
8. Bxf6	Bxf6
9. Bd5	

And White won.

Noah: Exactly.

Pat: So is there any hope for me? Or am I gonna lose games in less than 19 moves?

Noah: Not if you take the opening more seriously than you do now.

And I don't mean by buying a bunch of $27 books or downloading every 1. d4 game ever played.

Pat: Then what...?

Noah: You need to change the way you think in the opening. Come back to the club tomorrow and I'll show you what I mean. Okay?

In which Pat learns the value of comparisons and common sense — and that memory does matter.

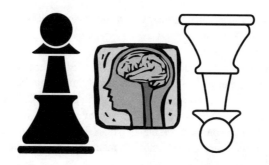

Pat: Okay, I decided to come back.

Noah: I never doubted you would.

Pat: But I did. The thing I wanted to know is this – if I did want help on my openings, where would we start?

Noah: We'd start by realizing that you have to think differently in the opening.

Pat: You mean I have to think differently from the way other players think?

Noah: No, differently from the way you think.

Different from the way you think in the middlegame or in the endgame. Opening-think is a different animal.

There are three basic elements of opening-think:

No. 1 – Memory
No. 2 –Logic / Common sense
No. 3 –Analogy

Pat: I thought you weren't supposed to memorize at all, that it was much better to understand everything.

Noah: That wasn't even true in Paul Morphy's day – he was one of the most booked up players of his century.

Nowadays memory plays a much greater role than it ever did. Two of the worst defeats Garry Kasparov suffered as world champion were pure memory lapses.

Pat: I remember reading something about one of them.

Noah: One of them is Diagram 16, where Kasparov blundered even though he had compiled the biggest vault of prepared openings ever. He reached a Sicilian position he had analyzed extensively and sacrificed a ♝.

"It's all written down in my notebook," he said afterwards.

Pat: So what happened?

Noah: Instead of the move in his notebook, 16. e5!, he played something else and lost.

The world champion simply forgot.

Pat: World champions must be human, too. I guess.

Noah: And he proved it again a few years later with another memory meltdown. That's it in Diagram 18.

Pat: But that's a middlegame, not an opening.

Noah: Actually, it was still book to Kasparov. That makes it an opening.

The first 14 moves had been heavily investigated since a famous draw in the 1953 Candidates tournament. Masters who played either side of the Nimzo-Indian's main line after that knew all about it.

Pat: Doesn't sound like anyone I know.

Noah: In any event when Kasparov was only ten years old he and his trainer came up with a big discovery, 21... Kf8!, which gives Black an advantage.

But when he finally had the position in a real game, 26 years later, Kasparov forgot his analysis and quickly blundered, losing by force.

"We often hear about chess books which emphasize ideas as opposed to variations. I would suggest that, strictly speaking, the idea in chess is the move."
– John Watson.

Kasparov-Lautier
Amsterdam 1995

1. e4	c5
2. Nf3	e6
3. d4	cxd4
4. Nxd4	Nc6
5. Nc3	Qc7
6. Be3	a6
7. Bd3	Nf6
8. 0-0	Ne5
9. h3	Bc5
10. Kh1	d6
11. f4	Ned7
12. a3	b5?
13. Bxb5!	axb5
14. Ndxb5	Qb6
15. Bxc5	dxc5

16

Now 16. e5!, gives White a strong attack, e.g. 16... Ba6 17. a4 Bxb5 18. Nxb5 Ne4 19. Qf3 f5 20. exf6 Ndxf6 21. Nc3 Qb7 22. Rae1.

16. Nd6†?	Ke7
17. Nxc8†?	Rhxc8
18. e5	Ne8
19. Qh5	h6

17

20. Rae1	f5!

And Black wins because the attack is over after 21. exf6† Ndxf6 22. Qg6 Kf8 or 21. Rf3 Qxb2.

I. Sokolov-Kasparov
Wijk aan Zee 1999

1. d4	Nf6
2. c4	e6
3. Nc3	Bb4
4. e3	0-0
5. Bd3	d5
6. Nf3	c5
7. 0-0	Nc6
8. a3	Bxc3
9. bxc3	Qc7
10. Qc2	dxc4
11. Bxc4	e5
12. Bd3	Re8
13. e4	exd4
14. cxd4	Bg4

The stem game, *Bronstein-Euwe, Candidates Tournament 1953*, went 15. Qxc5 Nxe4 16. Bxe4 Rxe4 17. Ng5 with great complications.

15. e5	Bxf3
16. exf6	Nxd4
17. Bxh7†	Kh8
18. fxg7†	Kxg7
19. Bb2	Rad8
20. gxf3	Rh8
21. Kh1	

18

Kasparov's analysis ran 21... Kf8! 22. Qe4 f5 23. Qh4 Rxh7, with advantage to Black.

21. ...	Rxh7?
22. Rg1†	Kh8
23. Rg3	

This stops 23... Qxh2# and prepares a powerful Rag1.

23. ...	Qe5
24. Rag1	Rh4?

And Black resigned after 25. Qc1! Kh7 26. Qb1†! Kh8 27. Qf1 Qe6 28. Qg2.

He saw it was hopeless after 28... f6 29. Rh3 or 28... Qf6 29 Rg8† Kh7 30 Qg7†.

Grandmaster Secrets: Openings

"You don't need to test trainers' analyses. You need to simply reproduce them at the board"
– Kasparov's reply

"Sometimes you have to test old analyses"
– Jan Timman to Kasparov after he lost to Sokolov.

Pat: There's no way I'm gonna memorize half that much book.

Noah: You don't have to. But you need to memorize a fair amount to compete successfuly. It's a simple fact of tournament life.

The real problem with memori-zation is that it becomes a crutch – a substitute for thinking.

Pat: Yeah, really.

Noah: And that crutch ends up cost-ing you when you remember enough to get yourself into a cru-cial position – but you don't re-member how to get out of it.

Pat: Isn't remembering a little better than remembering nothing?

Noah: No, it's often worse. You react the wrong way because of what you think you're supposed to do, as in Diagram 19.

To avoid the Benko Gambit, White played 4. Nc3 – rather than 4. c4 b5 – and found himself in a position after four moves that was new to him. But he had a vague memory of what to do.

Pat: How vague?

Noah: Fairly. He remembered an old Smyslov game in which White played a thematic maneuver, Nd2-c4. Black countered with ...Nc7/ ...b6 and ...Ba6 so he could play ...Bxc4 followed by ...a6 and ...b5.

Lautier's clearest memory was that White got an edge by inserting the key move, b3. That discourages ...Bxc4 because then bxc4!, with play along the b-file, would be strong.

Pat: What didn't he remember?

Noah: He didn't remember what to do before b3.

Lautier-Ponomariov
Enghien-les-Bains 1999

1.	d4	Nf6
2.	Nf3	c5
3.	d5	d6
4.	Nc3	g6
5.	e4	Bg7
6.	Be2	0-0
7.	0-0	Na6
8.	Nd2	Nc7
9.	a4	b6
10.	Nc4	Ba6

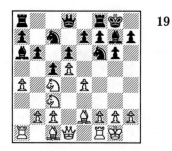

19

11. Bg5?!   Qd7!
12. b3?   e6!

In the Smyslov game White played 11. Bf4! and then 11... Rb8 12. b3! — when ...e6 would have just lost a ♟ after dxe6. And 12... Bxc4 13. bxc4! favors White.

13. Qd2

Now, however, 13. dxe6 Qxe6 14. Qd3 Nxe4! 15. Nxe4 d5 is great for Black.

13. ...   exd5
14. exd5   Rfe8

Black threatens 15... Ne4!.

20

15. Bf3   Ng4

And ...Ne5! at least equalizes for Black.

Pat: Okay, I always suspected memory was a biggie, despite what everyone says. But what's the deal with logic?

Noah: Logic is indispensible in the opening, especially because it acts as a counterbalance to memory.

Every player relies to some extent on memory of moves played previously. But often those moves are just ludicrous. And it's logic — or simple common sense — that should you tell when they're ludi-

crous, as in Diagram 21.

Pat: That can't be Kasparov playing Black.

Noah: It is. This is a classic case of someone following book moves — book that he himself had created — but not recognizing how silly the moves were.

It doesn't take a 2800 rating to recognize how suspicious Black's last few moves were. But the world champion relied on a previous game he had played that turned out well.

Pat: Where does common sense come in?

Noah: Common sense should have told Black that moves like ...a5 and ...Ra6 are likely to be punished tactically.

And logic did tell White that bizarre moves by one player can be answered by bizarre moves from his opponent. In this case, 17. Nd8!.

Topalov-Kasparov
Amsterdam 1996

1. e4	c5
2. Nf3	d6
3. d4	cxd4
4. Nxd4	Nf6
5. Nc3	a6
6. Bc4	e6
7. Bb3	Nbd7
8. f4	Nc5
9. 0-0	Ncxe4
10. Nxe4	Nxe4
11. f5	e5
12. Qh5	Qe7?

Better than 12... Qc7? 13. Ne6! but much worse than the logical 12... d5!.

13. Qf3	Nc5
14. Nc6!	Qc7
15. Bd5	a5

In a game with Spanish TV viewers Kasparov got a strong position as Black after 16. Be3 Ra6 17. Nd4 exd4 18. Bxd4 Kd8.

16. Bg5

21

16. ...   Ra6??

Black had to play 16... Bd7 and hope he isn't lost following 17. Bxf7† Kxf7 18. Qh5†.

17. Nd8!

And White won easily after 17... f6 18. Nf7 Rg8 19. Be3 g6 20. Ng5 Rg7 21. fxg6 Rxg6 22. Bf7† Qxf7 23. Nxf7.

Pat: Is there a more practical use of logic? I mean, I'm not gonna get a chance to play 17. Nd8 against Kasparov next week.

Noah: Logic should always kick in when you get an unfamiliar position. Take Diagram 22 for example.

"The thing I find most surprising is that such a stupid-looking move can be so strong."
– Michael Adams on 5. f3 in the Benko Gambit (1. d4 Nf6 2. c4 c5 3. d5 b5 4. cxb5 a6)

Pat: I don't have the Pirc Defense gene. Help me out here.

Noah: You don't have to know much about the Pirc to realize that White is making a lot of non-developing moves, in fact three in a row with ♖-pawns.

The logic of chess suggests that Black should be able to do something in the center.

Pat: Like 7... d5, you mean.

Noah: Exactly. In a few moves White is fighting for equality – and losing the fight. Black's common sense trumped White's fancy ♙ moves.

Piket-Glek

Wijk aan Zee 1997

1. d4	d6
2. e4	Nf6
3. Nc3	g6
4. Be3	a6
5. h3	Bg7
6. a4	0-0
7. a5	

22

7. ...   d5!

Now 8. exd5 Nxd5 9. Nxd5 Qxd5 is fine for Black.

8. e5	Ne4
9. Nxe4	

Or 9. Bd3 Nxc3 10. bxc3 c5 and ...Nc6xa5.

9. ...	dxe4
10. Bc4	c5!
11. dxc5	Qc7
12. e6	f5!
13. c3	f4

WHY LOGIC MATTERS

The strongest openings are the ones that can't be easily handled by common sense. For example:

(1) The Queen's Gambit (1. d4 d5 2. c4) is strong because the most logical defense, 2... Bf5 and 3... e6/...c6, allows White to seek favorable complications with 3. cxd5!.

(2) The Ruy Lopez (1. e4 e5 2. Nf3 Nc6 3. Bb5) is strong because the natural defenses, 3... d6 or 3... Nf6, have tactical problems. For example,

3.	...	Nf6
4.	0-0	Nxe4
5.	d4	

24

And now 5... exd4? 6. Re1 d5 7. Nxd4 loses for Black because both 8. Nxc6 and 8. f3 are threatened.

So Black must try lines that have to fight for equality, such as 5...Nd6 6. Bxc6 dxc6 7. dxe5.

(3) The most logical defense to 1. e4 e5 2. Nf3 is 2... Nf6, responding to an attack with an attack. But after 3. Nxe5:

25

Black cannot safely reply 3... Nxe4 because of 4. Qe2!.

So he has to accept a slight inferiority in the center with 3... d6 4. Nf3 Nxe4 5. d4 d5.

(4) The Italian game, 1. e4 e5 2. Nf3 Nc6 3. Bc4, was the strongest opening for more than a century, largely because the logical defense:

3.	...	Nf6
4.	Ng5	d5
5.	exd5	Nxd5

26

... kept losing to 6. Nxf7! Kxf7 7. Qf3† (or 6. d4!), the Fried Liver Attack.

Only the introduction of 5... Na5! – a weird-looking move – by Polerio in 1560 saved the Two Knights Defense.

"Not being familiar with the position, I played mechanically and just tried to put my pieces on reasonable squares. Larsen said after the game that 'White's plan seems natural and strong' – but that he has never faced it before."
– Michael Wilder on getting a big opening edge against Bent Larsen.

23

14. Bd4   Nc6
Soon Black had a clear edge.

Pat: I never thought there was much common sense in the openings, just a lot of fancy moves that seem to work.
Noah: Actually there's a huge amount of logic lying under the surface in opening-think. Common sense moves refute most bad openings.
Pat: I'll buy that.
Noah: But did you realize that the strongest openings are the ones that can't be countered with logical moves?

Pat: How's that?
Noah: Because in the strongest openings for White, the logical defenses by Black fail tactically. So Black has to resort to somewhat illogical moves – and that's why White gets a longterm initiative.
Pat: How am I supposed to use logic in the opening?
Noah: Logic is a great asset when you land in a position you've never seen before.
Pat: I land there all the time.
Noah: Get used to it. It's part of competitive chess. Check out Diagram 27.
Pat: This one's new to me. Where do I begin?
Noah: A good way to start is to ask yourself what's good about Black's last move.
Pat: Hmm. Looks like he's gonna go after White's ♗ with ...Nb6. And if White repeats to b3, Black can play ...Ne5 or ...Na5 and plant a ♘ on c4. Goodbye kingside attack.
Noah: You might know that this is

similar to a real variation that goes 8... 0-0 9. Qd2 Nd7.
Pat: I might know – but I don't.
Noah: In any case you can also figure out – logically – what's bad about 8... Nd7.
Pat: It's a retreat. Retreats are often bad. And it wastes time.
Noah: And it's played before Black has completed his usual developing moves such as castling. That's why 9. Bb5! is punishing.
Pat: But is it common sense for White to gain an edge by moving the ♗ again, right after developing it on c4?

1.	e4	c5
2.	Nf3	d6
3.	d4	cxd4
4.	Nxd4	Nf6
5.	Nc3	g6
6.	Be3	Bg7
7.	f3	Nc6
8.	Bc4	Nd7

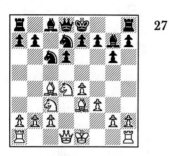

27

9. Bb5!

The threat of 10 Nxc6 is strong because Black cannot defend c6 with normal moves (9... Qc7? 10. Nd5).

Exchanging on d4 just helps White (9... Nxd4 10. Bxd4 and now 10... Bxd4 11. Qxd4 0-0 12. 0-0-0.

In fact, Black's best is to retreat one of the Knights to b8. No good is 9... Na5 10. b4! Nc6, and then not 11. Nxc6?? Bxc3† but 11. Nd5! Ndb8 12. Bg5, with an obvious advantage.

Noah: Remember what I said ear-

lier – often the best answer to a bizarre move is another bizarre move.

Of course, logic is also important in the middlegame. But it's often easier to handle in the opening?

Pat: Why?

Noah: Because in the opening you can determine the exact point where you left your book knowledge and had to start thinking.

Pat: So?

Noah: And you can be reasonably sure that the moves leading up to that position weren't just blunders.

After all, they've been played by a lot of good players before.

Pat: I repeat – so?

Noah: So, you can also be reasonably sure that your position is sound – until your opponent played a new move. If that's all true, you can try to find a logical use of your pieces.

They must be on the squares you put them for a good, book reason – even if you haven't figured out the

reason yet.

A good illustration of that is Diagram 28. What does this position remind you of?

Pat: Looks like a French where White plays 3. e5. Except that here White has Nd2 and Black has that dorky move with the a-♟.

Noah: True. But unless White has just refuted a serious opening, there must be a good move for Black.

1. e4	e6
2. d4	d5
3. Nd2	a6

This a standard variation that has appeared in many GM games.

4. e5!?

28

In the Advance Variation (3. e5 c5 4. c3 Nc6 5. Nf3 Qb6) or 3... Nf6 Tarrasch (3. Nd2 Nf6 4. e5 Nfd7 5. Ngf3!? c5 6. c3 Nc6 7. Bd3 Qb6) Black has useful pressure on d4 and wouldn't waste a tempo on ...a6.

4. ...   Bd7!

Black finds a logical way of using ...a6. He prepares 5... Bb5, exchanging off his problem ♗. For example, 5. Ndf3 Bb5 6. Bxb5† axb5 7. Qd3 Qd7 8. Ne2 b6 and 9... c5. And if White stops that idea with:

5. a4

Black has:

5. ...   c5!

29

And gets a favorable version of the Advance because White's a4 turns out to be a weakening move after 6. Ndf3 Nc6.

"Karpov stopped playing 1. e4 or now rarely plays it because he does not trust his energy any more. When you play 1. d4 you are sometimes able to play the opening using only common sense."
– Viktor Korchnoi

Also 5. c4 could have been answered by 5... dxc4 6. Bxc4 Bb5! 7. Ne2 Nc6 with at least equality.

Pat: Neat. Black's ...a6 went from useless to useful.
Noah: Precisely. We'll get back to the problem of landing in an unfamiliar position on another day because it's such an important topic.

But today I just want to add that logic and common sense can work hand in hand with the third basic component of opening-think.
Pat: Remind me.
Noah: Reasoning by analogy.
Pat: If you're gonna start using SAT words on me...
Noah: Relax, "analogy" just means comparison. Thinking by analogy means comparing your position with others you recall that resemble it – as in Diagram 30.
Pat: What's the score here?
Noah: Neither player was in familiar territory in this anti-book opening. When there's no memory to

rely on, you're essentially left with logic and analogy.

In this case, Black recognized that the position after 5. e4 was very much like a French Defense. So he was ready to play it like a French and reply to 6. Bh4 with 6... dxe4 7. Nxe4 Be7.
Pat: So far, I'm with you.
Noah: But White wasn't thinking that way. He was familiar enough with French positions to know that dxc5! followed by Nd4 is a standard plan.

But he came up with two moves, 11. g4? and 12. Bg2? that just didn't fit the circumstances. He didn't think by analogy.
Pat: If I'm supposed to think that way, how do I start?
Noah: You start by recognizing when there is a similarity between the position on the board and some other opening you're more familiar with.

What often happens, even in grandmaster games, is that one

player sees the similarity but the other doesn't. That was the case in Diagram 31.

Yermolinsky-Kaidanov
Hudson 1993

1. d4	d5
2. Nc3	Nf6
3. Bg5	Nbd7
4. Nf3	e6
5. e4	h6
6. Bxf6	Nxf6
7. Qe2	Be7
8. e5	Nd7
9. 0-0-0	a6
10. h4	c5

30

Best now is 11. dxc5! followed

by Nd4 and f4 with a good game.

11. g4?   b5

Black gives White another chance for dxc5 and Nd4. Better was 11... c4! and ...b5-b4.

12. Bg2?   b4

Now 13. Nb1 Qa5 or 13. Na4 c4 are horrible for White.

For example, 13. Na4 c4 14. Nd2 Rb8 15. f4 Qa5 16. b3 c3 17. Nf3 Nb6 and Black wins.

In the game White played 13. Nxd5?! and lost soon after 13... exd5 14. dxc5 Nxc5.

Pat: What's this one all about?

Noah: Both players were well aware that this is a common position that arises with colors reversed in the Tarrasch Defense of the Queen's Gambit Declined.

Pat: Colors reversed?

Noah: Sure. Black has the same basic position in the diagram that White normally does in the Tarrasch – you know, after 1. d4 d5 2. c4 e6 3. Nc3 c5 4. cxd5 exd5 5. Nf3 Nc6

6. g3 Nf6 7. Bg2 Be7 8. 0-0 0-0.

Recognizing the similarities between positions with colors reversed is an invaluable asset when thinking by analogy.

In this case, it's like White has an extra move in the position Black usually gets in the Tarrasch.

Pat: You're really confusing me now.

Noah: All you have to realize here is that in the diagram both players could have followed the ideas of a distantly-related opening, the Tarrasch.

But only one of them did.

**Dzhindzhikashvili-
D. Gurevich**

U.S. Championship 1992

1. d4	**Nf6**
2. c4	**c5**
3. e3	**g6**
4. Nc3	**Bg7**
5. Nf3	**0-0**
6. Be2	**cxd4**
7. exd4	**d5**
8. 0-0	**Nc6**

31

9. Re1

This is a solid, common sense move.

9. ...   b6?

In the comparable colored reversed position of the Tarrasch, White has a choice between Bf4, Bg5, b3 and cxd5 – so Black should have tried one of the solid ideas here, such as 9... Bf5.

Instead, he played a move that made 9. Re1 more effective, since White now has:

10. Ne5!   Bb7

Or 10... Nxe5 11. dxe5 Nd7 12. Qxd5 and 11... Ne4 12. Bf3.

11. Bf3   Na5

12. Bg5!   h6

13. Bh4   Rc8

Another bad thing about Black's ninth move: with the white ♖ on f1 he could have played 13... dxc4 14. Bxb7 Nxb7.

But here that's bad because of 15. Nc6.

32

14. cxd5

And White stood better, after either 14... Nxd5 15. Bxd5 Bxd5 16. Bxe7! Qxe7 17. Nxg6 or 14... g5 15. Bg3 Nxd5 16. Bxd5! Bxd5 17. h4!.

Pat: Why is reasoning by analogy supposed to work?

Noah: It works because there are certain ♟-structures, piece developments and plans that occur over and over.

And if you don't understand how the position on the board resembles others, it can cost you dearly – as in Diagram 33.

Pat: Who's doing what here?

Noah: White's eighth move avoided the loss of material from a ...b5 fork.

But Black should have appreciated that 8... b5! was still a good move from a positional point of view. Black would then expand on the queenside and exert pressure on the center after ...c5/...Bb7 and possibly ...b4.

As the game went Black paid the price of getting a very passive middlegame.

Pat: And this has something to do with analogy.

Noah: Yes, because ...b5, after ...dxc4, is a common theme in all sorts of QGD positions, including the Meran Variation. Black knew that – but didn't make the proper comparison.

Kasparov-Short
PCA Championship 1993
3rd "quick" game

1. Nf3	d5
2. c4	e6
3. d4	Nf6
4. Nc3	dxc4
5. Qa4†	Nbd7
6. e4	a6
7. Bxc4	c6
8. Qd1!	

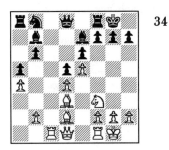

8. ...   **Be7?!**
Correct was 8... b5! followed by

9 Bd3 c5 or 9... Bb7.

9. 0-0	**0-0?**
10. a4!	

Black has no active plan of development now.

10. ...   **b6**
Not 10... b5 11. axb5 cxb5 12. Bxb5.

11. Bd3	**Bb7**
12. e5!	**Nd5**
13. Nxd5	**cxd5**
14. Bd2	**a5**
15. Rc1	**Nb8**

The ♞ had no future on d7.

16. Bb5
White won after 16... Na6 17. Qb3 Rc8 18. Rc3! Nc7 19. Bd3

Bb4? 20. Bxh7†! Kxh7 21. Ng5† Kg8 22. Rh3, threatening 23. Rh8†! and mates.

"You can permit yourself any liberty in the opening except the luxury of a passive position."
– World correspondence champion Grigory Sanakoev

Pat: That was pretty ugly for a so-called world championship game.

Noah: Failing to reason by analogy can be pretty embarrassing. We'll talk about traps some other day but let me ask you: Ever hear of something called the Tarrasch Trap?

Pat: Nope.

Noah: No disgrace. It was a big deal once – but that was more than 100 years ago when the Steinitz Defense to the Lopez was in fashion.

Then Siegbert Tarrasch won a game by introducing a new trap. That's it in Diagram 35.

Pat: Still don't know it.

Noah: But you can appreciate that all of Black's moves make sense. That's another reason why the Lopez is so strong.

Usually a trap exploits a player's greed or naïvete. But the Tarrasch Trap exploited the most logical defense against the Ruy anyone had come up with.

The game was reprinted all around the world and became so

well known that nobody fell for it – for about 82 years.

Pat: I see what you mean. The Tal game is the same thing.

Noah: Except for the extra move ...a6, which is meaningless.

Black, a strong grandmaster who must have known of the Tarrasch Trap, never thought he was falling into it when he reached Diagram 36.

What happened is that over the years everyone forgot about the discredited Steinitz Defense and theory endorsed the "much improved" Steinitz Defense Deferred. The similarities between the two were largely forgotten.

Pat: That must be a pretty extreme case.

Tarrasch-Marco
Dresden 1892

1. e4	e5
2. Nf3	Nc6
3. Bb5	d6
4. d4	Bd7

5. 0-0	Nf6
6. Nc3	Be7

And now:

7. Bxc6	Bxc6

35

8. Re1

Rule of thumb: When White protects his own e-♙ in the Ruy, he's probably threatening Black's.

8. ...	0-0?

Correct was 8... exd4 even though it gives White a superior center.

9. dxe5	dxe5
10. Qxd8	Raxd8
11. Nxe5	

White wins a ♙ because 11... Bxe4 12. Nxe4 Nxe4 13. Nd3! costs

more (13...f5 14. f3 Bc5† 15. Nxc5 Nxc5 16. Bg5! ♖-moves 17. Be7 and White wins).

Tal-Ivkov
USSR-Yugoslavia match 1974

1. e4	e5
2. Nf3	Nc6
3. Bb5	a6
4. Ba4	d6
5. 0-0	Bd7
6. d4	Nf6
7. Bxc6	Bxc6
8. Re1	Be7
9. Nc3	0-0?

36

10. dxe5!

And White won the endgame.

Noah: Extreme but it shows how important reasoning by analogy is, particularly when you're out of book.

Comparisons help take the mystery out of many openings when you find yourself in a new position around move ten.

Pat: Make that move five for me.

Noah: Actually move five isn't a bad time to start thinking analogously. That's what White did in the next game.

Pat: What's the message there?

Noah: Well, you can start by appreciating the words "by transposition."

Pat: I see them all the time. What's the point?

Noah: The point is that the game started out looking like one opening but then changed into another.

It began as a Sicilian but after 5... e5 the position really became a double e-♟ opening, much like a Ruy Lopez. It transposed.

Pat: So far I'm with you. What about

diagram 37?

Noah: Well, by move 11 White began relying on tried-and-true Lopez strategy. He chose a plan that works in a lot of main-line Ruys – closing the center with d5 and attacking on the queenside with b4.

By the time he reached Diagram 38 it looked like a classic lesson in Lopez strategy.

Nisipeanu-Kempinski
Medellin 1996

1.	e4	c5
2.	c3	d6
3.	d4	Nf6
4.	Bd3	Qc7
5.	Nf3	e5
6.	h3	Be7
7.	0-0	0-0
8.	Be3	a6
9.	a4	b6
10.	Nbd2	Bb7

37

11. d5!   Ne8

Black prepares ...f5 but better was 11... Nbd7.

12. b4   Nd7
13. a5!   b5

Black didn't like the appearance of 13... bxa5 14. Rxa5 – although that would have given him better chances for counterplay (after 14... f5 15. exf5 Bxd5 16. Qa4 or 15... Nef6 16. Ng5) – than in the game.

14. c4!   bxc4
15. Nxc4   f5

Or 15... cxb4 16. Nb6! and Black is severely cramped.

16. bxc5   fxe4

Worse is 16... Nxc5 17. Bxc5 or 17. Nb6 Rb8 18. exf5.

17. Bxe4   Nxc5
18. Bxc5

38

With a major edge for White (18... dxc5? 19. d6 or 18... Qxc5 19. Nb6 Rd8 20. Qb1! and 21. Rc1).

Pat: So the trick here is to find some other similar opening – something that I'm supposed to know well enough to remember what to do.

Noah: Sort of. Sometimes it's the differences between the opening you have on the board and the one you recall that help you. That's what probably occurred to White in Diagram 39.

Pat: What's it different from?

Noah: From a line in the Boleslavsky Sicilian – which comes about by way of 1. e4 c5 2. Nf3 Nc6 3. d4 cxd4 4. Nxd4 Nf6 5. Nc3 d6 6. Be2 e5 7. Nb3 Be7 8. 0-0 0-0.

Pat: Looks like something I saw once in a book.

Noah: White probably did, too. And he probably knew that in the Boleslavsky position, the desirable move – from a positional point of view – is 9. Bg5, so that Bxf6 will win control of the d5-hole.

But in the Bolelsavsky, 9. Bg5 fails tactically to 9... Nxe4, a common simplifying trick.

Pat: And here?

Noah: Here there's a difference: the a-♟s are advanced.

That might not seem like much to you. But White checked to see if it did – and he noticed that in this position the ...Nxe4 trick fails.

And that made Bg5 strong.

Kamsky-Short
PCA semifinals 1994

1. e4	c5
2. Nf3	d6
3. d4	cxd4
4. Nxd4	Nf6
5. Nc3	a6
6. a4	Nc6
7. Be2	e5
8. Nb3	Be7
9. 0-0	0-0

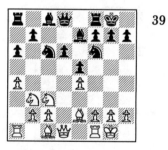

39

10. Bg5!

Now 10... Nxe4? 11. Bxe7 Nxc3 12. Bxd8 Nxd1 13. Bc7 Nxb2 and White traps the ♘ with 14. Rfb1.

10. ...	Bxe6
11. Bxf6!	Bxf6

12. Nd5	Bg5
13. a5!	Rc8
14. Bg4!	

40

And White had a clear positional edge (c3, Nb6).

Pat: Even I could play White in Diagram 40.

Noah: Think by analogy and you may get a chance. But bear in mind that analogy plays a much greater role in 1. d4 openings than 1. e4.

Pat: Why's that?

Noah: Because the various members of the 1. d4 family are more closely related to one another, in ♟-structure especially, than the 1.

e4 openings.

Pat: Is that why I get into trouble faster after 1. d4?

Noah: It could be. There are a lot of little finesses that you need to recognize through analogy – like Diagram 41.

Pat: Looks simple enough.

Noah: Here you have a run-of-the-mill, symmetrical version of the Queen's Gambit Declined.

Pat: Where Black can equalize with just about anything.

Noah: Not true. In fact, the natural – and logical – 6... Be7 can lead to a poor game for Black.

Pat: And this is analogy because...?

Noah: Because Black can understand the position by asking himself what the point of 6. a3 was. If he does that, he may realize it leads the opening into a Queen's Gambit Accepted, with colors reversed.

And once he sees that he'd realize 6... Be7 is weak.

Pat: Again with the colors reversed business.

1. d4	d5
2. c4	e6
3. Nc3	Nf6
4. Nf3	c5
5. e3	Nc6
6. a3	

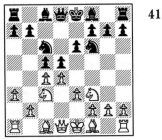

41

But 6... Be7 allows 7. dxc5! and White gets a reversed version of the Queen's Gambit Accepted – with two extra tempi (7... Bxc5 8. b4 Bb6 9. Bb2).

Better is 7... dxc4 8. Qxd8† Kxd8 9. Bxc4 Bxc5 but White still has the edge after 10. b4.

Noah: Yes, colors reversed. As I said – a useful concept in analogy think-ing.

Pat: Do you ever have to reason by some far out analogy – like decid-ing to play a Scheveningen Sicilian position like, oh I don't know, like a King's Gambit?

Noah: If the ♟-structures are simi-lar you can make some pretty dis-tant jumps from one opening to another.

Pat: I'll bet you have an example somewhere. Maybe in Diagram 42?

Noah: That'll do for a start. The moves could place the position under the heading of Réti Open-ing, or English Opening – by trans-position.

Or you could call it a "Queen's Indian Defense Deferred." Or even a "Double Fianchetto." But the ♟-structure puts it in the Benoni family.

Pat: But Black doesn't play it like a Benoni.

Noah: No, he finds a way of getting something a bit better, a very good version of the Benko Gambit.

1. Nf3	Nf6
2. c4	b6
3. g3	c5
4. Bg2	Bb7
5. 0-0	g6
6. Nc3	Bg7
7. Re1	Ne4
8. Nxe4	Bxe4
9. d4	0-0
10. d5	

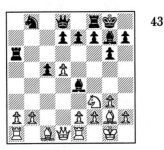

42

Black could continue like a Modern Benoni with 10... e6 and ... exd5, or one of the older Benoni forms with 10... d6 and ...Nd7-f6.

But in *Summerscale-Adams, Brit-ish Championship 1997* Black recog-nized he could get a nice form of a Benko Gambit with:

10. ...	b5!
11. cxb5	a6
12. bxa6	Rxa6

43

Black stood well after 13. Nd2 Bxg2 14. Kxg2 d6 15. Nc4 Nd7 16. e4 Qa8 and ...Ra4 followed by ...Qa6.

Pat: Cool. From a boring English to a Benko.

Noah: Analogy isn't supposed to be cool. It's just another weapon, like logic. But you might enjoy Dia-gram 44. It's almost as much of a jump.

Pat: From where to where?

Noah: From a QGD that was popular in the 1990s into a Gruenfeld. White came up with a new idea, a TN, by way of analogy.

He explained that he visualized the position after 11. Bd3 and compared it with another position he knew.

Pat: Which was?

Noah: Which was a common Gruenfeld line that runs 1. d4 Nf6 2. c4 g6 3. Nc3 d5 4. Nf3 Bg7 5. Bg5 Ne4 6. cxd5 Nxg5 7. Nxg5 e6 8. Nf3 exd5 and is considered okay for White. But "White can only dream" of reaching Diagram 45 from there, he said.

Pat: So that meant if he could get into something like the dream position, the b4 plan had to be good, right?.

1. d4	d5
2. c4	c6
3. Nc3	Nf6
4. Nf3	e6

5. Bg5	h6
6. Bxf6	Qxf6
7. e3	Nd7

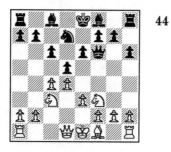

44

Now 8. Bd3 is a standard plan. But in *Piket-Dreev, Wijk aan Zee 1996* White found a new one:

8. a3	g6
9. b4!	Bg7
10. cxd5	

Also good is 10. Qb3 0-0 11. Rc1 Qe7 12. cxd5 exd5 13. Bd3 Nb6 14. 0-0 Be6 15. a4.

10. ...	exd5
11. Bd3	0-0
12. 0-0	

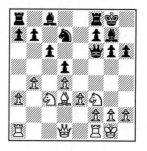

45

And White had an excellent game with Qb3, Rab1 and Rfc1.

Noah: Right. Reasoning by analogy means you have to be very conscious of any changes in ♙-structure, like White's cxd5.

Pat: Are you just talking about changes you should make – or changes that you don't want your opponent to make?

Noah: Both. Diag. 46 is a splendid example of one player reasoning by analogy – but not his opponent. Does anything about the position stand out to you?

Pat: Should it?

Noah: Well, it isn't obvious but it looks like a King's Indian Defense (KID) or a Modern Benoni – with colors reversed, of course.

Pat: Of course.

Noah: I'm serious. With his 10th move Black begins to reorganize his center with ...f6 and ...e5 to resemble a Saemisch Variation of the KID.

You know the one that goes 1. d4 Nf6 2. c4 g6 3. Nc3 Bg7 4. e4 d6 5. f3. Then if Black plays ...c5 White pushes his ♙ to d5. After ...e6xd5 and cxd5 you get a nice Saemisch ♙-structure.

Pat: I think I see all that.

Noah: And since the Saemisch is recognized as a powerful setup in the KID, White would like to stop Black from getting the same ♙-structure from Diagram 46.

Pat: Which he can't.

Noah: Right, he can't. So, instead, he should avoid a cramped position by simplifying exchanges.

In the Benoni – with colors re

versed from what we have here – Black usually does well by trading a pair of ♘s with ...Ne5.

Pat: And here White should be trading ♘s with 11. Ne5!.

Shcherbakov-Khenkin
Borzhomi 1988

1.	c4	e6
2.	Nf3	d5
3.	b3	Nf6
4.	g3	c5
5.	Bg2	Nc6
6.	0-0	Be7
7.	e3	0-0
8.	Bb2	d4
9.	exd4	cxd4
10.	Re1	Ne8!

46

Here 11. Ne5! Nxe5 12. Rxe5 f6 13. Re1 e5 14. d3 and Nd2 is best and gives White a reasonable game.

11.	a3	a5
12.	d3?	f6!
13.	Nbd2	e5
14.	Nf1	

White has no good places for his ♘s, e.g. 14. Ne4 Nc7 15. Nfd2 or 15. Nh4 would have been met by 15... f5!

14.	...	Nc7
15.	h4	Na6!
16.	N3d2	

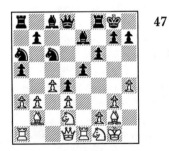

47

Too late White sees that 16. N1h2 Nc5 and ...Qb6 is bad for him.

He hopes for 16...Nc5 17. Ne4, which might finally exchange a pair of ♘s. But:

| 16. | ... | Bf5! |
| 17. | Ne4 | Qd7 |

And after 18. Nh2 Bh3 19. Bh1 h6! Black, with ...f5, had the edge and eventually won.

Noah: A lot of analogy is about ♟-structure, but not exclusively. Often it's where a piece should go the second time you move it.

Pat: Why the second time?

Noah: The first time you move a piece you're usually relying on book memory. In Diagram 48, for example, Black is still in his book and has moved most of his pieces once.

Then he recalled that there was a similar position in the Exchange Variation of the Slav Defense.

Pat: That's a bit of a jump from a Torre Attack, or whatever this is.

Noah: A bit. The point here is that in the Exchange Slav, Mikhail Botvinnik used to get serious coun-

terplay by attacking White's ♗ with ...Nh5 when it was developed on f4 and capturing there or on g3 if it retreats.

Pat: I get it now. Black saw that he could get an improved version of Botvinnik with ...Ne4 and ...g5.

Malaniuk-Piket
Gröningen 1993

1.	d4	Nf6
2.	Nf3	e6
3.	Bg5	h6
4.	Bh4	c5
5.	c3	cxd4
6.	cxd4	Qb6
7.	Qc2	Nc6
8.	e3	d5

The Botvinnik plan came about in a similar position: 1. d4 d5 2. c4 c6 3. cxd5 cxd5 4. Nc3 Nf6 5. Nf3 e6 6. Bf4 Nc6 7. e3 and now 7... Nh5 8. Bg5 Qb6 9. a3 h6! 10. Bh4 g5 11. Bg3 Nxg3 12. hxg3 Bg7.

| 9. | Nc3 | Bd7 |
| 10. | Be2 | |

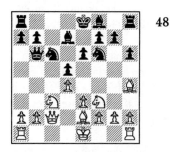

48

10. ...   Ne4

Black's last move is based on 11. Nxe4 dxe4 12. Qxe4 Qxb2 or 12. Nd2 Rc8 with good play for Black.

11.	0-0	Rc8
12.	Rfc1	g5!
13.	Bg3	Nxg3
14.	hxg3	g4
15.	Ne1	h5

49

16. Na4   Qd8

With a fine game for Black.

Noah: That's enough analogy. But, there's one other important area we need to touch on today and it's more about feeling than thinking.

Pat: Feeling?

Noah: Yes, a feeling for how much you should be able to get out of a position. It's like a sense of how much you deserve.

Pat: I'm not getting this.

Noah: Look at it this way – do you think Black is better after White makes a "bad" first move, like 1. a3 or 1. h4 ?

Pat: Of course.

Noah: Actually he shouldn't be. Take a look at the following.

Black doesn't try to overwhelm his opponent after 1. a3. He just wants a solid position and from there he builds a platform for playing to win in the middlegame.

Miles-Almasi
Biel 1996

1. a3

A waiting move that is not wasted if Black replies 1... e5 or 1... d5 and then 2. c4!.

1. ...   Nf6

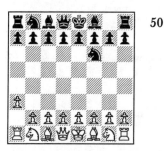

50

A common sense decision.

Black plans a simple development he could also have used against 1. g3 or 1. Nf3.

2.	Nf3	d5
3.	d4	c6
4.	e3	Bg4
5.	h3	Bh5
6.	g4	Bg6
7.	Ne5	Nfd7
8.	Nxg6	hxg6
9.	c4	e6

White's a3 is somewhat useful but he has no advantage.

10.	Nd2	Be7
11.	Bg2	Na6
12.	b3	Nc7

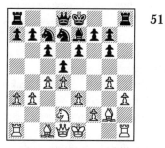

51

13. Bb2   b5!

14. cxd5   cxd5

And Black, who is now at least equal, won on the 55th move.

Pat: But some openings are awful.

Noah: True, but not quickly refuted. After all, the worst thing you can say about 1. a3 is that it wastes time.

The easiest way to make an awful opening turn out well is to try to crush it. In Diagram 52 you see how Black's sloppy play appears to put him on the ropes by move 10.

Pat: Lame-o. Three straight retreats to the first rank.

Noah: But looks are deceiving. White has a huge lead in development – yet Black has no real weaknesses. As a result it is White who is psychologically vulnerable.

Pat: Because?

Noah: Because he thinks all it takes is a few sharp moves and Black's position will collapse. But it doesn't.

Dückstein-Sigurjonsson
Siegen 1970

1. e4   g6
2. d4   d6
3. Nc3   Bg7
4. f4   Nc6
5. Nf3   Nf6

Black could have punished White's failure to play 5. Be3 by pinning him now with 5... Bg4. But the real mistakes are coming up.

6. Be2   Bg4
7. d5   Nb8?

Black stands well after 7... Bxf3 8. Bxf3 Na5.

8. e5!   Ng8
9. Ng5!

Now 9... Bxe2 10. Qxe2 makes e6 a stronger threat.

9. ...   Bc8

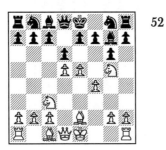

52

On 10. Bb5† (hoping for 10... Bd7? 11. e6!) Black has 10... c6 11. dxc6 bxc6.

And then if 12. Qd5 Nh6! he has excellent compensation after 13. Bxc6† Nxc6 14. Qxc6† Bd7.

10. e6   Nh6
11. f5?

Based on 11... Nxf5?? 12. Nxf7 or 11... gxh5 12. Bh5.

But it's not nearly as good as 11. exf7† Nxf7 12. Ne6 Bxe6 13. dxe6 Nh6 14. Ne4 or the no-risk 11. Bg4 followed by exf7† and Be6.

11. ...   0-0
12. 0-0   gxf5
13. Bh5   fxe6
14. dxe6   Nc6

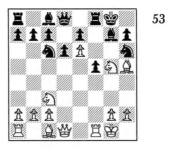

53

White's last chance for an edge was 15. Bf7† Kh8 16. Qh5 (or 15... Nxf7 16. exf7† Kh8 17. Qh5).

But he played for more with 15. Nf7 and after 15... Nxf7 16. Bxf7† Kh8 17. Qh5 Ne5 18. Rf4 Bf6 19. Nd5 Nxf7 Black drew comfortably.

Pat: How does this help me think?

Noah: It helps you when you have choices. That's what chess is all about – choices.

Pat: Choices like chocolate or vanilla?

Noah: More like whether to go for a big edge or a small one as White.

Pat: I'll settle for any.

Noah: The right choice will depend on what your position deserves. In Diagram 54 White could have reasoned by analogy that he has an edge.

Pat: What analogy?

Noah: Analogy with the Nimzo-Indian Defense or some QGDs. But since Black rarely plays ...Ba5 in those positions, White figured he was a tempo ahead and he deserved something out of the opening.

The question is how big a something.

Pat: And he chose too big.

Conquest-Rozentalis
Hastings 1996/7

1.	c4	e6
2.	Nc3	Bb4
3.	Qb3	Ba5

More common is 3... Nc6. But not 3... c5 4. Nb5!.

4.	Nf3	Nf6
5.	d4	d5
6.	Bg5	dxc4

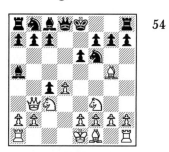

54

7. Qa4†?

Here 7. Qxc4 is good because 7... Qd5 is probably best and then 8. Qxd5 Nxd5 9. Bd2 is a promising endgame for White.

But White concluded that forcing moves promised more (7... c6 8. Bxf6! Qxf6? 9. Qxa5).

7.	...	Nc6
8.	e4	Bd7
9.	Qxc4	h6!

Now 10. Bh4 g5 wins the e4-♙.

10. Bxf6   Qxf6

And Black had signficant counterplay, e.g. 11. Be2 b5 12. Qd3 b4.

The game actually went 11. a3 0-0-0 12. Be2 g5! 13. e5 Qg7 14. 0-0? Bb6 – and Black was much better.

Noah: Correct. He thought he should get a terrific game with a quick e2-e4. But his feeling about what he deserved out of the opening was wrong.

Pat: Way wrong.

Noah: And it's not just White who

tries for too much in the first hour.

In Diagram 55 Black tried to get a great diagonal for his ♗ – and maybe an edge – by setting up 10... Ba6, so that White couldn't reply 11. b5.

Pat: What's wrong with that?

Noah: Well, ambition is fine – if it works. But in this case it prompted White to reassess how much of an edge he should get out of the opening.

After the modest 9... Bb7 White would have been content with a small advantage, such as after 10. Rc1.

But after 9... c6 White's sense of what he deserves led him to find 10. g4!.

Komarov-Razuvaev
Reggio Emilia 1996/7

1.	Nf3	Nf6
2.	c4	e6
3.	Nc3	Bb4
4.	Qc2	0-0
5.	a3	Bxc3

6.	Qxc3	d5

More common is 6... b6.

7.	b4	dxc4
8.	Qxc4	b6
9.	Bb2	c6

55

10. g4!   a5

Black needs counterplay and 10... Ba6 11. Qc3 followed by 12. g5 isn't enough. No better is 10... Qd5 11. Qc3 and if 11... a5 then 12. Rc1! and 13. g5

11. g5   Nd5?

Black misses his chance to curtail White's initiative with 11... Qd5! (12. Qc3 axb4 13. axb4 Rxa1† 14. Bxa1 Qa2).

12. Rg1   axb4

13. Qd4   f6
14. gxf6   Qxf6?

56

15. Rxg7†! Kxg7
16. Qg4†

And White won. Somewhat better was 14... Rxf6 15. axb4 Rxa1† 16. Bxa1 Qf8! but 17. Qh4! clearly favors White.

Pat: But what if Black had...?
Noah: Maybe we shouldn't overdo it on the first day. Let's talk again tomorrow. There's an awful lot of ground to cover in the opening.
Pat: Same time?
Noah: Same time.

"I was thinking about how to start my game in the next round."
– **David Bronstein replied after Bronstein had thought 40 minutes over his first move in one game and he was asked why.**

In which Pat learns that White isn't Black, that Black isn't White and equal isn't always equal.

Noah: Pat, why don't we start today with you choosing the subject?

Pat: Okay. There's something I always wanted an honest answer to.

Noah: Shoot.

Pat: How much do I really need to know in the opening? I mean, there's so much "book" out there. I'm sure there's a lot of it I can ignore – but how much do I need to know?

Noah: Not that much, actually. For starters, you need to know how to play at least one good defense to 1. e4 and one to 1. d4.

You might want to have two: a solid defense to use against stronger players and when you don't mind a draw – and a sharper one, when winning is a high priority.

Pat: Isn't it always?

Noah: Not always. I'm sure you've seen GMs who meet 1. d4 with 1... Nf6 when they need a full point. But they use 1... d5 – to play a Slav or some other QGD line – when they're just trying to equalize in the opening.

Or they play the Sicilian when going for a kill but 1... e5 when they can afford to draw.

Pat: And that's all I need when I have Black?

Noah: What you need is what you can comfortably handle.

You don't need to know how to play the Scheveningen Sicilian and the Caro-Kann and the Alekhine's and the Modern.

Pat: What about junk like 1. g3 ?

Noah: For all the closed systems – 1. Nf3, 1. c4, 1. g3, 1. b3, and so on – you can get away with one answer to each. Maybe less.

Pat: How can it be less?

Noah: Because of that magical word transposition. For example, you can use a system based on ...d5 and an early ...Bf5/...c6/...e6 against 1. Nf3 as well as against 1. g3 and 1. c4.

You can even use it against 1. b3 and 1. f4.

57

Black can set up this formation against a variety of move orders. For example:

1. Nf3	d5
2. g3	c6
3. Bg2	Nf6
4. 0-0	Bf5
5. d3	e6

Or

1. c4	c6
2. Nf3	d5
3. b3	Nf6
4. g3	Bf5
5. Bg2	e6
6. Bb2	Nbd7

Pat: Not bad. What else do I have to know?

Noah: You need to know one opening system as White, either 1. e4 or 1. d4 or 1. c4 – but not two or all three.

And whether with White or Black you need to know the basic goals of each opening you play.

"A chessplayer cannot and must not play all the openings known to theory"
– Mikhail Botvinnik

Pat: You mean like whether to attack on the kingside or queenside.

Noah: Even simpler. For example, there's a line in the French, called the Alekhine-Chatard Attack. For decades it was a minefield for Black. The key position is shown in Diagram 58.

Pat: Don't know it.

Noah: You don't have to, unless you play a Classical French as Black.

The point here is that for decades 6. h4 kept getting White great positions no matter what Black did. He tried almost everything. The book moves were 6... c5, 6... h6, 6... f6 or 6... a6.

Pat: What am I missing. Why can't Black win a ♙?

Noah: Accepting the gambit was considered – unacceptable.

1. e4	e6
2. d4	d5
3. Nc3	Nf6
4. Bg5	Be7
5. e5	Nfd7

6. h4

White gets an edge in most lines now, e.g. 6... h6 7. Be3! followed by 8. Qg4.

Also 6... c5 7. Bxe7 Kxe7 8. f4! (or 7... Qxe7 8. Nb5! and Black should sack the Exchange with 8... 0-0, because 8... Na6 9. Nd6† Kf8 10. c3 is much worse).

6. ...	Bxg5!
7. hxg5	Qxg5
8. Nh3	Qe7
9. Nf4	

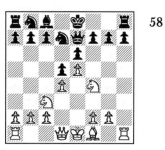

58

White, with Qg4 and 0-0-0 coming up, appears to have more than enough compensation for the ♙. For example, 9... a6 10. Qg4 Kf8

11. Qf3! (threatening 12. Ng6†) Kg8 12. Bd3 c5? was one disaster (13. Bxh7† Rxh7 14. Rxh7 Kxh7 15. 0-0-0 and wins, *Keres-Wade, London 1954*).

Another went 9... a6 10. Qg4 g6 11. 0-0-0 c5 12. Qg3! (threatening 13. Ncxd5!) Nb6 13. dxc5 with a big advantage for White (*Bogolyubov-Spielmann, Stockholm 1919*).

9. ...	g6
10. Qg4	Nc6!

59

Black stands well after ...Nb6, ...Bd7 and ...0-0-0.

Pat: Because Black doesn't get counterplay? That's why I usually

lose when I try the French.

Noah: Black doesn't need counterplay after 7... Qxg5. After all, he's a ♙ ahead.

What he needs is safety. Attacking the center with ....c5 is the opposite of safety.

Once someone figured out that Black's real goal in the opening was to castle queenside quickly, the Alekhine-Chatard became almost a museum piece.

Pat: So far, so good. What else do I need to know?

Noah: You also have to know this –

BLACK ISN'T WHITE

Pat: Duh.

Noah: No, this is important. This means that Black doesn't have to necessarily do anything in the opening – except get out of it.

In Diagram 60 you see White playing the Sicilian so passively that Black made the mistake of thinking he deserved an advantage. And that turned out to be fatal.

Pat: It looks like Black just overlooked 9. Nxe5.

Noah: I'd say there was a reason he overlooked it. Remember what I

"Your only task in the opening is to reach a playable middlegame."
– Lajos Portisch – who nevertheless was a leading authority on getting an edge with 1. d4.

said about developing a feel for whether or not you deserve an edge?

Well, in this case Black felt he deserved the advantage – and the only way to get one was to preserve his extra ♙ with 8... e5.

Balashov-Filippov
Seversk 1998

1. e4   c5
2. Nf3   e6
3. Nc3   Nc6
4. Be2!?   Nf6
5. 0-0

Since White has made no aggressive moves, particularly avoiding d4, Black could just play 5... Be7 and 6... 0-0, or 5... d6 and ... Bd7, with a good game in either case.

5. ...   d5?!
6. exd5   Nxd5

White has a fine position after 6... exd5 7. d4!. Black, however, hopes to dominate the center with ...e5.

7. d4   cxd4
8. Nb5

60

8. ...   e5?

White has only a small edge after 8... Bc5 9. Nbxd4.

9. Nxe5!   Nxe5
10. Qxd4   f6
11. Qxd5!

And White won the ♙ up endgame after 11... Qxd5 12. Nc7† Kf7 13. Nxd5 Bc5 14. Be3 Bxe3 15. Nxe3 Nc6 16. Bc4† Be6 17. Rad1 Rhd8 18. Bxe6† Kxe6 19. Rfe1.

Pat: I don't understand why Black can't play like White. Didn't you just say the other day that I should

think by analogy?

And what about those colors reversed positions?

Noah: The problem is that most openings favor White at least slightly because he gets to move

*"It has long been known that if the game of chess could talk, it would say: 'Love me with **Black!** Anyone will love me with **White.'** "*
– David Bronstein

first. If White forfeits that privilege – if he plays 1. e3 and then meets 1... e5 with 2. e4, for example – then Black is perfectly entitled to play like White.

But most openings aren't like that. And Diagram 61 is an example.

Pat: Looks like Black was doing okay.

Noah: He was. Usually when Black gets in ...d5 safely in a Maroczy Bind ♟ formation he's in good shape.

The problem is that good doesn't mean great. Black began to think he was in great shape and getting the better of it.

Pat: But it looked like he was out of danger after 14... Bxc6.

Noah: Well, you're right that Black managed to liquidate the center and grab a nice diagonal for his B/c6.

But this cost him time. When he finally got around to castling he walked right into a crushing sacrifice.

Kamsky-Lautier
Dortmund 1993

1. e4	**c5**
2. Nf3	**d6**
3. d4	**cxd4**
4. Qxd4	**a6**
5. Bg5	**Nc6**
6. Qd2	**Nf6**
7. Bd3	**e6**
8. c4	**h6**
9. Bf4	**d5!**
10. exd5	**exd5**
11. 0-0	**Be7**
12. Nc3	

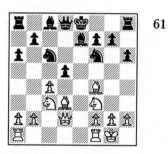

61

12. ... **Bg4?**

After 12... Be6 White has only a minor advantage. For example, 13.

cxd5 Nxd5 14. Be4! and now 14... Nxf4 15. Qxf4 0-0 16. Bxc6 bxc6.

13. cxd5

Black may have chosen 12... Bg4 because 13. Ne5 Nxe5 14. Bxe5 fails to 14... dxc4. But his loss of time hurts now.

13. ... **Bxf3**

14. dxc6

Unclear is 14. d6 Bxd6 15. Qe3† Qe7.

14. ... **Bxc6**

15. Rad1

Now 15... Nd5 16. Be4! or 15... Qb6 16. Rfe1 are poor for Black.

15. ... **0-0**

62

16. Bxh6! **gxh6**

17. Qxh6

And White's threat to bring a Rook to the kingside was decisive. Black lost soon after 17... Re8 18. Bc4 Bd7 19. Rd4.

Pat: I suspect now you're also going to tell me that White isn't Black.

Noah: That's right:

WHITE ISN'T BLACK

Pat: Which means?

Noah: Which means White wants more than dead even equality out of the opening. Otherwise his opening is a failure – and he can get the worst of it, as in Diagram 63.

Pat: White sure seems okay there.

Noah: Not quite true. Remember I told you that most openings take their character from White having the right to move first.

In this opening Black needed to offset that advantage and he decided to do it with ...dxc4, followed by a nice expansion on the queenside with ...b5.

Pat: What's wrong with that?

Noah: Nothing. In fact, it would have given him the better of it – except that it makes him vulnerable to a4! at some point.

Pat: Like move eight.

Noah: Or nine. The point is White didn't do it at any point. He played passively, as if he didn't have to do anything in the opening except castle and connect his ♖s.

And the result is that Black ended up with the better of a symmetrical position.

Andersson-Belyavsky
Pärnu 1997

1.	d4	Nf6
2.	c4	e6
3.	Nf3	d5
4.	Nc3	c6
5.	Qb3	dxc4
6.	Qxc4	b5
7.	Qd3	a6
8.	Bg5	c5
9.	e3?!	

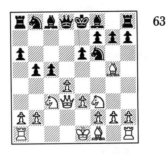

63

Better was 9. a4!. Then 9... cxd4 10. Nxd4 b4 allows White to get a slight edge with 11. Ne4 Bb7 12. Bxf6.

9.	...	Nbd7
10.	Be2	Bb7
11.	0-0	Be7

Black threatens to seize the advantage by putting his ♕ on b6 and ♖s at c8 and d8.

12.	dxc5	Nxc5
13.	Qxd8†	Rxd8
14.	Rac1	0-0

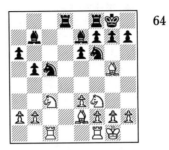

64

And by default, Black is superior. He was steadily improving his position after 15. Nd4 Rc8! 16. f3 Ncd7 17. Rfd1 Bc5 18. Bh4 Nd5!.

Pat: Okay, so I have to know what I'm playing for. But let's get back to my first question – **how much book do I need to know?**

Noah: The bare minimum is: You need to know the traps that come up in your openings.

Pat: But there are all these books that say studying traps is like playing for cheapos.

Noah: I'm not saying you should try to spring traps. But you do need to

know how to avoid traps in the lines you play.

Traps aren't just cheap tactics. They are based on good-looking, reasonable moves and that's why so many good players fall into them, such as in Diagram 65.

Pat: Sure doesn't look like a trappy position.

"To play for a draw, at any rate with White, is to some degree a crime against chess."
– Mikhail Tal

Noah: But it is one because ...Ng4 is a strong move in similar positions. When Black reaches this one he often wonders, "Doesn't White have to play f3 or h3 around here? So, why isn't ...Ng4 a good move?"

Pat: I get it. After ...Ng4, White can't move the B/e3 because the ♘ would hang on d4.

Noah: And the capture on c6 is just bad. So Black's move was logical – it just had a huge tactical hole in it.

That's also the case with Diagram 66, which must have set a record for victims over the years.

1. Nf3	Nf6
2. c4	c5
3. Nc3	Nc6
4. d4	cxd4
5. Nxd4	g6
6. e4	d6
7. Be2	Bg7
8. Be3	0-0
9. 0-0	

65

9. ...	Ng4??

Now 10. Nxc6 Nxe3! is bad for White. But:

10. Bxg4!	Bxg4
11. Nxc6!	

Black loses a piece. He resigned in *Korchnoi-Liardet, Baden 1997* – for one of many examples.

Black played on far as 11... Bxd1 12. Nxd8 Bxc3 13. Rfxd1 Resigns in *Akesson-Heidenfeld, Pula 1997*.

1. e4	g6
2. d4	Bg7
3. Nf3	d6
4. Bc4	Nd7??

66

5. Bxf7†	1-0

Black loses his ♛ after 5... Kxf7 6. Ng5† Ke8 7. Ne6 and his ♚ after 6... Kf6 7. Qf3†. This game was *Dadiani-Durbov, Kiev 1896*.

But it was also *Hamlisch-NN, Vienna 1899; Bogolyubov-Meister, Kiev 1912; Luzgin-Ioffe, Minsk 1962;* and *Arnason-I. Pribyl, Yurmala 1990*.

In a different move order:

1. e4	d6
2. d4	Nd7
3. Bc4	g6
4. Nf3	Bg7??
5. Bxf7†	Kxf7
6. Ng5†	1-0

It was *Tal-Shtreicher, Riga 1950*.

And in another:

1. d4	d6
2. Nf3	Nd7
3. e4	

67

3. ...	g6
4. Bc4	Bg7??
5. Bxf7†	1-0

It was *Ibragimov-Zhelnin* (rated 2490!), *Russia Cup, Moscow 1998*.

Pat: But those are dinosaur traps. Everyone must know them by now.

Noah: Dinosaurs still find their victims today – and strong ones. Besides, there are relatively new and unknown traps that you also have to beware.

Pat: Show me what a new trap looks like.

Noah: Okay. Cast your eyes on Diagram 68.

Here you see the spectacle of the world's No.4 ranked player, rated 2725, in what up to then was the most important game of his life.

Pat: How important?

Noah: It decided a Candidates semifinals match. Yet Black blundered into a trap on the fifth move and lost.

If that isn't a warning against being complacent about traps, I don't know what is.

Gelfand-Kramnik

Candidates semifinals,
final game, 1994

1. c4	c5
2. Nc3	Nf6
3. g3	d5
4. cxd5	Nxd5
5. Bg2	

68

5. ...	e6?

Black confuses this position with similar ones, such as 1. c4 c5 2. Nf3 Nf6 3. Nc3 e6 4. g3 d5 5. exd5 Nxd5 when 6. Bg2 Nc6 gives Black a nice position.

6. Nxd5	exd5
7. Qb3!	

White wins either the d-♟ or the b-♟. Black tried 7... Nc6 8. Qxd5 Qxd5 9. Bxd5 Nb4 10. Be4 f5 11. Bb1 and eventually lost.

Pat: Okay, so I have to know the traps that I might fall in. But besides that, don't I have to know a lot of sub-sub-variations?

Noah: That depends on how sharp the openings you use are.

Pat: Why? It seems like you need to memorize 20 moves to play the Ruy Lopez – and that's not really tactical.

Noah: Not quite true. If you don't know the book at move 20 in a Lopez, it won't kill you – unless it's a sharp line like the Marshall Attack. The main Lopez variations are relatively quiet so the risk is only that you'll make a second-best move, a minor sin.

Another example is the Slav Defense. If you defend with the Slav you don't have to know the Exchange Variation much beyond the seventh move – because the cost of ignorance or being surprised is relatively cheap.

But you must know some serious book in the gambit lines like 1. d4 d5 2. c4 c6 3. Nf3 Nf6 4. Nc3 dxc4 5. e4!?. Not knowing how to get out of the opening in those variations you can get destroyed before your

second Pepsi.

Pat: I guess you're right.

Noah: Another way of putting it is:

The amount of book you need to know depends on how well you understand the basic tactics of your openings.

Pat: How's that?

Noah: Look at it this way. The Queen's Gambit Declined is a fairly simple opening in terms of tactics. Only a few tactical ideas recur, such as the freeing maneuvers ...Ne4 or ...dxc4/...Nd5.

But you can lose very quickly if you don't understand them, as Black failed to do in Diagram 69.

Pat: Where's this from?

Noah: You'd be surprised. It was the very first game Tigran Petrosian played in a Soviet Championship.

1. d4	d5
2. c4	e6
3. Nc3	Nf6

4. cxd5 exd5
5. Bg5 Be7
6. e3 c6

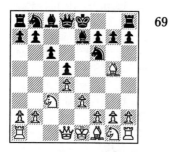

69

The move ...Ne4 is an excellent equalizing move after 7. Nf3 and is a fine move at some later point in the main line of 7. Qc2 0-0 8. Bd3 Nbd7 9. Nf3 Re8 10. 0-0 Nf8.

7. Qc2 Ne4??

But not here. Petrosian's game (as Black) ended in minutes.

8. Bxe7 Qxe7
9. Nxd5! cxd5
10. Qxc8†

The rest was 10... Qd8 11. Bb5† Nc6 12. Bxc6† bxc6 13. Qxc6† Resigns.

Pat: Okay, the sharper the opening, the more book I have to know.

Noah: And the more certain you need to be about the accuracy of what you memorize.

A mistake in a quiet, book line of the English isn't going to hurt you much.

Pat: You mean if the books say it's slightly advantageous for you as White but it's really dead even.

Noah: Correct. But when you believe the book about an explosive position – and it turns out to be wrong, you pay the price big time, such as in Diagram 70.

1. d4 d5
2. c4 dxc4
3. Nf3 Nf6
4. e3 e6
5. Bxc4 a6
6. 0-0 c5
7. Bb3 b5
8. a4 b4
9. Nbd2 Bb7
10. e4 cxd4

11. e5 Nfd7
12. Nc4 Nc5
13. Bg5

Informant 64 pointed out that 13... Qc7 14. Nxd4 favors White slightly. It claimed further that:

13. ... f6
14. exf6 gxf6
15. Nfe5

... loses for Black because of the threat of 16. Qh5†.

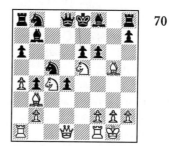

70

But in *Slipak-Spangenberg, Buenos Aires 1996*, Black chose the obvious defense.

15. ... h5!

And Black won in 30 moves (16. Ng6 Qd5 17. Nd6† Qxd6 18.

Nxh8 Nxb3 19. Qxh5† Kd7 20. Qf7† Be7 21. Bxf6 Nxa1, etc.)

Pat: But don't you have to trust book? At least most of the time?

Noah: Sure, you can trust published analysis for almost all lines that have been around for a while and have withstood the test of time.

But if you think you've come up with a strong new move, think twice.

Pat: I take it that's what happens in Diagram 71.

Noah: Yes. This was known to favor Black since 1975 because of a high-profile example of 13... e4!. Yet in this game White – facing the world champion, no less – plunged forward with 14. Nxe4.

> **If you think you've come up with a strong new move, think twice.**
> —GM N. Tall

Pat: Maybe he thought he had an improvement.

Noah: Sure, and maybe he thought he'd also refuted 1... c5. Not very likely.

That suggests another must-know:

You need to be know how to evaluate published opening analysis.

Yudasin-Kasparov
Ljubljana 1995

1. e4	c5
2. Nf3	d6
3. Bb5†	Nd7
4. d4	Ngf6
5. Nc3	cxd4
6. Qxd4	e5
7. Qd3	h6
8. Nd2	Be7
9. Nc4	0-0
10. Bxd7	Bxd7
11. Nxd6?	Qc7

Now 12. Ndb5 Qc6 favors Black.

12. Nf5	Bxf5
13. exf5	e4

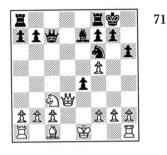

71

In the previous game Black's pressure grew after 14. Qe2 Rfe8 15. Bd2 Rac8.

14. Nxe4?	Qe5
15. f3	Rad8
16. Qc3	

Or 16. Qe2? Nxe4 17. fxe4 Bb4† 18. Kf2 Rd4 and 17. Qxe4 Bh4† 18. Ke2 Rfe8, which both favor Black.

16. ...	Qxf5
17. 0-0	Nxe4
18. fxe4	Qxe4

Black was always winning after this.

Pat: How in the world am I supposed to evaluate stuff appearing in the *Informant?*

Noah: I'll say it once more: Use your common sense.

Ask yourself if you feel comfortable playing the recommended line – regardless of how many exclamation points the moves are given.

You'll realize you really hate some positions that are supposed to be great.

Pat: I hate a lot of them.

Noah: You'll also realize that not all "equal" positions are really equal. That's an unfortunate result of *Informant*-speak.

Pat: What do you mean?

Noah: Well, using an equals sign to assess a position can mean "both sides have equal chances of winning." Or it can mean "with best play White can't do much." There's a big difference.

Pat: I'll bet that's what Diagram 72 shows.

But before we go there, what's the deal with 6... Bb4 – and then 7... Bd6 ?

Noah: It gives White an extra tempo, a3, but it's less than useful because b3 becomes weak. We'll get around to the value of extra tempi another day.

Pat: But the point you're tying to make here is that the evaluation is wrong, right?

1. d4	d5
2. c4	e6
3. Nc3	Nf6
4. Nf3	c6
5. e3	Nbd7
6. Bd3	Bb4
7. a3	Bd6
8. 0-0	0-0
9. e4	dxe4
10. Nxe4	Nxe4
11. Bxe4	

Now 11... Nf6 12. Bc2 and Qd3 or Bg5 favors White. But the position has been called "equal" because of the key line:

11. ...	e5
12. dxe5	Nxe5
13. Nxe5	Bxe5

14. Bxh7† Kxh7
15. Qh5† Kg8
16. Qxe5 Qd3!

"...there are two kinds of equal positions. Equal positions you like to play and equal positions you can't stand the sight of."
— Viswanathan Anand

72

Black has excellent drawing chances because of the ♗s-of-opposite-color and White's weak light-squares, such as b3 and c4, (thanks to 7. a3).

Noah: Right. Black has excellent drawing chances. But excellent drawing chances don't make the position "equal."

It's like the *Informant* giving an endgame with ♔ + ♖ + ♗ vs. ♔ + ♖ and concluding with an "=".

Pat: You mean because if he finds the right moves, the guy with the ♔ + ♖ can draw.

Noah: Yes, it's drawable with best play. But that ain't equal.

The same goes for Diagrams 73 and 74.

Pat: I kind of like White in both positions.

Noah: It's easy to feel that way. Yet the books sometimes give them as equal. True, White's winning chances are relatively few in the endgame of Diagram 73. But he's the one who has them, not Black. Same story in Diagram 74.

Pat: And Diagram 75?

Noah: This is an about-to-be endgame that is supposed to be equal even after White plays Nd5.

Pat: But you think it isn't equal.

Noah: Let me put it this way: When a Maroczy Bind position is rated as = it usually means the annotator doesn't think White is winning, yet.

"EQUAL" – BUT ONLY IN BOOKS

Example I

1. c4 e5

2. g3 g6?!
3. d4 exd4
4. Qxd4 Nf6
5. Nc3 Nc6
6. Qe3†! Qe7
7. Qxe7† Bxe7

73

Example II

1. d4 d5
2. c4 e6
3. Nc3 Nf6
4. cxd5 exd5
5. Bg5 c6
6. e3 Bf5

And now the only way for White to get an edge is:

7. Qf3 Bg6

8. Bxf6	Qxf6
9. Qxf6	gxf6

74

EXAMPLE III

1. e4	c5
2. Nf3	Nc6
3. d4	cxd4
4. Nxd4	g6
5. c4	Nf6
6. Nc3	d6
7. Be2	Nxd4
8. Qxd4	Bg7
9. 0-0	0-0
10. Qe3	Be6
11. Bd2	Qb6

75

> *"Long experience has taught me the secret of playing Maroczy Bind positions for a win: remember always to be White.*
> *– IM David Strauss*

Pat: But even a goofy equals has got to be better than a real plus-over-equals (±) for your opponent.

Noah: Not necessarily. Usually you're better off with a plus-over-equals position as Black – provided you have counterplay – than to have Diagram 74, which may mean hours of thankless defense to reach a draw.

Pat: Okay, we're back to my question of the day: What else do I have to know?

Noah: You also have to learn to be suspicious about positions that your common sense tells you are ugly – but they end up in the *Informant* because they were used to win some big game. For example, it took six years before someone showed how awful Black's position in Diagram 76 really is.

Pat: Why would somone play this line – and retake with the ♛ at move 12?

Noah: Because 12... Qxd6 was played in a 1991 game that Black

won quickly.

It was only after the 1997 game that people realized how awful Black's position was by move 12.

Shabalov-Browne
Las Vegas 1997

1. e4	c5
2. Nf3	d6
3. d4	cxd4
4. Nxd4	Nf6
5. Nc3	a6
6. Bg5	e6
7. f4	Nc6
8. e5	h6
9. Bh4	

76

| 9. ... | g5?! |

10. fxg5   Nd5
11. Nxd5   exd5
12. exd6   Qxd6?

Black is worse – but still breathing – after 12... Bxd6! 13. Qe2†
Kf8.

13. Qe2†   Be7
14. Nxc6   bxc6
15. Bg3   Qg6

The previous game had gone 16. gxh6? Bg4 17. Qe5 Qxc2! with advantage to Black (since 18. Qxh8† Kd7 19. Qc3 loses to 19... Bb4! 20. Qxb4 Re8†).

In fact, Black's position looks awful – and appearances aren't deceiving.

16. Qe5!   Rg8

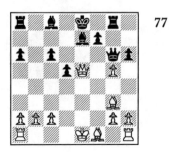

77

17. gxh6!

Now 17... Qxh6 18. Bf4 Qg6 may be best although 19. 0-0-0 is still bad for Black.

17. ...   Qxc2
18. Be2   Rg5
19. Qh8†   Kd7
20. Qc3   Qxc3†
21. bxc3

And White won the endgame.

Pat: What if I look at more than one book and compare the analysis?

Noah: That's better, but if it's new analysis you'd be better off checking everything with a computer.

Once faulty analysis appears in print it often develops a life of its own. A good illustration of that is Diagram 78:

Pat: What am I looking at?

Noah: This comes from a celebrated book by Isaac Boleslavsky back in the 1960s. White has the edge, Boleslavsky declared – and this conclusion was still being quoted in other books in the 1980s.

But his analysis contains two holes large enough to drive a pair of SUVs through.

Pat: You mean because Black is really winning after 14. Qxf6.

Noah: And because White missed a win of his own a move earlier. Bear in mind that Boleslavsky was the foremost opening theoretician of the last half of the 20th century.

1. e4   c5
2. Nf3   Nc6
3. d4   cxd4
4. Nxd4   Nf6
5. Nc3   d6
6. Bg5   e6
7. Nxc6   bxc6
8. e5   dxe5
9. Qf3   Bd7
10. 0-0-0   Be7
11. Bxf6   Bxf6
12. Ne4   0-0

78

13. Rxd7?   Qxd7
14. Qxf6

Black has the strong 14... Rad8! threatening mate in one as well as 15... gxf6, e.g., 16. Qf3 f5!

Moreover, White had a real win with 13. Nxf6† gxf6 14. Qd3.

Pat: Okay, I'll have to check new stuff with my computer. But suppose a book says one thing and another says something else – and the computer doesn't find any holes. Who do I trust?

Noah: That's "whom." And the answer is – you can usually trust reputation.

DANGER SIGNS

How to recognize a suspicious opening book

• It's Biased

Watch out if the author tries to prove "1. h4 wins!"

• It's Dated

The book is about a hot new opening but doesn't include any games played in the past three years.

• It Relies On Old Reputations

For example, 1. e4 e5 2. Nc3 Bc5 was called dubious for years on the basis of 3. Nf3 Nc6? 4. Nxe5!. In fact, Black's position is fine after the simple 3... d6.

Also, for decades the tricky 3... d5 in the Ponziani (1. e4 e5 2. Nf3 Nc6 3. c3) was given an ! – but in fact it's worse than 3... Nf6.

And the Bishop's Game (1. e4 e5 2. Bc4) was ridiculed because of 2... Nf6 3. d3 d5 (which, in fact, favors White after 4. exd5 Nxd5 5. Nf3).

• It's An Ego Trip

The author quotes more of his own games than of any grandmaster's.

• It Ignores Transpositions

Some players recognize the Maroczy Bind trap of Diagram 65 when the position comes about by way of the Dragon Sicilian. But they fall into it when it arises by way of the English.

• It's Dogmatic

Siegbert Tarrasch was the bestknown writer of his day but he said, for example:

Hypermodern openings like 1. Nf3 were a "petty and cowardly strategy."

4. Ng5 in the Two Knights was "a typical example of a bungling move."

"All lines of play which lead to the imprisonment of a Bishop are on principle to be condemned!" – such as ...d6 in a main line Ruy Lopez.

And 1. d4 Nf6, is "certainly not correct."

A game played by Kasparov is more credible that one played by Neverhurdovich.

Pat: You mean GMs don't lie?

Noah: They don't lie in their games. There's too much at stake.

The only time they fudge the truth in the games they play is in grandmaster draws.

Pat: How does that work?

Noah: Well, as you probably suspect when a game ends after 15 moves between two guys rated over 2600 it often has nothing to do with the position. There's a cautionary tale here in Diagram 79.

Pat: This one is hard to believe. I'm like, Anand lost in six moves?

Noah: What happened is that a GM game with 5... Bf5, which had been agreed drawn in advance, was mentioned in the latest *Informant*. Readers concluded 5... Bf5 was playable.

Pat: It wasn't.

1. e4	e5
2. Nf3	Nf6

3. Nxe5	d6
4. Nf3	Nxe4
5. Nc3	Bf5??

79

As played in *Miles-Christiansen, San Francisco 1987,* which was drawn in 20 moves after 6. Nxe4 Bxe4 7. d3 Bg6 8. Bg5 etc. But in *Zapata-Anand, Biel 1988,* a draw wasn't agreed in advance, so:

6. Qe2!	1-0

Because 6... d5 7. d3 or 6... Qe7 7. Nd5 wins material.

Noah: Not even close. That's an extreme case, but there have literally been dozens of phony GM games that ended in a handshake

after Diagram 80, which weren't at all equal.

Pat: Looks pretty even to me.

Noah: Yes, but if you play this position as Black in the real world you'd better be prepared to be squeezed by a White who sees 12. Qb3!?.

Black may eventually equalize – but there's a lot more to the position than the downloads would indicate.

1. c4	c5
2. Nc3	Nc6
3. g3	g6
4. Bg2	Bg7
5. e3	e6
6. Nge2	Nge7
7. 0-0	0-0
8. d4	cxd4
9. Nxd4	Nxd4
10. exd4	d5
11. cxd5	Nxd5

80

The most common move here, at least in GM games, is 12. Nxd5 and then 12... exd5, draw agreed. But more promising is:

12. Qb3!?

White has a small edge after:

12. ...	Bxd4
13. Bh6	Bg7
14. Bxg7	Kxg7
15. Rfd1	

Regaining the pawn.

Pat: But you're saying that the moves played in most GM games are legitimate.

Noah: Of course, because in real games the GMs want to play the

"Chess is not skittles."
– **Garry Kasparov's only comment in *BCO*, after concluding that 1. c4 g5 is a winning position for White.**

best moves. Anyone does.

But published analysis is a different story.

Pat: Why?

Noah: Well, Tarrasch wasn't the only great opening authority who was dogmatic. A lot of big names make snap judgments and get them into print – because they're big names.

Also, just because a GM's name is on the cover doesn't mean he's staking his reputation on the analysis. Look at Diagram 81.

Pat: What do we have here?

Noah: This is from a 1986 Batsford book on the King's Gambit – with Viktor Korchnoi listed as one of the authors. They examined an offbeat line that leads to the diagram and concluded the position was "unclear" (∞) after 10... Qg3†.

Pat: It's unclear to me.

Noah: It may be – but the other check wins outright.

1. e4   e5
2. f4   exf4

3. Nf3   d6
4. d3   g5
5. h4   g4
6. Nd4   Qf6
7. Nb5   Na6
8. Bd2   f3
9. Bc3   Qf4
10. Bxh8

81

The book considered 10... Qg3† and 11... fxg2 "unclear."

But 10... Qe3†! 11. Be2 fxg2 wins on the spot, e.g. 12. Rf1 Be7 13. Qd2 g1=Q.

Pat: Isn't that rare?

Noah: I wish it were. But some of the blunders that appeared in print are

just ridiculous, such as Diagrams 82 through 86.

And my favorite is Diagram 87. (See the next two pages).

Pat: Why that one?

Noah: Because the author was trying to prove that Black's ♛ wasn't being trapped. He was looking for a trap that was staring him in the face.

Pat: Amazing.

Noah: But more often, a bad book will mislead you with superficial evaluations.

Pat: The snap judgments you were talking about.

Noah: Sure. In an endgame, a position can be analyzed to death – and there are only three conclusions: White wins, Black wins or, draw.

In openings, however, an analyst can get away with saying a position is plus over minus (±), or plus over equals (⩲) – with little or no supporting evidence.

Pat: I always suspected the GMs were just guessing when they did

BAD ANALYSIS MULTIPLIED

A Complete Defence to 1. P-K4 (1967) gave 1. e4 e5 2. Nf3 Nf6 3. d4 Nxe4 4. Bd3 d5 5. Nxe5 Be7 6. 0-0, a standard position, and now 6... Nd7! 7. c4 Nxe5 8. dxe5 Be6 9. cxd5.

82

It said that Black could play either 9... Bxd5 or 9... Qxd5 10. Qe2 Nc5.

But after 9... Qxd5?? White wins the ♘ with 10. Qa4†.

Die Sizilianische Verteidigung analyzed the Four Knights Variation (1. e4 c5 2. Nf3 e6 3. d4 cxd4 4. Nxd4 Nf6 5. Nc3 Nc6) and now 6. Nxc6 bxc6 7. e5 Nd5 8. Ne4 into a line that went 8... Qa5† 9. Bd2 Nb4 10. f4 Qd5 11. Nf2 Bc5 12. c3 Na6 13. Qg4 with advantage to White.

83

But the simple 13... Bxf2†! wins a piece.

In the first edition of *ECO's Volume C*, the analysis of the Siesta Variation of the Ruy Lopez (1. e4 e5 2. Nf3 Nc6 3. Bb5 a6 4. Ba4 d6 5. c3 f5) ran 6. exf5 Bxf5 7. 0-0 Bd3 8. Qb3 b5 9. Qe6† Nge7 10. Ng5 bxa4 11. Qf7† with the conclusion that White has perpetual check.

84

But after 10... Bc4 there is no perpetual and Black keeps a full ♖.

ECO's Volume D, first edition, copied an old analysis that ran 1. d4 d5 2. c4 dxc4 3. Nf3 Nf6 4. e3 g6 5. Bxc4 Bg7 6. Nc3 Nfd7 7. h3 — without mentioning that 7. Bxf7† wins.

Also in that edition. a main Meran line went 1. d4 d5 2. c4 c6 3. Nc3 Nf6 4, Nf3 e6 5. e3 Nbd7 6. Bd3 dxc4 7. Bxc4 b5 8. Bd3 a6 9. e4 c5 10. e5 cxd4 11. Nxb5 Ng4 12. Qa4 Rb8 13. Nd6† Bxd6 14. exd6 Qb6 15. Qxd4 with the verdict that White has good chances.

85

But several strong players have lost quickly after 15... Nde5! (16. Nxe5 Qxd4 and 16. Qxb6 Nxd3†).

In annotating Fischer-Polugayevsky, Palma de Mallorca 1970 (which began 1. c4 Nf6 2. g3 c6 3. Bg2 d5 4. Nf3 Bf5 5. Qb3 Qb6 6. cxd5 Qxb3 7. axb3 cxd5) the *Informant* said White would have been better after 7... Nxd5 because of 8. Nc3 Nb4 9. Nd4 Bg6 10. Ra4 N8a6 11. Nxc6!.

86

When this was tested in *Sumiacher-Polugayevsky, Mar del Plata 1971,* Black played 9... e5! and White was lost.

1.	e4	d6
2.	d4	Nf6
3.	Nc3	c6
4.	f4	Qa5
5.	Bd3	e5
6.	Nf3	Bg4
7.	Be3	exf4
8.	Bxf4	Qb4

In "A Complete Black Defensive System with 1... d6" a main line goes this way saying "The trappy 9. a3 Qxb2 10. Na4 backfires" because of:

9.	a3	Qxb2??
10.	Na4	Bxf3
11.	gxf3	Qxd4

87

But 12. c3 wins the ♕.

that.

Noah: Often they are. Alexander Khalifman said he won two games in 1997 when he adopted a King's Indian line that had been mis-evaluated as merely a plus over equals – and therefore not too bad for Black – but was really plus over minus.

Another example is Diagram 88.

Pat: What's the deal here?

Noah: You're looking at a very risky move by Black. The ♛ is badly placed on b6 because it is lined up against the B/e3. Also, the ♛ can be kicked back by Na4 any time White wishes. And the immediate effect of ...Qb6 is to prompt White to put his a-♖ on its best square, b1.

Pat: I would have played 10... Nef5 instead. But what do I know?

Noah: You'd know enough. The point is that a snap judgment about 10... Qb6, coupled with what a Russian analyst called "the hypnotic effect of an exclamation point in the *Informant,*" made it look good.

1. e4	c5
2. Nc3	Nc6
3. g3	g6
4. Bg2	Bg7
5. d3	d6
6. f4	e6
7. Nf3	Nge7
8. 0-0	0-0
9. Be3	Nd4
10. e5	Qb6?

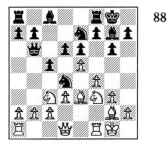

88

Given an exclamation point in an *Informant.*

11. Rb1	Nef5
12. Bf2	Nxf3†
13. Qxf3	dxe5
14. fxe5	

This is an obvious move, but in the *Informant* 14. Na4? Qc7 15. fxe5 Bxe5 16. Bxc5 Bd7! 17. Bxf8 Rxf8 and ...Bd4†/...Ne3 was given instead.

14. ...	Bxe5
15. Ne4!	

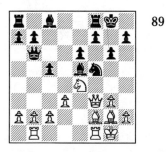

89

And White is better as Yuri Balashov showed in two games that went 15... Bd7 16. Bxc5 Bd4† 17. Kh1! and 15... Nd4 16. Qd1 f5 17. Nd2 Qc7 18. c3!.

Pat: Seems like this is more about middlegame positions than evaluating the opening.

Noah: That's because the more the opening phase is explored, the later

in the game we can say the opening ends.

And the more the opening is explored, the more superficial evaluations can be tossed out. That's what happened in Diagram 90.

Pat: I kinda like White.

Noah: So did the books – until recently. As late as ten years ago this type of position would be routinely given a plus-over-minus sign.

Pat: Because of the lead in development, right?

Noah: And because of that ♘ on e5. And because White can capture the light-squared ♗ with that ♘ when he wants. And because he can get his ♖s to the best-looking files.

Pat: Looks like White is just waiting for the kill. Like after Black castles, he can sack on h6.

Noah: But he waits in vain. The position simply isn't as good as it looks.

There's a limit to what White can do with his development and Black should equalize.

Ivanchuk-Karpov
Dortmund 1997

1. e4	c6
2. d4	d5
3. Nd2	dxe4
4. Nxe4	Nd7
5. Ng5	Ngf6
6. Bd3	e6
7. N1f3	Bd6
8. Qe2	h6
9. Ne4	Nxe4
10. Qxe4	c5
11. 0-0	Nf6
12. Qh4	Qc7
13. Re1	Bd7
14. Bg5	Be7
15. dxc5	Qxc5
16. Ne5	Bc6

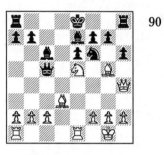

90

White gets nothing from 17. Nxc6 Qxg5! or 17. Rad1 Nd5 18. Bxe7 Qxe7.

17. Qh3   Rd8!

Black prepares to castle since he can meet a sacrifice on h6 with ...Rxd3!.

18. Rad1

Not 18. Nxf7 Kxf7 19. Qxe6† Kf8 20. Bg6 Bd5! and Black wins.

18. ...   Ne4!

Black liquidates into an even endgame (19. Bxe4 Rxd1 20. Bxc6† bxc6 21. Rxd1 Qxe5).

The vital tactical point is that 19. Bxe7? allows 19... Qxf2† 20. Kh1 Qxe1†! and ....Nf2†/...Nxh3†.

Pat: So the moral for all this is what – that there's a lot of bad analysis out there and I don't have to know it?

Noah: And that you can get away with knowing fewer openings and a lot less book knowledge than you think you do.

But come back tomorrow and we'll talk about which openings.

"Trust in authority is what I have to thank for many a defeat."
– Siegbert Tarrasch

In which Pat discovers cult, category and long-weekend openings, and that variations can be fragile, low-risk or low-maintenance.

Chapter
Four:

PICKING
AND
CHOOSING

Noah: You know I've been thinking about that first game you showed me.

Pat: That terrible Nimzo-Indian I lost in 19 moves? Don't remind me.

Noah: I want to because I think I know when you made your first mistake.

Pat: Gimme a hint. Move six? Seven? Eight?

Noah: No, move one – I suspect you may be playing the wrong openings.

Pat: I play the ones I like.

Noah: But they may not like you. Or you may have outgrown them.

Beginners tend to like all openings equally. It's a sign of maturing when you realize that some openings are just right and some just wrong for you.

Pat: How do you pick the right ones?

Noah: You can start with today's rule number one:

STAY IN CHARACTER

Pat: Which means...

Noah: Which means you already know what types of positions you do well with. When you select an opening it should fit naturally into your chess character.

Pat: I never thought I had one.

Noah: Everyone does. It's the sum of the personality traits a player reveals in his or her moves. Sometimes even a world-class GM, with a very distinct chess character, can wander into the wrong opening, as in Diagram 91.

This is from the first round of an Olympiad team tournament when Mikhail Tal decided he could experiment against an obscure Australian master.

Pat: Looks like Tal just didn't know the book move.

Noah: But that's bound to happen when you play something new. Tal's real mistake was not 6... Qc7, but his decision to adopt an un-Tal-like line of the Caro-Kann Defense.

Jamieson-Tal
Nice 1974

1. e4	c6
2. d4	d5
3. Nc3	dxe4
4. Nxe4	Nf6
5. Nxf6†	gxf6
6. Bc4	

91

Black should play 6... Bf5 so he can continue ...e6. Tal played a natural, but in this position, dreadful move:

6. ...	Qc7?

And after his B/c8 was locked in ...

7. Qh5!	e6
8. Ne2	Na6

9. Bf4

White has an obvious edge. The former world champion was lucky to draw.

"I have never in my life played the French Defense, which is the dullest of all openings."
– Wilhelm Steinitz, revealing a bit of his chess character

Picking and Choosing

"I play for a draw in the Sicilian Defense, but for a win in the Caro-Kann!"
– an unrepentent Tal, after he rejected a draw as Black in a Caro-Kann in 1977

Noah: The same goes for Diagram 92. You're right if you say White lost because he made an oversight. But there's a deeper reason.

Pat: Which you're going to tell me.

Noah: I will. But first, let me explain that this came from an alternating simultaneous exhibition.

Pat: Translation, please.

Noah: That means the two players handling White, Alexander Alekhine and Salo Landau, gave a joint simul. Alekhine played one move and Landau played the next one.

Pat: What went wrong?

Noah: What went wrong is that they ended up in a typical Sicilian Defense position – the type that would fit in well with Alekhine's aggressive character.

But it didn't fit in with Landau's, a conservative 1. d4 player.

Alekhine & Landau - NN
Blindfold simul 1934

1. e4	c5
2. Nf3	e6
3. d4	cxd4
4. Nxd4	Nf6

92

5. Bg5??	Qa5†
6. Qd2	

Or 6. Bd2 Qb6, winning a ♟.

6. ...	Bb4
7. c3	Nxe4!

Pat: It's not hard to guess which guy played 5. Bg5.

Noah: Not very. That leads us to rule number two:

IGNORE FASHION

Pat: You mean the openings that the GMs are playing now? But I like

"If you're afraid of the move a4-a5, don't play the Benoni."
– Garry Kasparov, on staying in character after 1. d4 Nf6 2. c4 c5

OUT OF CHARACTER

Other great players had out-of-character quirks in their opening repertoire. For example, **Anatoly Karpov** played conservative systems against almost all Sicilian Defense variations — but when facing 1. e4 c5 2. Nf3 d6 3. d4 cxd4 4. Nxd4 Nf6 5. Nc3 e6 he regularly adopted the sharpest, most double-edged move, 6. g4!?.

Also, **Tigran Petrosian** was devoted to the dubious Najdorf Sicilian variation that goes 1. e4 c5 2. Nf3 d6 3. d4 cxd4 4. Nxd4 Nf6 5. Nc3 a6 6. Bg5 Nbd7?!. He continued to play it even after getting lost positions by move 20 — including a key game in his loss of the world championship.

"It is always advisable to avoid openings that cover more than four pages in an Informant!"
— Viswanathan Anand

some of the popular stuff.

Noah: So does everyone else. The trendier the opening, the more likely your opponent will know as much about it as you. Or more.

Pat: Some strange stuff is going on from move 16 to 24.

Noah: It's all heavily analyzed book – up to a point. The point comes at the 28th move.

Pat: The first new thing in this game is move 28?

Noah: Yes, and that's part of the psychological trap you fall into in a lot of fashionable openings.

You think because all sorts of high-Elo players have endorsed the first 20 or so moves of an opening, that you're on solid ground by following the notes in the latest computer download.

In fact, that often means you end up losing a game without ever being in it.

Relange-Sadler
Hastings 1997/1998
1. e4 c5 2. Nf3 d6 3. d4 cxd4 4. Nxd4 Nf6 5. Nc3 a6 6. Bg5 e6 7.

That's bound to happen in the lines you see over and over in the *Informant*. Take Diagram 93.

f4 Be7 8. Qf3 Qc7 9. 0-0-0 Nbd7 10. g4 b5 11. Bxf6 Nxf6 12. g5 Nd7 13. f5 Bxg5† 14. Kb1 Ne5 15. Qh5 Qd8.

There are a few, very few, alternatives to be considered in moves of this supersharp line, such as 15... Qe7 or, after 15... Qd8, 16. Rg1. The players are still relying on memory.

16. Nxe6 Bxe6 17. fxe6 0-0 18. Rg1 Bf6 19. exf7† Kh8 20. Nd5 g6 21. Qh3 Rxf7 22. Nf4 Qd7 23. Qb3 Qc6 24. Bh3 Bg7 25. Rgf1 Raf8 26. Ne6 Rxf1 27. Bxf1 Rf2.

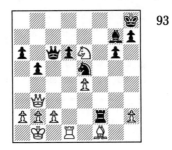

93

28. a4??

This position had been reached

several months before – by Sadler, who was Black in that game, too. But then he replied 28... b4?? and lost.

28. ...   bxa4!

And Black won quickly: 29. Qb8† Bf8 30. Nxf8 Qxc2† 31. Ka2 Nc6!.

Then 32. Nxg6† Kg7 33. Qb7† (33. Qc7† or 33. Qh8† are met by 33... Kh6!) Rf7! and wins.

For example, 34. Qb6 a5, threatening 35... Nb4† (35. Rb1 Nb4† 36. Ka1 Qxb1†! 37. Kxb1 Rxf1#).

Pat: But I thought the reason some openings are played over and over by the GMs is because they're the best openings.

Noah: Rubbish. For a century nobody played the Evans Gambit. People thought it was refuted or that the players who used to use it were just weak – patzers like Paul Morphy and Mikhail Chigorin.

Then Garry Kasparov played the Evans in 1995 and it suddenly be-

"The words 'best defense,' 'best move,' 'strongest move' make me afraid. Oh, I say them myself. But do you notice how often the strongest move is only the strongest move today and considerably weaker tomorrow?"
– Mikhail Chigorin

came a serious opening again.

Pat: So, the moral is I should play something like the Evans?

Noah: No, the moral is rule number three:

FIND YOUR OWN WEAPONS

You don't have to invent something to have a solid and strong opening arsenal. You need something that you feel comfortable with – that was rule number one, if you remember.

Pat: I haven't forgotten it – yet.

Noah: And it helps if your weapons are also ripe for revival, if they're little-known openings that aren't as bad as they're supposed to be.

Pat: But there are just so many openings. How do I know what I want?

Noah: Ask yourself some questions. Such as:

Do I need an advantage from the opening or just a position I can play in the middlegame?

If the answer is *just a position* you might do perfectly well with 1. Nf3 and 2. b3 followed by Bb2 and e3.

Or with 1. d4, 2. Nf3, 3. Bf4, 4. e3 followed by Nbd2, Bd3, and 0-0 almost regardless of what Black does.

Pat: Not me. I want to feel I've gotten something out of all the time I've spent going blind looking at opening books.

Noah: Then you need to find openings that promise a good chance of getting an edge, at least as White. So the question is, how much edge?

Pat: Shouldn't I want the most I can get?

Noah: That depends on how much you want to work at the board – or study away from it.

Diagram 95 shows what happened once when a Polish IM played 1. Nc3 against Tal. Tal figured he deserved only a good position, not a refutation. Remember: Black is not White.

Pat: I've heard.

OPENINGS OVERDUE FOR BEING REDISCOVERED

After 1. e4 e5 2. Nf3 Nc6 instead of the Ruy Lopez, consider 3. Bc4 since the Two Knights (3... Nf6 4. Ng5) virtually forces Black to sacrifice a ♙. Lots of theory that nobody remembers.

The French is filled with choices for Black that haven't been studied seriously for decades. Among them are the McCutcheon Variation (3. Nc3 Nf6 4 Bg5 Bb4), Tartakower's 3. Nc3 Nf6 4. Bg5 Be7 5. e5 Ne4 (6. Bxe7 Qxe7 7. Nxe4 dxe4 and ...b6) and the Tarrasch with 3. Nd2 Nc6, 3... Ne7 or 3... Be7. Or even 3. Nc3 Be7.

Also the virtually un-booked neo-Rubinstein — 3. Nd2 or 3. Nc3 and now 3... dxe4 4. Nxe4 Qd5.

94

Black has active play after 5. Bd3 Nf6 6. Nxf6† gxf6 7. Nf3 Rg8 or 5. Nc3 Bb4 6. Nf3 Nf6 7. Bd3 Ne4.

There's still plenty of room for new ideas after 1. d4 d5 for Black in the Chigorin QGD. Or the Slav with 3. Nc3 dxc4 or 3. Nf3 dxc4 — which you won't find in books like *MCO*.

The non-Exchange and non-Qb3 lines of the Gruenfeld have plenty of good ideas for White that have been out of fashion for decades— but never refuted.

The Antoshin Variation of the Dutch — 1. d4 f5 followed by 2... Nf6, 3... d6, 4... c6, 5... Qc7 and 6... e5. Sound but virtually unknown today.

"To be able to avoid what everyone knows in the opening it's necessary to know what nobody knows."
— Mikhail Botvinnik

Picking and Choosing

Noah: Tal's decision to play 1... c5, rather than 1... e5 or 1... d5, was partly psychological. He thought

"People looked at me like I needed a doctor."
– **Alexey Shirov when he played 1. c4 e5 2. Nc3 Bb4 3. Nd5 Be7 at Manila 1990, before it became popular.**

that if someone plays 1. Nc3 they probably don't want to get into an orthodox Sicilian line – even though it means playing the best move, 2. e4!.

Pat: And in the end, Black got an advantage after all – even though he wasn't looking for it.

Sydor-Tal
Lublin 1974

1. Nc3   c5

Black declines the adventures of 1... d5 2. e4 d4 3. Nce2 e5 4. f4 or 2... dxe4 3. Nxe4 e5 4. Nf3.

2. Nf3   Nc6
3. d4   cxd4
4. Nxd4   Nf6

(board diagram, labeled 95)

In his effort to avoid book White played:

5. Bg5?   e6
6. e3   Bb4!
7. Qd2   h6
8. Bxf6

Not 8. Bh4 g5 9. Bg3 Ne4.

8. ...   Qxf6
9. a3   Ba5
10. Be2   d5

With a clear edge for Black.

Noah: That often happens. Another case of modest development paying off is the Budapest Defense. When it was young, in the 1920s and 1930s, White tried to crush 3... Ng4 with the most aggressive lines.
Pat: Like what?
Noah: Like kicking the ♘ around with 4. e4 Nxe5 5. f4.

Or by keeping the extra ♙ with 4. Bf4 Nc6 5. Nf3 Bb4† 6. Nc3.
Pat: What's wrong with those lines?
Noah: Nothing really. But they require White to accept a fair amount of risk. That stands to reason when

you accept a gambit or push all your center ♙s to the fourth rank.

But around 1970, when the Budapest was more than 50 years old, attitudes changed about how much advantage White needed. After it was realized he could get a small but risk-free edge with 4. Nf3, that became a main line.

1. d4   Nf6
2. c4   e5
3. dxe5   Ng4
4. Nf3

Considered a bad move for decades because Black now locks in White's B/c1.

4. ...   Bc5

Or 4... Nc6 5. Bg5! with a superior game for White (5... Be7 6. Bxe7 Qxe7 7. Nc3 and Nd5. And 5... Bb4† 6. Nbd2 Be7 7. Bf4!.

5. e3   Nc6
6. a3   a5
7. b3   0-0
8. Nc3   Re8

LOW MAINTENANCE, LOW RISK

With 1. e4:

The 3. Bb5† **Sicilian** (after 1. e4 c5 2. Nf3 d6)

3. exd5 exd5 4. c4 versus the **French** (after 1. e4 e6 2. d4 d5)

Delayed Exchange Variation of the Lopez (1. e4 e5 2. Nf3 Nc6 3. Bb5 a6 4. Ba4 Nf6 5. 0-0 Be7 6. Bxc6 dxc6 7. d3 and Nbd2-c4)

The **Bishop's Opening/Vienna Game** in which White plays Nc3, Bc4 and d3 (1. e4 e5 2. Bc4 Nf6 3. d3 Nc6 4. Nc3 and now 4... Bc5 5. Nf3 d6 6. Na4!?, e.g. 6... Bb6 7. c3 Be6 8. Bb5 00 9. Bxc6 bxc6 10. Bg5)

On 1. d4:

Meeting the **King's Indian** with 1. d4 Nf6 2. Nf3 g6 3. Nc3 and 4. Bf4, or

Playing b3 in the **Fianchetto Variation** (such as 1. d4 Nf6 2. c4 g6 3. g3 Bg7 4. Bg2 0-0 5. Nf3 d6 6. 0-0 Nbd7 7. Nc3 e5 8. e4 c6 and now 9. b3, rather than the main line 9. h3)

Against a **Benoni/Benko** player, trying 1. d4 Nf6 2. Nf3 c5 3. e3 with the idea of 3... g6 4. dxc5! and then 4... Qa5† 5. Nbd2 Qxc5 6. a3 and 7. b4

2. Nc3 and Bg5 against the **Dutch** (1. d4 f5)

And why go into the complex **Meran** after 1. d4 d5 2. c4 c6 3. Nc3 Nf6 4. e3 e6 when you can play simply and solidly a la Yusupov — with 5. b3 and 6. Bb2 ?

With Black:

The 5... exf6 **Caro-Kann** (1. e4 c6 2. d4 d5 3. Nc3 dxe4 4. Nxe4 Nf6 5. Nxf6†)

The Botvinnik line in **Richter-Rauzer** (1. e4 c5 2. Nf3 d6 3. d4 cxd4 4. Nxd4 Nf6 5. Nc3 Nc6 6. Bg5 e6 7. Qd2 h6 8. Bxf6 gxf6 — another serious opening White can hardly avoid after 6. Bg5 but you won't find it in encyclopedic books like *MCO*)

The **Queen's Gambit Accepted** (1. d4 d5 2. c4 dxc4) with 3. Nf3 Nf6 4. e3 Bg4 is supposed to be inferior. But there's only a tiny edge for White — and in only a few, little-known lines.

The **Bogo-Indian** (1. d4 Nf6 2. c4 e6 3. Nf3 Bb4†) rarely gives Black an edge but assures him at worst a very slight inferiority with easy to find moves.

Picking and Choosing

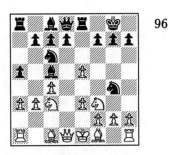

96

9. Be2	Ncxe5
10. Nxe5	Nxe5
11. 0-0	

And Bb2, with an excellent game for White at very little risk.

Pat: I guess I'm not too crazy about taking risks in the opening.

Noah: Then what you should do when shopping around for a new system is to check the books – and look carefully for the sharpest, most dangerous reply that your opponent might choose. Then see if you're comfortable playing against it.

Pat: Isn't the scariest line obvious?

Noah: No, that changes with theory. The Exchange Variation of the Ruy Lopez with 5. 0-0 was a terrific, no-risk weapon for White when Bobby Fischer began using it more than 30 years ago.

It was virtually unknown and all the lines, such as 5... f6 or 5... Bg4 or 5... Bd6, ended in plus-over-equals signs for White – at least.

Pat: Then what happened?

Noah: Then Black discovered 5... Qd6 and ...0-0-0 and suddenly there was a way White could lose. The Exchange Ruy was no longer no-risk.

Pat: So I should be looking for openings where I won't have to go ♟-grabbing or risk hanging my King.

Noah: If that's what your chess character calls for. But remember, the amount of risk attached to an opening may change as theory changes.

For example, the Gruenfeld used to be considered much more solid than alternative 1.d4 defenses such as the King's Indian and Benoni.

But today the Gruenfeld may force Black to accept a risky gambit if White plays the Modern Exchange line.

Pat: White has to sacrifice and Black has to accept?

Noah: More or less. If White plays differently after 9. Be2 he has no edge, and if Black doesn't grab the ♟ he's just worse. Diagram 97 is something you absolutely have to know if you're playing the Gruenfeld today.

1. d4	Nf6
2. c4	g6
3. Nc3	d5
4. cxd5	Nxd5
5. e4	Nxc3
6. bxc3	Bg7
7. Nf3	c5
8. Rb1	0-0
9. Be2	cxd4

Playing to win a ♟. After 9... b6 10. 0-0 Bb7 White has an advantage with 11. d5 or 11. Qd3 (11... Ba6 12. Qe3 cxd4 13. cxd4 Qd7 14.

"Capablanca was right when he said that fashionable openings are just copied from other players (just like children do at exams)..."
– Leonid Yudasin

d5!).

As a *New In Chess* writer put it, "It is always pleasant... when one's opponent does not take the a-♙. After all, now only White has chances."

10. cxd4   Qa5†
11. Bd2

In the early 1990s it was found that 11. Qd2 Qxd2† 12. Bxd2 e6 isn't much for White so...

11. ...   Qxa2

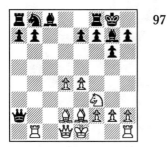

97

Typical play would be 12. 0-0 and 13. Bg5 with compensation for a ♙.

Pat: Maybe the Gruenfeld isn't for me.

Noah: Maybe not. But the risk takers are often the players who are rewarded in the opening. Check out the games of Bent Larsen, Tony Miles and Oleg Romanishin for proof.

But you have to determine your own risk-tolerance level.

Pat: You mean I can't trust the books on that?

Noah: Definitely not. The priority of most opening literature is to establish the truth about lines: Who's better and by how much?

The books measure openings in terms of advantage or disadvantage, not risk. For instance, there's a dicey line in the Accelerated Dragon that comes to mind.

Pat: How dicey?

Noah: You'll see how much in Diagram 98. The books have worked out all sorts of lines that favor White. On paper it looks like it's worth a shot.

But virtually no one is willing to

OTHER LOW-RISK, LOW-PROFILE LINES FOR WHITE

After 1. d4:

4. a4 versus the **Benko Gambit** (1. d4 Nf6 2. c4 c5 3. d5 b5 and then 4. a4 bxc4 5. Nc3 followed by e4 and Bxc4, or 4... b4 5. Nd2 and 6. e4)

7. f3 against the **Modern Benoni** (1. d4 Nf6 2. c4 c5 3. d5 e6 4. Nc3 exd5 5. cxd5 d6 6. e4 g6 and now 7. f3 Bg7 8. Bg5)

5. h3 versus the **King's Indian Defense** (1. d4 Nf6 2. c4 g6 3. Nc3 Bg7 4. e4 d6 and now 5. h3 0-0 6. Bg5 followed by Bd3)

Spielmann's 4. Qb3 in the **Nimzo-Indian** (1. d4 Nf6 2. c4 e6 3. Nc3 Bb4 and now 4. Qb3 c5 5. dxc5)

4. Bf4 in the **Queen's Indian** (1. d4 Nf6 2. c4 e6 3. Nf3 b6 and now 4. Bf4 Bb7 5. e3 Be7 6. h3 and Nc3).

After 1. e4:

3. Nc3 versus the **Alekhine's** (1. e4 Nf6 2. e5 Nd5 and now 3. Nc3 Nxc3 4. bxc3 d5 5. d4 or 4... d6 5 f4)

2. d3 versus the **Caro-Kann** (1. e4 c6 and now 2. d3 d5 3. Nd2 as in a **King's Indian Reversed**).

try it over-the-board.

1.	e4	c5
2.	Nf3	Nc6
3.	d4	cxd4
4.	Nxd4	g6
5.	Nc3	Bg7
6.	Be3	Nf6

The books indicate White has moderate opportunities for an edge after 7. Nb3 or 7. Bc4. But there is also:

7.	Nxc6	bxc6
8.	e5	Nd5

White appears to get an edge from 8... Ng8 9. Bd4.

9.	Nxd5	cxd5
10.	Qxd5	

98

With immense complications, such as 10... Rb8 11. Bxa7 Rxb2 12. Bd4 or 11. 0-0-0 (and if 11... 0-0 then 12. Bxa7!).

Pat: Looks way too risky for me.

Noah: That's for you to determine. But consider what happens after 1. e4 c5 2. Nf3 Nf6.

You can avoid the theoretical debate with 3. Nc3 – and almost certainly transpose into a normal Sicilian after 4. d4.

Pat: I have a feeling you're about to say "but."

Noah: But experience indicates White's best chance lies in 3. e5 Nd5 4. Nc3 even though his ♙-structure is damaged after 4... Nxc3 5. dxc3.

He's betting that Black's cramped position will count more in the middlegame than Black's superior ♙-structure. That's a different kind of gambit and a different kind of risk.

Pat: I thought a gambit meant sacrificing a ♙.

Noah: That depends on how you look at it. Larsen said it was a kind of gambit for Black to play 1. d4 g6 2. Nf3 d6 3. g3 Bg7 4. Bg2 Nf6 5. 0-0 and now 5... Nc6 6 d5 Nb8.

Instead of material, Black gives up time and part of the center – but he gets control of squares such as c5 and lures White into an unfamiliar position in which he can go too far.

Pat: Are there any other low-risk opening that aren't well known?

Noah: Not only low-risk but low-maintenance.

Pat: Meaning?

Noah: Meaning they don't require the devotion of studying like a Talmudic scholar.

There's relatively little theory about them and the theory that exists changes very slowly. Several examples come to mind (page 64).

There's another good question you should be asking yourself:

Do I usually try to score big in the opening? Or do I like to defer making decisions, and the heavy thinking, until the middlegame?

Pat: I never thought about that.

Noah: Well, then you should be aware that some openings, like the Sicilian, Gruenfeld, and King's Indian, start the fight in the opening. There are major decisions by move 10, and the margin of error is narrow. One bad move can be fatal.

Other openings, such as the Caro-Kann, QGD, and Queen's Indian, more or less postpone the battle of ideas until the middlegame.

Pat: Or to the endgame. Some of those Caro-Kann positions put me to sleep.

Noah: Perhaps. But even in sharp openings there are ways to put off the heavy thinking until well after you've finished development.

In the Sicilian you play the Closed with 2. Nc3, and even without much book knowledge you won't have to think until move 10.

Or the Ruy Lopez with 5. d3

instead of the main line 5. 0-0. But an even better way of avoiding a memory battle after 1. e4 e5 is to adopt the Pseudo Lopez.

Pat: What's that?

Noah: That's 1. e4 e5 2. Nf3 Nc6 3. Bc4 and 4. d3 followed by handling White's pieces like in a Ruy Lopez with c3, Bb3, 0-0 and Re1, Nbd2-f1-g3 and eventually d4.

It's the Ruy without having to know yesterday's innovation in the Marshall Gambit or today's TN in the Open Defense – or tomorrow's new idea in the Schliemann.

Pat: I get the picture.

Noah: The bottom line is – don't take up an opening that will require more study than you're capable of.

Pat: Even if I like it?

Noah: You'll like winning more.

So, don't play the Dragon or Najdorf Sicilian, the Marshall Gambits in the Ruy Lopez or Semi-Slav or the Botvinnik line of the Semi-Slav if you don't have the free hours to keep up on theory. Ask yourself how much time you can spend – and budget it.

Pat: Okay. What else should I be asking myself when I choose an opening?

Noah: A good question that's related to the last one is:

Do I like openings I can prepare extensively?

Or at least that I can be sure I'm better prepared in than a typical opponent?

Pat: I guess the answer is – sort of.

Noah: If you really mean it, then consider the Dilworth or Riga Variations of the Open Ruy Lopez. Some of the main lines have been analyzed past move 30.

Pat: Doesn't that mean a lot of study?

Noah: You can ace them in a long weekend. And there are a couple of good features to these lines.

First, the theory on them hasn't changed much since Viktor Korchnoi was a fourth-grader – and it's unlikely to change much in the future. Once you've mastered one

"Frankly, the King's Indian Defense is a riskier undertaking for Black than the King's Gambit is for White."
–David Bronstein

"One must choose openings systems of small popularity because the positional themes of these systems are not well known."
–Mikhail Botvinnik

of these lines you probably won't have to look them up in an *Informant* for years.

Pat: What's the second good thing?

Noah: Secondly, White doesn't have much choice until you steer the position into your preparation.

The Ruy Lopez is by far the most popular 1. e4 e5 opening. And after 5... Nxe4 White has no chance of an advantage if he doesn't play 6. d4.

Pat: So if White plays 1. e4 you have a pretty good chance of getting to play the 6... exd4 Riga positions.

Noah: Right. And unless White really knows his theory, he has to find some remarkable moves, such as 10. Kh1 and 11. Rxe4† and 12. Qd8†. In fact, he has to find about 10 "only" moves to reach an advantage in Diagam 101 – and it's not clear that it's much of an advantage.

Pat: And in the Dilworth?

Noah: Once Black takes on e4 at move five, White's only real way of

---

TWO VARIATIONS WORTH A LONG WEEKEND #1

The Dilworth Variation
1. e4 e5 2. Nf3 Nc6 3. Bb5 a6 4. Ba4 Nf6 5. 0-0 Nxe4 6. d4 b5 7. Bb3 d5 8. dxe5 Be6 9. c3 Bc5 10. Nbd2 0-0 11. Bc2

11.   ...   Nxf2
This is Dilworth's move.
12. Rxf2   f6

99

White is more or less forced to try 13. exf6 Bxf2† 14. Kxf2 Qxf6 15. Nf1 Ne5 16. Be3.

Then 16... Rae8 leads into equal positions after 17. Bc5 Nxf3 18. gxf3 Rf7! or 17. Kg1 Nxf3† 18. gxf3 Qxf3.

---

avoiding the Dilworth – if he wants an advantage – is with 9. Nbd2 or with 10. Qd3, neither of which you'll see much.

Pat: So what you're saying is that if I adopt the Dilworth I have very good chances of reaching the position after 16... Rae8 – or a better one for Black.

Noah: That's what I meant about budgeting your study time.

Pat: You mean because these long-weekend lines are like an investment in the future.

Noah: Very much so. There's another one that comes to mind in the Petroff Defense. Black can get it if White plays 3. d4. That's not as popular as 3. Nxe5 but it's still played a lot.

Pat: What's the similarity to the Riga and Dilworth?

Noah: The Petroff line also gets you into an endgame – and it's one you can be 99% sure that you will know better than your opponent. Also, it's filled with "only" moves for White. That's it in Diagram 102.

1. e4	e5
2. Nf3	Nf6
3. d4	Nxe4
4. Bd3	d5
5. Nxe5	Bd6
6. 0-0	0-0
7. c4	

White's fourth, fifth and sixth moves were more or less automatic. Black can handle 7. Nc3 with 7... Nxc3 8. bxc3 Nd7 and 7. Nd2 with 7... Bxe5 8. dxe5 Nc5 and ... Nxd3.

TWO VARIATIONS WORTH A LONG WEEKEND #2

THE RIGA VARIATION
1. e4 e5 2. Nf3 Nc6 3. Bb5 a6 4. Ba4 Nf6 5. 0-0 Nxe4 6. d4 exd4!?

100

Only one line has been found to give White any edge at all. Believe it or not, it goes:

7. Re1   d5

Now 8. Bg5 Be7 9. Bxe7 Kxe7! is fine for Black (10. Bxc6 bxc6 11. Nxd4 Kf8).

8. Nxd4

The other alternatives are 8. Ne5 Bd6! 9. Nxc6 Bxh2† as in the main line and 8. c4 dxc3 9. Nxc3 Bb4!.

8. ...   Bd6!
9. Nxc6

Here 9. Qh5 0-0 gives Black the better of it after 10. Nxc6 bxc6 11. Bxc6 Rb8.

Also 9. Nd2 Bxh2† 10. Kf1 0-0 11. Nxc6 Qh4!.

9. ...   Bxh2†

Now 10. Kxh2 Qh4† 11. Kg1 Qxf2† is perpetual check.

And 10. Kf1 Qh4! gives Black fine chances (11. Nd4† b5 12. Be3 0-0 13. Nf3 Qh5 and 14... Bg4 or 11. Be3 0-0 12. Nd4 Bg4).

10. Kh1!   Qh4
11. Rxe4†!

The only move: 11. Nd4† Kf8 favors Black as does 11. Bg5 Qxg5 12. Qxd5 Qxd5 13. Nb4† Kd8!.

11. ...   dxe4
12. Qd8†   Qxd8
13. Nxd8†   Kxd8
14. Kxh2   Be6
15. Be3

Not 15. Nc3 c5, threatening 16... b5 17. Bb3 c4, when Black may be better.

15. ...   f5
16. Nc3   Ke7
17. g4   g6

101

The poor reputation of this opening is due to a single game, *Capablanca—Ed. Lasker, New York 1915*, which White won after 18. Kg3 h5 19. gxf5 h4†? 20. Kh2.

But 19... gxf5 gives Black a fine game.

7. ...	Bxe5
8. dxe5	Nc6

Now 9. f4 Bf5 or 9. Bf4 Nb4 give Black easy equality. There is only one bid for superiority, 9. cxd5.

9. cxd5	Qxd5
10. Qc2	

Otherwise the e-♟ is lost (10. f4 Qc5† or 10. Qe2 Nc5).

"The true Dragon player will analyze six Exchange sacrifices on c3 before breakfast."
– John Nunn

10. ...	Nb4!
11. Bxe4	Nxc2
12. Bxd5	Bf5!

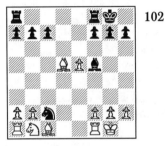

102

The key variation – known by only a few fanatics – is 13. g4! Bxg4 14. Be4 Nxa1 15. Bf4 f5 16. Bd5† Kh8 17. Rc1 c6 18. Bg2 Rfd8 19. Nd2 Rxd2! 20. Bxd2 Rd8, with roughly equal chances.

Pat: What else do I have to worry about in picking an opening?

Noah: You have to recognize when an opening is "fragile."

Pat: Fragile?

Noah: Yes, when it's highly vulnerable to a TN that will change its status. One strong novelty by Black can put the Velimirovic Attack out of business in the Sozin Sicilian, at least for awhile.

Or one strong TN for White might retire the Polugayevsky or Poisoned Pawn Variations of the 6. Bg5 Najdorf. The newer or more tactical the line, the more fragile it may be.

That's a far cry from the Maroczy Bind or the QGD, which are almost TN-proof. If you play a fragile line you have to spend a lot more time on research.

Pat: What else do I have to be scared of?

Noah: Beware of being seduced by pretty analysis that you may never get a chance to play.

For instance, if you look up the Belgrade Gambit, you'll find all sorts of exciting variations that White would enjoy.

Pat: Here's where you're going to say "but," right?

Noah: But the real test of the Belgrade is the dull 5... Be7. It's dull but

simple for Black to play and to equalize with. Even if you love the four other lines at move five as White you may hate the main line.

1. e4	e5
2. Nf3	Nc6
3. Nc3	Nf6
4. d4	exd4
5. Nd5	

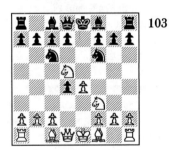

103

Among the wild variations are 5... Nxe4, 5... Nxd5, 5... Bb4† and 5... Nb4.

For example, 5... Nxe4 6. Qe2 f5 7. Ng5 and now 7... d3! 8. cxd3 Nd4 is necessary.

5. ...	Be7!

White has nothing better than regaining his ♙ with:

6. Bf4   d6
7. Nxd4

After which 7... 0-0 and 8... Nxd5 followed by ...Ne5/...Bf6 gives Black easy equality.

Pat: Okay, I've decided I don't like to take much of a risk, I want a real edge with White and I can't study 20 hours a week. What else should I know about myself?

Noah: Another question to ask is:

Do I like having the main choices in the opening?

That's worth asking because some whole openings give one player all or most of the major choices.

Pat: The player with the choices must be in good shape.

Noah: No, it's a matter of taste. For example, White has the key decisions in the Nimzo-Indian at move four.

But that doesn't mean the Nimzo-Indian is busted. Quite the con-trary.

1. d4   Nf6
2. c4   e6
3. Nc3   Bb4

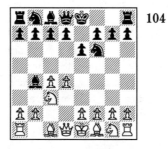
104

White has a huge choice that in-cludes:

the sharp attacking 4. a3,
the relatively unbooked 4. f3,
the positionally double-edged 4. Bg5,
the conservative 4. Qc2,
the largely forgotten 4. Qb3,
the transpositional 4. Nf3,
and finally,
the main line, 4. e3.

Pat: Where else does White have the choices?

Noah: In the Benko Gambit, the Queen's Indian Defense, the Mod-ern Benoni, the King's Indian De-fense and the Queen's Gambit Accepted at moves three, four and five.

Pat: Sure, White should have the choices. As somebody once told me, White isn't Black.

Noah: You're right, he isn't. Never-theless, it's Black who has most of the choices in other openings, such as the Ruy Lopez.

So, whether you feel comfortable giving your opponent the main op-tions is a matter of taste. There are a lot of players who are never going to feel at home as Black after 1... g6 because it leaves White calling the tune.

Pat: Sounds like me. What else?

Noah: Another question is:

Do I like to have a ready-made plan, one that begins right in the opening?

In certain lines, White's game plan starts very early, such as the kingside attack in the Saemisch Var-iation of the Nimzo-Indian. Or the Yugoslav Attack – you know, Be3, f3, Qd2 and Bc4 – of the Dragon Sicilian. Or the Minority Attack in the Exchange Variation of the QGD.

Pat: Are we done with the questions I have to ask?

Noah: No more questions. But there is a warning. There are certain classes of openings that are not for everybody.

Pat: Why not?

Noah: Because they're not meant to be. For example, there are what I call fanatic openings.

Only true believers who want to prove something will willingly go into the Blackmar-Diemer Gam-bit, for example.

But since the opening books try to be encyclopedic, and give every-thing its due, the Blackmar is treated like a serious opening.

Pat: I'm not that serious a player –

but I'd never play the Blackmar.

Noah: You should feel the same way about the Vienna Game with 3. Bc4 Nxe4 – what Savielly Tartakower, who knew all about gambling, called "the poker variation."

It only gets played when White wants to test his memory of the crazy, sacrificial lines – and when Black tries to avoid the safe equality he would get from 5... Be7.

There's one final thing I wanted to suggest when you choose your openings—They should form a repertoire.

Pat: Another SAT word.

Noah: It's just a fancy name for an arsenal of lines, an arsenal that fits together.

A well-formed repertoire cuts down on the number of positions you have to learn – and also avoids surprises that land you in an opening you don't play.

Pat: What kind of surprises?

Noah: Surprises like Diagram 106. Black was 19-year-old Rafael Va-ganian and he was already a strong master. But like a lot of young players, he hadn't given much thought to transpositions – and the dangers of finding yourself OOR.

Pat: OOR?

"My third move"
– **Vasily Ivanchuk, when asked where he made his losing mistake against Anatoly Karpov at Tilburg 1993. (Their game began 1. e4 c6 2. d4 d5 3. e5).**

Noah: Out of Repertoire. You see, Vaganian grew up meeting 1. c4 with 1... c5. It was natural then for him to also answer 1. Nf3, with 1... c5. Then he would transpose into the English with 2. c4 or get into a related closed position after 2. g3.

But Vaganian, a devoted French Defense player when he faced 1. e4, was stunned when he found

> **OOR = Out of Repertoire**

himself in a Sicilian.

Pat: But there's nothing wrong with the position after 2. e4.

Podgaets-Vaganian
Vilna 1971

1. Nf3	c5??
2. e4!	Nc6
3. d4	cxd4
4. Nxd4	e6
5. Nc3	Qc7
6. g3	a6

FANATIC OPENINGS

The **Blackmar-Diemer Gambit** (1. d4 d5 2. e4). Insane complications arise in lines such as 2... dxe4 3. Nc3 Nf6 4. f3 exf3 5. Nxf3 Bf5 6. Ne5 e6 7. g4.

The **Vienna** with 1. e4 e5 2. Nc3 Nf6 3. Bc4 Nxe4, which can become incomprehensible after 4. Qh5 Nd6 5. Bb3 Nc6 6. Nb5 g6 7. Qf3 f5 8. Qd5 Qe7 9. Nxc7† Kd8 10. Nxa8 b6.

The **Sicilian Gambit** that runs 1. e4 c5 2. Nf3 Nf6 3. e5 Nd5 4. Nc3 e6 5. Nxd5 exd5 6. d4 Nc6— long memory and lots of confidence required.

Vaganian knew at least this far but not much further.

7. Bg2	Nf6
8. 0-0	Nxd4
9. Qxd4	Bc5
10. Bf4	d6
11. Qd3	

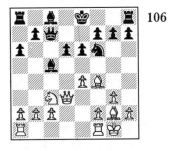

106

Now Black began to panic about 12. Bg5.

11. ...	h6?

12. Na4!	e5
13. Nxc5	exf4?
14. Nb3	fxg3
15. hxg3	0-0
16. Rad1	Rd8
17. e5	Ne8
18. Qe4!	

And White won.

Noah: There's something wrong with every position – if you don't know how to play it.

For example, suppose you want to play the Dutch Defense by way of 1. d4 e6 and 2... f5, because you're trying to avoid the Staunton Gambit – 1. d4 f5 2. e4.

But you'd better know what to do in a French Defense after 1. d4 e6 2. e4! – or you're OOR, big time.

Pat: It seems like there are lots of tricks like that in the 1. d4 openings.

Noah: Absolutely, and the good players know them from experience, rather than from books. For example, a lot of books say that the best answer to 1. d4 d5 2. Nf3 is 2... c5.

But Tigran Petrosian, for example, played 2... Nf6 – because on 2...c5 3. c4 he would have been OOR.

1. d4	Nf6
2. c4	e6
3. Nf3	

GRANDMASTER OPENINGS

Hugely popular at the international level but not useful to the vast majority of amateurs. They include:

Most **Petroff Defense** lines. GMs like them for their drawing ability — and at the GM level drawing with Black is a very good thing.

The old main line of the **Caro-Kann** (1. e4 c6 2. d4 d5 3. Nc3 dxe4 4. Nxe4 Bf5), a variation used by GMs and virtually no one else.

The **Catalan** for White, and particularly lines in which Black holds onto an extra ♙ with ...dxc4 and ...b5. A fine strategy — if you can defend like a grandmaster.

Decades ago the **Deferred Steinitz Defense** to the **Ruy Lopez** (1. e4 e5 2. Nf3 Nc6 3. Bb5 a6 4. Ba4 d6) was played by José Capablanca, Alexander Alekhine and Paul Keres — but hardly anyone below master. Today, no one does.

The opposite of GM openings are:

CATEGORY OPENINGS

That is, the lines played mostly by Class A, B and C players. Almost no GM would play the **Stonewall Attack** (1. d4, 2. e3, 3. Bd3 and 4. f4), the **Morra Gambit** (1. e4 c5 2. d4) or 1. b3, for example. Or goofy lines such as 1. d4 c5 2. d5 Nf6 3. Nc3 Qa5 followed by ...b5.

Also, the **Milner-Barry Gambit** in the **French** (1. e4 e6 2. d4 d5 3. e5 c5 4. c3 Nc6 5. Nf3 Qb6 6. Bd3 cxd4 7. cxd4 Bd7 8. 0-0 Nxd4) but it happens a lot at the 1600 level.

105

"Outplayed, and the game is only three moves long!"
– **An out-of-repertoire Yasser Seirawan, after his game with Kasparov at Barcelona 1989 went 1. d4 d6 2. e4 Nf6 3. f3!, leading him into a Saemisch KID, an opening he'd never played as Black.**

107

If you're a 1. d4 player who avoids the Nimzo-Indian (3. Nc3 Bb4) this way then you need to know more than the little about the Queen's Indian (3... b6).

You also need to have some knowledge of the Benoni (3... c5 4. d5) lines in which White plays Nf3 – rather than f4, f3 or Nge2.

You can avoid that by way of 4. e3 after 3... c5 – but then you need to know the Semi-Tarrasch (4... d5!) or you're OOR.

And you should know what to do in the Queen's Gambit Declined (3... d5) with a N/f3.

Pat: Besides avoiding transpositional tricks is there any real reason to have a repertoire?

Noah: Yes, a good repertoire can allow you to master similar types of ♟-structures and middlegames.

For example, a player who plays the Caro-Kann against 1. e4 might also use the Semi-Slav against 1. d4 and some ...d5/...e6 system against the English, Réti and related closed lines. They all employ the same ♟-structure.

Having a repertoire helps limit how much you need to know.

Pat: Don't the big names have big repertoires.

Noah: Some do, like Jan Timman and Garry Kasparov. But Bobby Fischer and Valery Salov did pretty well with a narrow range of openings.

Pat: I'm still not sure why I need a repertoire.

Noah: Well, consider how useful they were to some of the high-Elo players.

Vladimir Kramnik (page 78) fashioned a White system that began with 1. Nf3 but got him into the 1. d4 positions he wanted – while avoiding a lot of 1. d4 main lines he didn't.

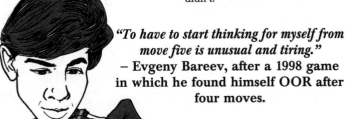

"To have to start thinking for myself from move five is unusual and tiring."
– **Evgeny Bareev, after a 1998 game in which he found himself OOR after four moves.**

SPECIALIZED REPERTOIRES

ISOLATED d-♙: If you like the active play you get in isolated d-pawn positions, you might open 1. e4 and use 2. c3 against **Sicilian** and the **Exchange Variation** of the **French** (3. exd5 exd5 4. c4).

As Black you might defend against 1. d4 with the **Tarrasch Variation of the Queen's Gambit Declined** and against 1. e4 with the **French** (and get an isolated d-♙ in the **Tarrasch** 3. Nd2 c5).

"BLACK" REPERTOIRE: With either color you give your opponent most of the decisions to make. As White you open 1. Nf3 and 2. g3—or just 1. g3. As Black, 1...g6.

TACTICAL: Sharp, sacrificial **Sicilian Variations** with Bc4 or Bg5 as White. **Benoni** and **Dragon** (or **Najdorf**) **Sicilian** as Black.

SOLID: As Black your first goal is equalizing, such as with the **Caro-Kann** or main line 1... e5 positions against 1. e4 and 1....d5 after 1. d4. José Capablanca, Vasily Smyslov and Anatoly Karpov were among the devotees of solid repertoires.

Tigran Petrosian (page 79) figured out a simple defense to 1. c4 based on his willingness to play the Slav Defense or the Makogonov QGD.

Pat: And what's the deal with Botvinnik's and 1. d4 ?

Noah: He (page 80) found a clever move order – 1. d4 d5 2. c4 e6 3. Nc3 c6 4. Nf3 Nf6 – that would get him into the Meran Defense of the Slav that he had analyzed to death. But it avoided the drawish Exchange Variation of the Slav because he didn't play 2... c6.

Also, after 3. Nf3 c6 4. Nbd2 he could get a nice version of the Dutch with 4... f5 – and the Dutch was also part of his repertoire, while the move Nbd2 was usually not part of his opponent's.

Pat: You're not making this easy – OOR and cult openings and long weekend variations.

Noah: And don't forget the keys like staying in character, avoiding fashion and finding your own weapons.

"Varying one's repertoire keeps the mind fresh."
– Jan Timman

But at least you have a better picture today of what kind of openings you should play and the choices you have.

Pat: And tomorrow?

Noah: Tomorrow is another day.

SOME CELEBRATED REPERTOIRES

VLADIMIR KRAMNIK in the 1990s — Relatively narrow

As **White:**

He played **1. Nf3** chiefly, often reaching standard d- ♟ positions (1...d5 2. d4 or 1... Nf6 2. c4 e6 3. Nc3 d5 4. d4).

He was willing to reach belated **Nimzo-Indian** positions (such as 1...Nf6 2. c4 e6 3. Nc3 Bb4 4. Qc2 0-0 5. a3 Bxc3 6. Qxc3 b6 7. d4) or **Gruenfelds** (1...c5 2. c4 Nf6 3. Nc3 d5 4. cxd5 Nxd5 5. d4 Nxc3 6. bxc3 g6 7. e4).

He also reached **English** positions — while avoiding 1. c4 e5 — by way of 1. Nf3 c5 2. c4 Nf6 3. Nc3 Nc6 4. g3 d5 5. d4 (and now 5...e6 6. cxd5 or 5...cxd4 6. Nxd4).

He avoided the **Queen's Indian Defense** with 1. Nf3 Nf6 2. c4 b6 3. g3 Bb7 4. Bg2 e6 5. 0-0 Be7 6. Nc3 0-0 7. Re1.

As **Black:**

Against 1. e4 he used either a **Petroff** or one of two favorite **Sicilian Variations.**

Against 1. d4, he adopted the **KID, Nimzo-Indian** or **Tartakower-Makogonov QGD.**

SOME CELEBRATED REPERTOIRES

TIGRAN PETROSIAN in the 1950s/60s — Relatively broad but with emphasis on avoiding sharp lines

As **White:**

He played **1. d4, 1. c4** and **1. Nf3,** almost always with intent of reaching a standard **English** or d-△ middlegame. He also tried 1. e4 to reach a **King's Indian Reversed** (1... e6 2. d3) — or got there by way of 1. Nf3 Nf6 2. g3 g6 3. Bg2 Bg7 4. 0-0 0-0 5. d3 and 6. e4.

He didn't mind playing the **QGD** with **Nf3,** so he often answered 1. d4 Nf6 2. c4 e6 with 3. Nf3. And since he liked playing an e3 line against the **Queen's Indian Defense,** he also used the 1. d4 Nf6 2. Nf3 e6 3. e3 move order.

After 1. c4 Nf6 he usually played 2. Nc3 and if 2... e6, then the sharp 3. e4 c5 4. e5 against weaker players and 3. d4 against stronger ones.

As **Black:**

Against 1. e4 he adopted a **Najdorf Sicilian** or **Winawer French** when he needed a win, but the **Caro-Kann** or a main line **Lopez** when a draw was acceptable.

Against 1. d4 he used the **KID,** the **Czech Benoni** or some **Old-Indian**-like move order against weaker players. Facing stronger players he often chose the **Slav** or **Tartakower-Makogonov QGD** (but with move order 1. d4 Nf6 2. c4 e6 3. Nc3 d5 so he could meet 4. cxd5 with 4... Nxd5).

Against 1. c4 he chose 1...Nf6 2. Nf3 c6 or 1... c6. Or 2... e6 3. Nc3 d5.

SOME CELEBRATED REPERTOIRES

MIKHAIL BOTVINNIK in the 1940s/'50s — Fairly broad

As **White:**
He played both 1. e4 **(Four Knights Game** as well as **Ruy Lopez)** and 1. d4 with relatively solid and simple systems such as the **Exchange** variations of the **QGD** and **Slav,** and the **Fianchetto Variation** of **KID.**

He later added the **Catalan** (1. d4 Nf6 2. c4 e6 3. g3 and 1. c4 e6 2. g3 d5 3. Bg2), **Réti** and **King's Indian Reversed.**

As **Black:**
Against 1. e4 he played the **Winawer French** mainly but also experimented with the **Open Lopez** — and used the **Dragon** and other **Sicilian** lines when he needed points.

Against 1. d4, he adopted the **Nimzo/Queen's Indian** and **Dutch** by way of 1. d4 e6 2. c4 f5. But in the late 1940s he developed a new weapon in the **Meran Defense.**

In which Pat finds that holes are not always holes, tempi don't necessarily count and that there are some things more valuable than riches.

Pat: Let me start it off today. There's something that always bugged me about the opening.

Noah: Tell me.

Pat: The stupid rules. When I first started playing I read all sorts of, you know, 'Don't do this' but 'Don't avoid doing that' and all it did was confuse me.

Noah: You're right. There are quite a few rules or principles.

What makes chess hard – opening, middlegame or ending – is that after you've learned all the principles you realize so many of them contradict one another.

Pat: You got that right.

Noah: But you can't ignore them because there is always some truth in them.

Pat: Some truth?

REUBEN'S RULES

In **The Ideas Behind the Chess Openings,** Reuben Fine set down **10 rules** for choosing moves in the opening. But in real life — particularly among better players — most of the rules are ignored.

For example, in a "typical" world championship match, Kasparov-Karpov, Seville 1987:

Fine's **Rule No. 1,** that only 1. e4 or 1. d4 should be played — was violated in 13 of the 24 games.

Rule No. 3, that ♘s should be developed before ♗s — was violated 16 times, such as in the popular QGD move order of 1. d4 d5 2. c4 e6 3. Nc3 Be7. (This finesse avoids 3... Nf6 4. Bg5, which gives White more choices.)

Rule No. 4, that pieces should be developed on their best square and left there until the middlegame — was violated five times, including one game that saw 11. Qb3 followed by 12. Qc2 and two in which Black played ...Bf5, soon followed by ...Be6.

Rule No. 5 said there should be few ♙ moves in the opening. But there were 174 ♙ moves — not counting captures — out of a possible 480 in the first ten moves of the 24 games.

Rule No. 6, banning early ♛ moves, was violated in eight games, each with a ♛ move in the first ten moves. (Even in Fine's heyday, the 1930s, this rule was violated by 4. Qb3 in the Gruenfeld, which was thought to be nearly a refutation of the whole opening.)

Rule No. 7, which called for early castling, was not followed in the eight games in which castling occured after move 11.

Rule No. 9, which said you should keep at least one ♙ in the center, was violated in nine games, when Black gave up the center in the **Gruenfeld** or **Caro-Kann Defenses.**

Fine's other rules were "Whenever possible, make a good developing move which threatens something," "Play to control the center" and "Do not sacrifice without a clear and adequate reason."

Noah: Sure. Take that golden rule of the opening:

DEVELOPMENT IS BETTER THAN RICHES

Pat: I never heard it put quite that way.

Noah: No matter. The point is it's misleading because it's only partly true.

It isn't development itself that wins or loses games. But differences in the amount of development can.

For instance in Diagram 108 a serious development gap occurs when an uncastled White tries to attack a coordinated, well-developed Black.

Krasenkov-Psakhis
Polanica Zdroj 1997

1. Nf3	Nf6
2. c4	b6
3. Nc3	Bb7
4. d4	e6

5. a3	d5
6. Bf4	Bd6
7. Bg3	0-0
8. e3	c5
9. dxc5	bxc5
10. Qb3	Bc6
11. Rd1	

Castling queenside was actually safer.

11. ...	Bxg3
12. hxg3	Nbd7

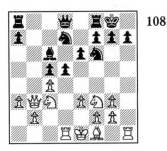

108

13. g4?	h6
14. g5	hxg5
15. Nxg5	Qa5!

Now 16. Nf3 Rfb8 17. Qc2 Rb6 favors Black's b-file pressure over White's slow-developing kingside attack.

16. Qc2?	**d4!**

And Black wins a ♘ (17. exd4 cxd4 18. Rxd4 Qxg5 or 17. Bd3 Rfd8 18. Bh7† Kf8).

Pat: That's so lame by White. But why is this rule only partly true?

Noah: Because it doesn't work in many positions, particularly ones with a closed ♙-structure. A player with all his pieces developed can find that they're just vulnerable to attack, like White's in Diagram 109.

Pat: How can Black get away with 9... Nc8 ?

Noah: He can because in a closed position having a key piece on the right square is usually more important than getting all of the pieces off the first rank quickly.

I. Ivanov-Gausel
Gausdal 1994

1. e4	e6
2. d4	d5
3. e5	c5

4. c3	Nc6
5. Nf3	Bd7
6. a3	c4
7. Bf4	Na5
8. Nbd2	Ne7
9. Be2	Nc8

Black discourages b4 because of ...cxb3 followed by ...Nb6-c4 or ...Na4. He also prepares ...Nb6/...Ba4.

10. 0-0	Nb6
11. Re1?	Be7
12. a4?	

109

12. ...	g5!
	0-1

After 13. ♗-moves g4 White loses a piece.

Pat: Yeah, but what about those games – not with closed centers – where GMs get away with taking 20 or so moves before touching a ♙?

Noah: GMs get away with it because they know the opening is just a means to an end – and that end is a good middlegame position.

So you have to evaluate your development in terms of what you're going to be doing past move 12 or so.

Black can sit back and play with only two or three pieces in Diagram 110 because his meager development is actually much more appropriate to his plan – an attack on the queenside – than White's development is to his plan, whatever that was supposed to be.

Evans-Suttles
San Antonio 1972

1.	e4	g6
2.	d4	d6
3.	Nc3	Bg7

4.	Be3	c6
5.	Qd2	b5
6.	0-0-0	Nd7
7.	f3	Nb6
8.	h4	h5!

White, denied an opportunity to play Bh6 now, needs a plan.

9.	Nh3	a5
10.	Nf2	b4
11.	Nb1	Rb8

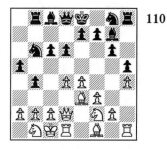

110

Here 12. Be2 is the necessary preparation for g4 but Black can still continue his undeveloped attack with ...Qc7 and ...c5.

12.	g4?	hxg4
13.	fxg4	Nf6
14.	Be2	Nxg4!

| 15. | Nxg4 | Bxg4 |

And Black won with his extra ♙ (because 16. Bxg4 Nc4 17. ♕-moves Nxe3 18. Qxe3?? allows 18... Bh6).

Pat: But isn't there an ideal development?

Noah: You mean the perfect places to put the ♞s and ♝s and ♜s?

People used to think that way – before games like the one in Diagram 111.

Pat: What's with 9... e6 ?

Noah: We'll get into holes later today. But let me just say here that Black can afford to weaken the dark squares – and at least bend a rule – to avoid a specific threat.

The main point is that White's development looks like it came out of a textbook.

Pat: Sure does.

Noah: And after the game Black said proudly that White had followed all of the rules advocated by writers such as Fred Reinfeld –

while Black broke them.

But White didn't have an edge because the center wasn't open and there was no direct contact between his pieces and Black's. And White later got the worst of it because Black has a nice tactical shot, 11... b5, that showed White's center was more of a target than anything on Black's side of the board.

Pat: I can't believe I can just leave my pieces on the first rank.

Kavalek-Suttles
Nice 1974

1.	e4	g6
2.	d4	d6
3.	Nf3	Bg7
4.	Be2	Nf6
5.	Nc3	a6
6.	a4	0-0
7.	0-0	b6
8.	Re1	Bb7
9.	Bc4	e6

This last move avoids e5-e6, e.g. 9... Nbd7? 10. e5 followed by 11. e6.

10. Bf4   Nbd7
11. Qd2

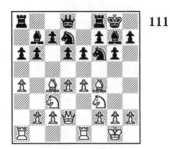

111

11. ...   b5!
12. axb5   axb5

Now 13. Bxb5 Rxa1 14. Rxa1 Nxe4 is fine for Black.

13. Rxa8   Qxa8
14. Bxb5   Bxe4!
15. Nxe4   Nxe4
16. Rxe4

Or 16. Qe2 Ndf6 17. Bd3 d5 18. Bxc7 Qb7!, which is great for Black.

16. ...   Qxe4
17. Bxd7   Ra8

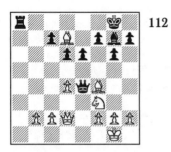

112

Material is roughly equal but Black's heavy pieces dominate (...Ra1† and ...Qb7/...c6 are threatened).

White was lost soon after 18. h4 Qb7 19. d5 e5! 20. Bh6 Qxb2 21. h5 Ra1† 22. Kh2 Qb1.

Noah: You can't for long. But you shouldn't move them at all unless you know where they belong.

It's like the problem the theoreticians used to agonize over in trying to find the right square for White's c-♗ in the Saemisch Nimzo-Indian. That's the key position in Diagram 113.

Pat: Even I can figure this one out – by elimination. On d2 the ♗ would just look like it's in the way. On b2 it just looks stupid.

Noah: And on h6 it's *en prise*.

Pat: That only leaves f4 and g5 – and Bg5 has gotta make more sense.

Noah: Actually, the ♗ is badly misplaced on g5, as the analysis shows. And f4 isn't much better.

Pat: So where does the the ♗ belong?

Noah: On c1, of course!

It's funny but White shouldn't do anything with the ♗ until at least move 10, when the center is clarified and Black has commited most of his pieces.

1. d4   Nf6
2. c4   e6
3. Nc3   Bb4
4. a3   Bxc3†
5. bxc3   d5

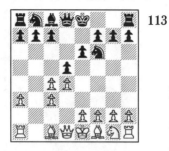

113

White used to play the natural 6. Bg5.

But after 6... c5 7. cxd5 exd5 Black is in fine shape with ...Qa5 coming up, e.g. 8. e3 Qa5 and 9... Ne4 or 8. f3 h6 9. Bh4 Qa5 10. Qd2 Nbd7 and ...b6/...Ba6.

Better is:

6. e3   c5
7. cxd5   exd5
8. Bd3   0-0
9. Ne2   Nc6
10. 0-0

"Castle because you will or because you must – but not because you can."
– attributed to both **Harry Nelson Pillsbury** and **William Ewart Napier.**

114

White can choose between 11. Bb2 and 11. a4/12. Ba3 – or delay any decision about the ♗ for several more moves.

Pat: So I guess the rule about "Develop Knights before Bishops" also makes sense – some of the time.

Noah: And figuring out when it doesn't make sense is another reason the opening is difficult.

But there's at least one bit of development advice that turns out to be true more often than any other.

Pat: Castle early?

Noah: Nope.

Pat: Don't go ♙ grabbing with your

♕?

Noah: That's better, but it doesn't work in a lot of good "poisoned pawn" lines. Guess again.

Pat: I'm out of guesses.

Noah: Okay, it's fairly simple –

LINE UP A ♖ AGAINST THE ENEMY ♕

That's particularly true if the only thing standing between the ♕ and ♖ is an enemy ♙ or piece, as in Diagram 115.

Pat: Why is 13... Rd8 so wonderful? There's a lot of other stuff on the d-file.

Noah: But the focal point of this position is d4 and there are all sorts of tactics involving ...cxd4 followed by a ♘ going to c5 or e5.

In this case White apparently didn't like the looks of 14. d5 Ne5! 15. 0-0.

Pat: So he tried to find a better place for his ♕.

Noah: And it died a horrible death

on f4 when he did.

Shaked-Kasparov
Tilburg 1997

1.	d4	Nf6
2.	c4	g6
3.	Nc3	d5
4.	cxd5	Nxd5
5.	e4	Nxc3
6.	bxc3	Bg7
7.	Be3	c5
8.	Qd2	Qa5
9.	Rb1	b6
10.	Bb5†	Bd7
11.	Be2	Bc6
12.	Bd3	Nd7
13.	Ne2	

115

13. ...   Rd8!

This stops 14. 0-0? because 14... cxd4 15. cxd4 Qxd2 16. Bxd2 Nc5! favors Black.

14. f3   0-0
15. h4   h5
16. Bg5   Rfe8

Black has sufficient pressure against d4 to equalize. White tried to ease the pressure by pushing the d-♟:

17. Rc1   Bb7
18. d5?   Ne5
19. Bb1   Nc4

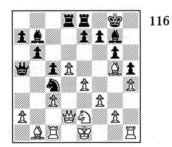
116

20. Qf4?   Be5
0-1

The ♛ is lost.

Noah: That reminds me a lot of Diagram 117, a position we used to see quite a bit in the 1960s and '70s.

Pat: You mean like, before PGN.

Noah: Before even *Fritz*. We played different lines then. Not worse, just different.

The idea here is the effectiveness of the same ♖-vs.-♛ lineup.

Pat: I can see it coming. Black is going to play ...Rd8 and then ...cxd4.

Noah: What's funny about this line is that White found a good counter-idea – 11. Rc1. Black was then reluctant to play ...cxd4 because that would expose his own ♛ to the R/c1.

1. d4   Nf6
2. c4   g6
3. Nc3   d5
4. cxd5   Nxd5
5. e4   Nxc3
6. bxc3   Bg7
7. Bc4   0-0
8. Ne2   c5

9. 0-0   Nc6
10. Be3   Qc7

117

Now 11. dxc5? Ne5! favors Black (12. Bb3 Ng4 13. Bf4 Qxc5).

11. Rc1

If White had anticipated 11... Rd8 by playing 11. Qc1 then Black would have lined up on the c-file, such as 11... Bd7 12. Rb1 cxd4 13. cxd4 Rac8 with about equal play.

11. ...   Rd8

Now if White gets off the hot file:

12. Qe1

Black can do the same:

12. ...   Qa5!

And if White defends the d-♟

"Why should I labor under antideluvian prejudices?" – IM James T. Sherwin when he violated the rule against playing ...Qxb2 (1. d4 Nf6 2. Nf3 e6 3. Bg5 c5 4. e3 Qb6 5. Nc3? Qxb2! and Black won).

with 13. Rd1 Black replies 13... cxd4 14. cxd4 Qxe1 15. Rfxe1 b6 with an equal ending.

Pat: Okay, development means something. But suppose I get a lead in development. How do I make it count?

Noah: There are a few rules, actually corollaries.

Pat: Don't you run out of these words eventually?

Noah: A corollary is just a natural consequence of a previous rule. In this case there are two corollaries to "Development is better than riches." They are:

DON'T TRADE ♕s WHEN AHEAD IN DEVELOPMENT*

and

DON'T ALLOW THE CENTER TO BE CLOSED WHEN AHEAD*

Pat: I guess that makes sense. When you've got more pieces out and the center is open you've got better chances of crushing somebody if you've still got a ♕.

And that's why you're showing me Diagram 118, right?.

Noah: That's right. White plays the opening sluggishly and then tries to open the center with 10. d5.

That would have been fine if Black closed the center – or if he had allowed a trade of ♕s, such as 13... Qxd5? You don't have to be José Capablanca to understand that.

Pat: I'll say.

Shaked-Kramnik
Tilburg 1997

1. d4	Nf6
2. c4	e6
3. Nc3	Bb4
4. e3	0-0
5. Ne2	d5
6. a3	Be7
7. cxd5	Nxd5
8. g3	Nxc3

9. Nxc3	c5
10. d5	Bf6!
11. Bg2	Bxc3†!
12. bxc3	exd5
13. Qxd5	

13. ...	Qe7!
14. Rb1	Nc6
15. 0-0	Be6

Now 16. Qd1 Rad8 loses even more time for White.

The game went 16. Qh5 Rad8 17. e4 Ba2 18. Ra1 Bc4 19. Re1 Ne5, after which Black dominated the key squares, such as d3, and won quickly.

Pat: But... were those asterisks?

Noah: They were. They mean you have to add these words to the corollaries: "without a good reason."

As in, "Don't trade Queens when ahead in development – without a good reason."

Pat: I never heard anyone actually speak with *asterisks.*

Noah: I do, so pay attention. The point is that there often are good reasons to violate these rules.

For example, you can afford to trade ♕s if it means you can cripple the enemy counterplay, as in Diagram 119.

Pat: Looks like another random Sicilian.

Noah: I know, all these Sicilian positions look alike. But as natural as 11... Qa5 was, it was virtually a losing blunder.

Pat: Weird. Instead of attacking with g4-g5, White jumps into an endgame.

Noah: But it worked. And bear in mind this was a big-deal game – the last, decisive round of a world championship Candidates cycle.

Anand-Kamsky
PCA Candidates finals
Las Palmas 1995

1. e4	c5
2. Nf3	d6
3. d4	cxd4
4. Nxd4	Nf6
5. Nc3	a6
6. Be3	e6
7. Be2	Be7
8. f4	Nc6
9. Qd2	Nxd4
10. Qxd4	0-0
11. 0-0-0	Qa5?

119

Behind in development, Black should counterattack with 11... b5.

12. Qb6!	Qxb6
13. Bxb6	

White's advantage increased with the ♛-trade, e.g. 13... Nd7? 14. Bc7 loses the d-♟ and 13... Bd7 14. e5! is strong (14... Ne8 15. Bc5! dxc5 16. Rxd7 or 14... dxe5 15. fxe5 Nd5 16. Nxd5 exd5 17. Bf3 and Bxd5).

In the game Black played the super-defensive:

13. ...	Ne8
14. e5!	d5

But that left the N/e8 locked out of play. White won easily after 15. f5 Bd7 16. Bg4.

Pat: That's so cool. Black's pieces don't get to play at all after 12. Qb6. But what's the deal about closing the center?

Noah: Sometimes it makes sense to close the center, at least partially, when you have more pieces out than your opponent.

In Diagram 120 White has a good move in 9. dxc5. But 9. d5 also works because it has a cramping effect that gives White great play on either wing. Also, 9. d5 stops Black's only counterplay, which comes about after ...cxd4.

Pat: And it's not like the center is frozen after 9... e5.

Noah: Right. White can always play f4xe5 – if he doesn't have an easier winning plan on the queenside.

Glek-Belitsev
Cappelle la Grande 1998

1. e4	c5
2. Nf3	d6
3. Bb5†	Nd7
4. d4	Ngf6
5. Nc3	a6
6. Bxd7†	Nxd7
7. 0-0	e6
8. Bg5	Qc7

120

9. d5!

White threatens to loosen the enemy center with 10. dxe6.

9. ...	e5
10. a4!	g6
11. Nd2	Bg7
12. Nc4	Nb6

Or 12... b6 13. f4 h6 14. fxe5! (14... hxg5? 15. Nxd6† is crushing and 14... Nxe5 15. Nxe5 Bxe5 16. Bf6 is poor for Black).

13. Nxb6	Qxb6
14. a5	Qc7
15. Qd2	

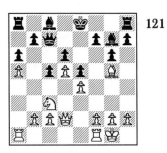

121

White can choose between a serious edge on the kingside with 16. f4 or on the queenside after 15... 0-0 16. Na4 f5 17. Nb6 Rb8 18. f3 followed by c4 and b4.

Pat: Does that do development? I mean are there any other corollaries or asterisks or whatever?

Noah: Not about development but there are quite a few other rules that work in the opening – and sometimes don't.

Pat: Such as?

Noah: Such as:

THE CENTER MATTERS

Pat: That's no state secret.

Noah: Perhaps not. But you'd be surprised how often some big-name GM is embarrassed by failing to pay attention to it.

Pat: That's what Diagram 122 is about, I'll bet.

Noah: You'd bet correctly. It must have been particularly awkward for Anatoly Karpov to be Black here because Tigran Petrosian had used the position with 4... b6? several years before in a famous lecture that every Russian schoolkid knew.

Yusupov-Karpov
Candidates semifinals
London 1989

1. d4	Nf6
2. Nf3	e6
3. Bg5	c5
4. e3	

A very familiar position in the Torre Attack.

| 4. ... | b6? |
| 5. d5! | |

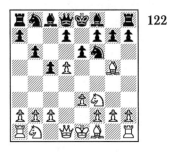

122

| 5. ... | exd5 |
| 6. Nc3 | Be7 |

The tactical point is that 6... Bb7 7. Nxd5 Bxd5 8. Bxf6 Qxf6 9. Qxd5 Qxb2 10. Rd1! is too strong for White. Black must accept White's domination of the center.

7. Nxd5	Bb7
8. Bxf6!	Bxf6
9. c3	0-0
10. Bc4	

And White had a substantial edge.

Pat: I've gotten squished like that – and I'm never gonna be world champion. But what about all those openings in which one guy lets the other guy run all over the center?

Noah: Giving up the center is a valid strategy – provided you get something in return.

What that something is can be counterplay against the center or on a wing. That's what the Gruenfeld and Nimzo-Indian Defenses are all about.

Failure to get that pressure can be disastrous, as in Diagram 123.

Pat: What was Black thinking?

Noah: He was thinking he could break up White's picture-perfect center with a mixture of ...cxd4, ...Bg4 and ...Nc6.

Pat: White put an end to that. He rules in the center after 7. h3.

Noah: True. But it might have been a shorter reign if Black had at least tried 8... Nc6.

Once he commited his ♘ to the passive d7, with no hope of pressuring d4, he was in serious trouble – although he probably didn't know it until Diagram 124.

KARPOV VS TORRE

Karpov also lost Torre Attacks to Viktor Korchnoi in the 1974 Candidates finals and to Viswanathan Anand in the 1998 FIDE world championship finals. After a few moves of a misplayed Torre in the 1993 Timman-Karpov world championship match, Korchnoi exclaimed, "He hasn't learned anything about the Torre Attack in 20 years!"

Leko-Strikovic
Cacak 1996

1. e4   g6
2. d4   Bg7
3. Nf3   d6
4. c3   Nf6
5. Bd3   0-0
6. 0-0   c5

Now 7. Nbd2 cxd4 8. cxd4 Nc6 gives Black pressure in the center.

7. h3!

This stops ...Bg4, which would have made ...cxd4 and ...Nc6 much stronger.

7. ...   cxd4?!

Black should try to complicate, such as with 7... d5, e.g. 8. e5 Ne4 or 8. exd5 cxd4.

8. cxd4

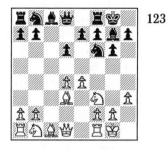

123

8. ...   Nbd7?

Too little pressure on the White center. Better was 8... Nc6 9. Nc3 e5 although 10. d5 Ne7 11. Be3 still favors White.

9. Nc3   e5
10. Be3!   a6
11. a4!

If Black takes aim at e4 with 11... Re8 White plays 12. d5, follows with a5 and b4, and increases pressure on the c-file.

11. ...   exd4
12. Bxd4   Re8
13. Bc4!

Now both 13... Nc5? (14. e5) and 13... Nb6? (14. Bxf7† Kxf7 15.

"Do you want to know how Tal wins? It's very simple. He arranges his pieces in the center and then sacrifices them somewhere."
– David Bronstein

Qb3†) fail tactically.

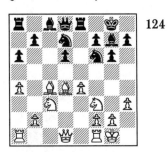

124

White can begin working against f7, with Ng5.

The game went 13... Nxe4 14. Bxg7 Kxg7 15. Nxe4 Rxe4 16. Bxf7! with advantage (16... Kxf7 17. Qd5† Re6 18. Ng5†) Qf6 17. Bd5 Rb4 18. Re1! Nb6 19. Rc1 Bd7 20. Rc7 and wins.

Pat: So that game was all about d4. Are some squares more important than others?

Noah: The center squares are born equal, but that doesn't last long. Some take on a much greater significance, such as e5 in the Sicilian.

For example, in Diagram 125 Black introduced a strong new move to win control of e5 for her ♞ and soften up other darken squares.

Pat: Looks crazy.

Noah: But the idea is sane. The best square for Black to occupy in the center is e5 so she eliminates the only enemy ♙ that controls it.

Pat: At the cost of nuking her kingside.

Noah: Yet once Black can play ... Ne5 it turns out that White's ♔ position is weaker.

This is clearer when you compare Diagram 125 with Diagram 126. Black goes from being powerless to a powerhouse in the center.

Shirov-(J) Polgar
Buenos Aires 1994

1. e4	c5
2. Nf3	e6
3. d4	cxd4
4. Nxd4	Nc6
5. Nc3	d6
6. g4	a6

7. Be3	Nge7
8. Nb3	b5
9. f4	Bb7
10. Qf3	

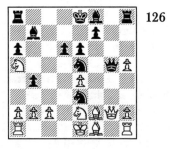

125

The book move was 10... Na5, after which White's powerful center enables him to launch a kingside attack with 11. 0-0-0 Nxb3† 12. axb3 Rc8 13. h4 and 14. g5.

10. ...	g5!

Now 11. 0-0-0 allows 11... gxf4 12. Bxf4 Ng6 and 13. Bg3 Nce5 or 13. Nc5 Qf6!?

11. fxg5	Ne5
12. Qg2	

Not 12. Qe2 b4!, winning the e-♙.

12. ...	b4
13. Ne2	h5!
14. gxh5	Nf5!
15. Bf2	Qxg5!
16. Na5	Ne3!

126

With a winning attack for Black (17. Qxg5 Nf3#).

Pat: So the bottom line is you have to control the center by occupying it.

Noah: Not exactly. Sometimes you exert better control by retreating.

For example, it's standard practice in the Dragon Sicilian to pull a well-developed, centralized ♞ back from d4. You see that in Diagram 127.

Overruled

Pat: I see it but I never understand it. It costs White a move to play Nb3 and it takes a good piece out of action.

Noah: But the retreat serves a higher purpose, controlling d5. By stopping ...d5, White reinforces his advantage in space.

Pat: The ♘ just looks dumb on b3.

Noah: Only temporarily. Thanks to 7.Nb3 White's other ♘ can occupy a much better outpost later on with Nd5!.

The same thing happens in the English Opening.

Pat: Let me guess – with colors reversed.

1.	e4	c5
2.	Nf3	d6
3.	d4	cxd4
4.	Nxd4	Nf6
5.	Nc3	g6
6.	Be2	Bg7
7.	Be3	Nc6
8.	0-0	0-0

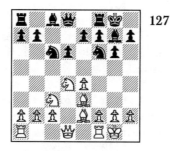

127

Now 9. Qd2 allows 9... d5 or the indirect attack on the center with 9... Ng4.

For example, 9... d5 10. exd5 Nxd5 11. Nxd5 Nxd4! or 11. Nxc6 bxc6 12. Rad1 Qc7 with equality.

9. Nb3

This stops both ...d5 and ...Ng4 and reinforces control of d5.

After the passive 9... Bd7? 10. f3 Rc8 11. Nd5! White stands better. He is also in good shape after the book 9... Be6 10. f4, preparing f5 and Bf3.

Similar to this is the colors reversed position from the English Opening: 1. c4 e5 2. Nc3 Nf6 3. g3

d5 4. cxd5 Nxd5 5. Bg2 Nb6!.

Noah: Good guess. Control of the center is so important that if you don't have it, you have to find counterplay somewhere else. Black missed that opportunity in Diagram 128.

Pat: But he was trying to win the d-pawn by attacking it with his ♛ and ♝.

Noah: You should be able to see from the diagram that Black's plan was doomed. White had too much strength in the center, so Black should have attacked on the wing.

Gulko-Vaganian
Erevan 1996

1.	c4	c5
2.	Nf3	Nf6
3.	Nc3	Nc6
4.	g3	d5
5.	d4	e6
6.	cxd5	Nxd5
7.	Bg2	Nxc3
8.	bxc3	cxd4

9.	cxd4	Bb4†
10.	Bd2	Be7

Black's last two moves are a little finesse to put pressure on d4 (...Bf6).

11.	Bc3	0-0
12.	0-0	Bd7

Black tries to quickly mobilize his queenside with ...Rc8 and ...b5-b4 or ...Na5, (13. e4 Na5).

The immediate 12... b5? allows 13. Ne5!.

13. Qd2

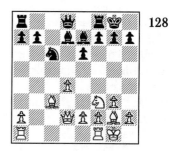

128

13. ...	Rc8?

Black misses 13... b5!, e.g. 14. e4 b4 15. Bb2 Na5 and ...Nc4.

14. e4	Bf6

15. Rac1   Qb6

16. d5!

And White had an obvious advantage after 16... Bxc3 17. Rxc3 exd5 18. exd5 Nb8 (18... Na5 19. Ne5) 19. Rb3 Qa6 20. Re1.

Pat: I get the picture. Black has to find counterplay somewhere.

Noah: It's not just Black. The center isn't a vacuum, so if White fails to control it, he can easily get locked out of it. You'll see that in the next game.

Pat: What's the deal here?

Noah: White plays very conservatively and tries to trick Black into seizing the center prematurely with ...f5 and ...e4.

Pat: But Black doesn't fall for that.

Noah: No. But you can't play conservatively forever.

When White missed his opportunity for 9. e4! he was headed downhill. By the time he failed to play 14. f4, his last chance to compete in the center, the trend was obvious.

Vera-Gulko

Lucerne 1993

1. d4	**d6**
2. Nf3	**Bg4**
3. c4	**Nd7**
4. Nc3	**e5**
5. e3	

Quiet center policy by White so far but not necessarily bad.

5. ...	**c6**
6. h3	**Bh5**
7. Be2	

Now 7... f5? is punished by 8. g4! fxg4 9. Nh2 and White will occupy f5 after hxg4 and Nf1-g3.

7. ...	**Be7!**
8. 0-0	**f5**

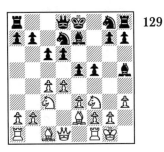

129

9. c5?

Here White needed to assert himself in the center with 9. e4! and if 9... f4 then 10. c5! (10... dxc5 11. dxe5!).

9. ...	**e4!**
10. cxd6	**Bxd6**

Black has the superior center and obtained an edge after:

11. Nd2	**Bxe2**
12. Qxe2	**Ngf6**
13. Nc4	**Bc7**
14. b3?	

White needed to play 14. f4!

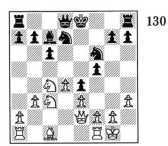

130

Black eventually gained a decisive edge with ...Nbd5 and ...f4.

Pat: Are there any, what'd you call them, corollaries to the rule about control of the center?

Noah: More than one. The first is:

♟s SHOULD CAPTURE TOWARDS THE CENTER*

Because it tends to unite them into fewer "islands" and concentrates their power towards the center.

In fact, even doubling your ♟s is often beneficial if it moves them towards the center. That's what happens in Diagram 131.

Pat: Before you get to that, why did White play 2. Nf3?

Noah: It's just a common-sense way of trying to control the course of the opening – by avoiding 2. d4 e5, which Black may have known better than White.

White was willing to tranpose into a normal 1. e4 e5 game, if Black had replied 2... e5.

Pat: Okay. And the point of 8. gxf3 was to avoid the loss of time after 8. Qxf3 Ne5, I guess.

Noah: True. In the game 8... Ne5 would have been answered strongly by 9. f4.

Onischuk-Miles
Wijk aan Zee 1996

1.	e4	Nc6
2.	Nf3	d6
3.	d4	Nf6
4.	Nc3	Bg4
5.	Be3	a6
6.	h3	Bh5
7.	d5	

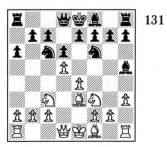
131

7. ...	Bxf3

8.	gxf3!	Nb8
9.	f4	c6
10.	Bg2	Qc7
11.	Qd4!	

White soon had an overwhelming advantage (11... cxd5 12. Nxd5 Nxd5 13. exd5 Nd7 14. c4 Nf6 15. Rc1 g6 16. c5).

Pat: And there's bound to be a reason for the latest asterisk.

Noah: You're right. It means there are major exceptions to the rule. One of the biggest is that you should capture away from the center when it really helps your ♖s or protects your ♔. In Diagram 132 it does both for Black.

Pat: What am I looking at?

Noah: You're looking at a typical situation that arises in the Slav, the Caro-Kann and some Frenches. Black retakes with the f-♟ for two reasons.

Pat: One must be to open the file for his R/f8.

Noah: And the other is to eliminate

the only mating threat — after ... hxg6 White could have put a ♘ on g5 and gone in for Qg4-h4-h7#

But after ...fxg6! Black can stop the mate with ...h6!.

1.	d4	d5
2.	c4	c6
3.	Nc3	Nf6
4.	Nf3	dxc4
5.	a4	Bf5
6.	e3	e6
7.	Bxc4	Bb4
8.	0-0	Nbd7
9.	Qe2	Bg6
10.	e4	0-0
11.	Bd3	Qa5
12.	e5	Nd5

132

Commenting on Paul Morphy's most famous game, which began 1. e4 e5 2. Nf3 d6 3. d4 Bg4 4. dxe5 Bxf3, Wilhelm Steinitz criticized Morphy's 5. Qxf3, saying that 5. gxf3!? was preferable — 5... dxe5 6. Qxd8† and 7. f4.)

13. Bxg6   fxg6!

Black has good play, for example 14. Ne4 c5 15. Neg5 Rae8 16. Qe4 cxd4 17. Nxd4 Nc5.

Pat: Are there any corollaries without asterisks?

Noah: Not many. There's another you must have heard before:

A ♘ ON THE RIM IS DIM*

This is true because a ♘ on the side of the board controls few squares – and fewer center squares in particular.

Pat: I suspect I know why there's an asterisk this time, because ♘s belong on the edge of the board when they do something good.

Noah: Correct. They serve a significant purpose, for example, in the Ruy Lopez when ...Na5 drives White's B/b3 off its best diagonal.

Or the significant purpose may be to hold onto a vital ♟, as in the

King's Gambit after 1. e4 e5 2. f4 exf4 3. Nf3 Nf6 4. e5 Nh5!.

Pat: And I see players as White trading off black ♗s on c5 or f5 with stuff like Na4 or Nh4.

Noah: Right. But you should also be aware that an edgy ♘ can be useful even when it doesn't threaten or protect anything. A good example of that is Diagram 133.

Pat: Before we go there, what's the story with Black's fourth move?

Noah: Black violates another rule with 4... Bd6 by blocking an unmoved center ♟. But it works because it solves the problem of defending the e5-♟ against the threat of Bxc6 – which would now be met by ...dxc6, unblocking the d-♟.

Sakaev-Sveshnikov
Gausdal 1993

1. b3	e5
2. Bb2	Nc6
3. e3	Nf6
4. Bb5	

Threatening Bxc6 and Bxe5. If 4... d6, White can try 5. d4.

4. ...   Bd6

If allowed, Black will continue ...0-0/...Re8/...Bf8/...d5, normalizing his development.

5. Na3

Now 6. Nc4 would be strong.

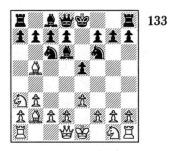

133

5. ...   Na5!

Black violates two rules, putting the ♘ on the edge and moving it a second time before completing development. But he takes the sting out of Nc4.

6. Be2   a6
7. Nc4

White was afraid that 7.... b5

would leave his ♘ on the rim indefinitely.

7. ...   Nxc4
8. bxc4   Qe7
9. a4?

With 9. Nf3 White is only slightly worse. The text stops ...Ba3 but wastes time.

After 9... 0-0 10. Nh3 Bc5 11. f4? Bxe3! White lost quickly (12. dxe3 Qb4† or, as the game went, 12. Bxe5 Ba7 13. Bb2 Re8 14. d4 d6 15. Nf2 Ng4! 16. Resigns).

Pat: Okay, does that do it for the rules of the opening?

Noah: Hardly. There are several other golden rules that the masters used to cite in the old days. For example:

EXCHANGES EASE A CRAMPED GAME

Pat: And that's still true?

Noah: It's generally true, as in Diagram 134.

Pat: Black does look a bit squeezed.

Noah: Right, and he can't free his position with ...exd4 because that just surrenders the center to White.

Pat: Does 8. dxe5 make sense then?

Noah: They used to think so 30 years ago. But now the masters prefer moves like 8. h3 to prevent the ...Bg4 pin, as we saw back in Diagram 123. The main point, though, is Black's recapture.

Pat: It looks like he's just messing up his chance for an equal center, I mean, with 8... dxe5.

Noah: Not really. White can't effectively avoid an exchange of ♘s on e5 after 8... Nxe5 and the result is that Black gets both an equal center and a ♘ trade that un-cramps his position.

1. e4	g6
2. d4	Bg7
3. Nf3	d6
4. c3	Nf6
5. Nbd2	0-0
6. Bd3	Nc6

"There are no rules any more, only the exceptions."
— **Alexey Shirov**

7. 0-0   e5

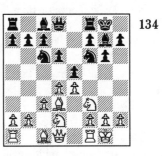

134

8. dxe5

Now 8... dxe5 9. Nc4 offers White a small edge after 9... Nh5 10. Bg5 or 9... Qe7 10. b4 and b5/Ba3.

8. ...   Nxe5!

This forces an exchange of pieces or a more favorable ♙ liquidation such as 9. Bc2 Re8 and if 10. Nd4 then 10... d5!.

9. Nxe5   dxe5

Black should have approximate equality after 10. Nc4 Nh5 or 10. Nf3 Qd6.

Pat: So if Black can simplify a

cramped position without loss of time he should do it.

Noah: Yes, and that's often true even when it costs a little time. In the Benoni Black is usually willing a give up a tempo or two to exchange a pair of ♘s.

A very typical case of that is Diagram 135. This is the same idea we talked about in Diagram 46, remember?.

Pat: Vaguely.

Noah: In this case 12... Ne5 is justified by a couple of things. One is that White took three tempi to get his ♘ to c4. So by trading it White is actually giving up on a piece he invested more time in than Black did on his Queen's ♘.

A second point is that Black's ♘ doesn't have a better square once he plays ...Nbd7. A third is that there's no better piece to defend the d6-♙ against the threats to it than the ♕ after ...Ne5.

Pat: But does 13. Na3 make sense ? I mean, it puts a ♘ on a dumb square and loses time.

Noah: I told you that the hard part of opening principles and rules is that they contradict one another, didn't I?

1. d4	Nf6
2. c4	c5
3. d5	e6
4. Nc3	exd5
5. cxd5	d6
6. Nf3	g6
7. g3	Bg7
8. Bg2	0-0
9. 0-0	Re8
10. Nd2	a6
11. a4	Nbd7
12. Nc4	

135

12. ...	Ne5

Not 12... Nb6 because then 13. Na3! is more effective – Black's N/b6 is badly misplaced.

13. Nxe5

Here 13. Na3!? may be best, to avoid trading pieces.

13. ...	Rxe5
14. Bf4	Re8

Black's game has been eased and he has fighting middlegame chances after 15. Qc2 Nh5 16. Bd2 f5.

Pat: You did. But why did you say generally exchanges are good?

Noah: Because the rule about exchanges deserves a smaller asterisk to cover exceptions in which trading pieces – with or without loss of time – violates some other, more important principle.

For example, in the Scotch 1. e4 e5 2. Nf3 Nc6 3. d4 exd4 4. Nxd4 it would be horrible for Black to trade ♘s and let White dominate the center after 4... Nxd4? 5. Qxd4.

Pat: But Black can kick the ♛ back with, you know, 5... c5.

Noah: That's even worse. There's something about holes you should know.

Pat: Like in "Avoid them"?

Noah: No, there isn't even a broad principle that works here. Chess thinking has changed too much in the last 100 years.

In the 19th century Wilhelm Steinitz coined the term "hole" for a key square unprotected by ♟s. Whenever Black played ...e6 and ...g6, and allowed a White piece to land on f6, the annotators would say "Tsk, tsk."

Pat: No one really says "Tsk, tsk."

Noah: Okay, allow me a little literary license. In any event there are times when holes are liabilities and there are times times when they are not. In Diagram 137 it's a liability.

After White allows 13... a4, b3 is a significant weakness. If White then pushes his b-♟ two squares Black takes *en passant* and piles up on the

isolated a-♟.

Pat: Looks convincing.

Seirawan-Karpov
Monaco 1994

1. d4	Nf6
2. Nf3	e6
3. Bg5	h6
4. Bxf6	Qxf6
5. e4	d6
6. c3	g6
7. Nbd2	Bg7
8. Bc4	Nd7
9. 0-0	0-0
10. Re1	e5
11. dxe5	dxe5
12. Qc2	a5

136

13. a3?

White explained that he tried to decide between 13. a4 and 13. b4, and then said to himself: "Why not just prepare b4 first?"

13. ...   a4!

And Black had a positional edge that grew after:

14. Nf1	Nc5
15. Ne3	c6
16. Rad1	h5
17. Ba2	Qe7
18. Nd2	Rb8
19. f3	b5
20. Ndf1	Be6

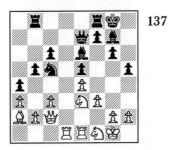

137

Black's superiority is undoubted (21. Bxe6 Nxe6 22. Qf2 Qc7 23.

Nc2 Rfd8).

Noah: But holes aren't holes if your pieces protect them sufficiently. Today you see systems such as 1. d4 Nf6 2. c4 e6 3. Nf3 b6 4. Nc3 Bb7 5. a3 g6 or 4. a3 Ba6 5. Qb3 g6 being used by GMs all the time.

Pat: Nobody cares about the hole at f6?

Noah: It's not a hole as long as there's a dark-squared black ♗ on the board.

Another good example is Diagram 138, a typical example of what happens when White's f-♗ is traded for a N/c6, as it so often is in the Ruy Lopez. Black can play ...f6!, despite the hole created at e6.

Pat: You mean, he can get away with it because he still has a light-squared ♗.

Noah: Pat, you're beginning to show some promise. Black, in fact, is stronger on the light squares than White so he can afford to give up a little of that strength to cover an

important dark-square – e5. It's as if e6 is a hole with an asterisk.

WHEN A HOLE ISN'T A HOLE

1. e4	e5
2. Nf3	Nc6
3. Bb5	a6
4. Ba4	Nf6
5. 0-0	Be7
6. Bxc6	dxc6
7. d3	Nd7
8. Nbd2	

138

White will attack the e-♟ with Nc4.

8. ...   0-0

9. Nc4   f6!

Better than 9... Bf6 10. b3 Re8 11. Bb2 followed by h3 and Nh2/f4, with advantage to White.

10. b3

Or 10. d4 exd4 11. Nxd4 Ne5! with good play for Black.

10. ...   c5!

And Black's N/d7 heads for d4 via b8 and c6.

A similar example is 1. e4 e5 2. Nf3 Nc6 3. Bb5 a6 4. Ba4 b5 5. Bb3 Na5 6. 0-0 d6 7. d4 Nxb3 8. axb3 and now 8... f6!.

And when Bobby Fischer came up with a new wrinkle in the Sicilian Defense in his 1992 rematch with Boris Spassky:

1. e4	c5
2. Nf3	Nc6
3. Bb5	g6
4. Bxc6	bxc6
5. 0-0	Bg7
6. Re1	

139

Spassky eventually responded with a clever counter:

6. ...   f6!

Followed by ...Nh6-f7 and ...0-0. Black doesn't commit himself in the center until after he's castled.

Pat: I think I've had enough asterisks for one day.

Noah: Let me hedge one last time, without an asterisk:

TEMPI DON'T (necessarily) COUNT

Pat: What's it mean?

Noah: It means that winning a tempo isn't always desirable because it doesn't mean you're gaining anything tangible.

Pat: But you've gained some time.

Noah: Not permanently. For example, there's a line in the Sicilian which is very simple to learn and doesn't have much new theory to worry about – and it begins with Black winning a tempo. You can see that in Diagram 140.

Pat: I've seen this line before, whatever it's called.

Noah: Call it whatever you want. It doesn't have a recognized name. The point is that even though Black seems to have gained time with his fourth move it doesn't matter much.

Pat: You mean because White can get the tempo back when he plays Be3, attacking the ♛.

Noah: And yet that only equalizes in, for example, the 5. Nb5 line.

Pat: And in the main line?

Noah: In the main line White retreats his ♘ to b3 but that turns out to be a useful move, as I've said

before.

And even though White could have played Be3 at any of several points, he didn't – because Black will usually retreat his ♛ to c7 anyway in order to prevent the e5 advance and create his own counterplay with ...b5.

Maybe Diagram 142 will make this tempo business clearer.

1. e4	c5
2. Nf3	Nc6
3. d4	cxd4
4. Nxd4	Qb6

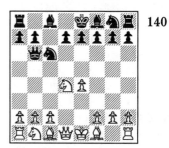

140

Now 5. Nb5 a6 6. Be3 gains a tempo.

Not everyone understood Spassky's 6... f6!. When Yasser Seirawan saw it he wrote:
"Huh? The only good thing about this move is that it won't win any prizes for novelty of the year."

But after 6... Qd8! 7. Nd4 Nf6 8. Nc3 e5! Black stands well (9. Nb3 Bb4).

5. Nb3	Nf6
6. Nc3	e6
7. Bd3	Be7
8. 0-0	a6
9. Kh1!	

White avoids Be3 since Black's ♕ is misplaced on b6 and he doesn't need to develop the B/c1 until he finds the right square. Typical play goes:

9. ...	d6
10. f4	0-0
11. Qf3	Qc7

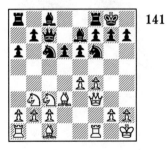

141

With good attacking chances for White.

1. d4	Nf6
2. c4	e6
3. Nf3	b6
4. g3	Ba6
5. b3	

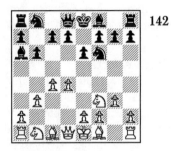

142

This was a popular line in the 1990s. Black's ♗ will retreat to b7, leaving White with an extra move, b3.

5. ...	Bb4†
6. Bd2	Be7

Black loses another tempo, with his ♗. But this leaves White's ♗ misplaced on d2.

Play might go 7. Bg2 c6 8. Nc3 d5 9. 0-0 Nbd7 10. cxd5 cxd5 11. a4 Bb7 with a fine game for Black.

Pat: I don't get it – Black loses two tempos.

Noah: That's tempi. And there are good reasons for why he does it.

First, Black's little dance with the ♗ from c8 to a6 to b7 gives White an extra move, b3. But that ♙ move restricts his options, such as by preventing his ♕ from going to the useful squares b3 and a4.

Pat: And the ♗ check?

Noah: It gives White another less-than-useful move, Bd2. The ♗ usually just gets in the way there.

In the end White ends up with two extra tempi – and both tend to hurt, not help.

Pat: And the point is...?

Noah: The point here is that gaining tempi – like controlling the center or getting an edge in development or most everything else we covered today – is a means to an end. And there are bound to be exceptions to the rules – and exceptions to the exceptions.

Pat: You're telling me.

Noah: I am. And the basic message is you have to be aware of the rules and general principles of the opening, and their corollaries and asterisks, so you'll be able to understand when breaking them is the best move.

That's what makes the opening hard. Come back tomorrow and we'll talk about ways to make it much easier.

Don't overlook the details of the Purdy Chess Library (see www.chessco.com). Here is what Grandmaster Paul Motwani had to say about "CJS Purdy's Fine Art of Annotation Volume 2:"

C.J.S. Purdy's Chess Jewels Selected Perfectly

Australia's late great IM Cecil John Seddon Purdy (1906-1979) was not only the first-ever World Correspondence Chess Champion and a four-times winner of his country's national championship, but also an extremely gifted writer who communicated his thoughts on the Royal Game with almost unsurpassed lucidity. Now, thanks to Thinkers' Press, their newly published 256-page Volume 2 of "C.J.S. Purdy's Fine Art of Chess Annotation and Other Thoughts" treats the reader to a magnificent collection of 120 instructive games and 13 further articles where Purdy poured out his pearls of wisdom, thereby allowing players of all standards to derive enormous benefit and enjoyment too.

In which Noah explains why safety may come second and that zugzwang doesn't occur just in the endgame — and why Pavlov is more important in the opening than Kasparov.

Chapter Six:

DECISIONS

Noah: Today I thought we'd get a bit further into some of the difficult choices players face every game regardless of opening.

Pat: Like what?

Noah: Like when to commit yourself – such as by pushing a ♟ – and when to sit on your hands.

Pat: I'm the type who always likes to do something now rather than put it off.

Noah: And that's part of the problem. Procrastination is often the better part of valor in the opening. Take Diagram 143 for example.

Pat: Does this have a name?

Noah: Most openings do. This position has been called the Janowsky Variation because a French-Polish master named David Janowsky used it a century ago.

The ...a6 move is almost always useful in the Queen's Gambit Declined because it prepares ...dxc4. After White retakes on c4 Black can expand with ...b5 and ...Bb7.

Pat: I like ...a6 for another reason – there are no scary ♗ checks on b5 after I play ...c5.

Noah: Yes, that's a valid point, too. But here the move is simply premature.

Pat: Because?

Noah: Because the position is too early for it. All White had to do to get an advantage is to reason – by analogy – and find a QGD variation in which ...a6 is a wasted move.

Pat: Which he did.

Noah: He did, the Exchange Variation – and in particular the Exchange with a kingside attack.

1. d4   d5
2. c4   e6
3. Nc3   a6

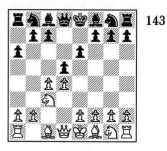

143

4. cxd5!   **exd5**

White has a favorable version of the Exchange Variation, since ...a6 is often irrelevent in that line.

5. Nf3   Nf6
6. Bg5   Be7
7. e3   Nbd7
8. Qc2   0-0
9. Bd3   Re8
10. h3!

If White castles kingside and plays the Minority Attack with b4-5, Black's ...a6 would be justified. Here it isn't.

10. ...   c6
11. 0-0-0   Nf8

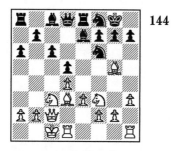

144

White is a tempo ahead of a normal Exchange QGD. In *Ståhlberg-Bohatyrchuk, Moscow 1935* he used it to develop a strong attack after 12. Bxf6 Bxf6 13. g4 and 14. Rdg1.

Pat: So 3... a6 is just a bad idea.

Noah: We're not talking about good and bad. A good idea may just be badly timed, as you see in Diagram 145.

Pat: Even I know something about this. It's the starting position of the Richter-Rauzer in the Sicilian.

Noah: And it's where White's decision-making starts. He has several good ideas he can use from move seven on.

And when the Richter-Rauzer was young White tried different ways of putting those ideas together.

Pat: I'm with you so far.

Noah: One of those ideas is f4. It controls the center and prepares to push the e-♙.

Pat: I feel a "but" coming up.

Noah: But at move seven it has a tactical flaw. White is not developed enough to play it safely. This is why you usually don't see f4 until move nine or later.

Pat: You said White had several ideas. What else?

Noah: Another good one is Nb3, which we talked about when we spoke of controlling the center. Here it does three things.

Pat: I count two – it discourages ...d5 and it prevents ...Nxd4.

Noah: Correct. Exchanges such as ...Nxd4 can ease Black's cramped game, as I mentioned yesterday.

But there's a third idea behind

Nb3: It prepares an attack on d6. White wants to play Qd2 and 0-0-0 which will threaten Bxf6 – because then ...Bxf6 would lose the d-♙.

Pat: Sounds simple enough. But there must be something wrong with Nb3 – or you wouldn't have brought it up.

Noah: It's a fine idea – but not at move seven. Again this is a matter of premature commitment, as Diagram 146 shows.

"Never make a good move too soon."
– James Mason

1. e4	c5
2. Nf3	Nc6
3. d4	cxd4
4. Nxd4	Nf6
5. Nc3	d6
6. Bg5	e6

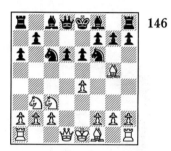

145

7. f4   h6!

The key point is 8. Bh4 is met by 8... Be7 and White cannot continue with the natural 9. Qd2 because of 9... Nxe4! (10. Nxe4 Bxh4† or 10. Bxe7 Nxd2).

And 8. Bxf6 Qxf6 is excellent for Black.

Alexander Alekhine introduced the Nb3 idea at Podebrady 1936 in

a game that went 7. Nb3 Be7 8. Qd2 0-0?! 9. 0-0-0 and White stood well.

But after 7. Nb3 Black can improve with

7. ...   a6!

146

8. Qd2   h6!

And now 9. Bf4 b5 or 9. Bh4 Nxe4!.

The right way of using the Alekhine idea was 7. Qd2 Be7 8. 0-0-0 0-0 and only then 9. Nb3.

Pat: It sounds like you're saying I should delay making any commitment until I'm castled and having my second soda.

Noah: No, the basic idea is to preserve your most important options until your opponent commits himself.

No less an authority than Miguel Najdorf said that 5... a6 in his Sicilian variation: 1. e4 c5 2. Nf3 d6 3. d4 cxd4 4. Nxd4 Nf6 5. Nc3 was basically a waiting move.

Pat: Waiting for what?

Noah: For a commitment. If White plays a non-commital move like 6. a4 or 6. Be3 or 6. Be2, Black can force matters with 6... e5, after which 5... a6 turns out to be very useful. Despite the hole at d5 Black gets good piece play, Najdorf found.

On the other hand, if White commits himself to sharper moves such as 6. Bg5 or 6. Bc4, Black will take on a different center, with 6... e6.

Pat: This is trickier than I thought.

Noah: That's why grandmasters are grandmasters. Some of the GMs of the older generation, like Bent Larsen, were terrific at tricking opponents that way. Take a look at

"Theory is a strange, speckled animal."
— **Bent Larsen**

Diagram 147.

Pat: What's happening here?

Noah: Several things happen from move five on. First, Black delays turning the opening into a kind of Dutch Defense until after White commits his N/g1. That's because he wants White to give up the possibility of Nh3-f4.

A move later makes all the difference. After 6... f5! Black stands well.

Pat: Yeah, but he shouldn't have gotten the edge.

Noah: That came about because of some more clever delaying tactics by Black, at move nine.

Rukavina-Larsen
Leningrad 1973

1. c4	g6
2. d4	Bg7
3. g3	c5
4. d5	d6
5. Bg2	Na6

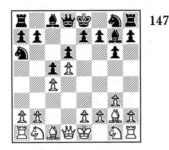

147

Black avoids 5... f5 because then 6. Nh3! and Nf4 exploits the e6 hole.

6. Nf3?!	f5!
7. 0-0	Nf6
8. Nc3	0-0

Now 9. b3? is met by 9... Ne4!.

9. Ne1	Rb8

Another good waiting move by Black – designed to meet 10. e4 Nxe4 11. Nxe4 fxe4 12. Bxe4 with 12... b5! and good queenside play.

10. Qd3

Here 10. a4 would invite 10... Nb4. White had to recognize he was in danger and play 10. Nc2 Nc7 11. a4.

10. ...	Bd7
11. b3	Ne4!

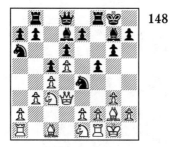

148

With great play for Black, e.g. 12. Bb2 b5! 13. cxb5 Nxc3 14. Bxc3 Bxb5 or 13. Bxe4 fxe4 14 Qxe4 Bf5.

In the game White lost after 12. Bxe4 fxe4 13. Qc2 Bh3.

Pat: But wasn't 5... Na6 pretty commital on Black's part?

Noah: Actually it's less commital than any other developing move at that point because the ♘ wasn't going anywhere else.

Pat: Because ...Nc6 was out of the question?

Noah: And because ...Nd7 would have left the ♘ with little to do and would also have made e6 more vulnerable. Putting the ♘ on a6 was actually a way of postponing the difficult decisions about other pieces and ♙s.

Another subtle point about delaying commitments arises in Diagram 149, in a more orthodox Dutch.

Pat: I don't get White's order of moves at all.

Noah: It's not that deep. White wants to play c4 to control the center. But he doesn't want to do it before ...Be7.

Pat: Why?

Noah: Because otherwise the ♗ check is good for Black, such as 4. c4 Bb4†. The check is not so worthwhile, however, if the ♗ has already spent a tempo to get to e7.

Pat: But Black checks anyway.

Noah: That's just a bit of psychology. He's trying to convince White to accept his "free tempo" – the

move c3 – and play something other than 7. c4. That's the best move but it would give the "free tempo" back.

But the real finesse occurs at move seven. Once Black decided to play a Stonewall formation, with ...d5 and ...c6, he could have played either pawn move first.

Pat: And you're saying 7... c6 is more accurate.

Noah: More accurate because it got White to commit his N/b1 prematurely.

1. d4	f5
2. g3	Nf6
3. Bg2	e6
4. Nf3	

White avoids 4. c4 Bb4† 5. Nc3 0-0 when Black stands well after 6. Nf3 Bxc3† 7. bxc3 d6 8. 0-0 Nc6 9. Qc2 e5 or 6. Bd2 d6 7. Nf3 Nbd7 8. 00 Bxc3 9. Bxc3 Ne4.

Also fine for Black is, 5. Bd2 Qe7 preparing ...e5, e.g. 6. Nf3 0-0 7. 0-0 Bxd2 8. Qxd2 Ne4 9. Qc2 d6

and ...e5 or 8. Nbxd2 d6.

4. ...	Bb4†!?
5. c3	Be7
6. 0-0	0-0

Now if White tries to avoid c4 with 7. Nbd2 Nc6 8. Qc2 Black has 8... d5!, stopping e4. Then White has nothing better than 9. c4.

7. c4

We're back to a normal position that could have come about with 4... Be7 5. 0-0 0-0 6. c4.

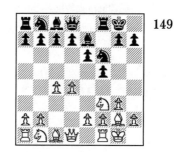

149

7. ...	c6

Another favorite move of Larsen's, delaying a decision about the d-♙.

8. Nc3	d5!

Now Black gets into Stonewall but avoids the best ♘ placement for White, which is Nbd2 followed by Ne5-d3! and Nf3.

Pat: Is there any rule of thumb about when to make commiting moves?

Noah: In general you want to delay them until after your opponent has exhausted his more dangerous options. A good example of this is the Winawer French, in Diagram 150.

Pat: I've seen this one. White's threatening to play c4, attacking the ♛. So at some point Black has to do ...c4.

Noah: Well, not exactly. White really isn't eager to play c4 because that undermines d4 and wrecks his center.

"The triumph of science in chess."
– Nikolai Riumin on 2. g3, rather than 2. c4, after 1. d4 f5)

And Black doesn't want to hurry ...c4 because that would kill his pressure on d4 and would allow White extra options of development that work best with a closed center.

Pat: You mean like putting a ♘ on g5 or h5.

Noah: That, as well as putting a Bishop on h3, which is a great way of anticipating ...f6.

1. e4	e6
2. d4	d5
3. Nc3	Bb4
4. e5	c5
5. a3	Bxc3†

"No, 1... e6 is not a forced win for Black – He only has a slight advantage!"
– John Watson

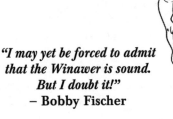

"I may yet be forced to admit that the Winawer is sound. But I doubt it!"
– Bobby Fischer

6. bxc3	Ne7
7. a4	Qa5
8. Bd2	

150

| 8. ... | Nbc6 |

Here 8... c4? is premature because of 9. Ne2 and Nf4-h5 or 9. Nf3 Nbc6 10. g3! and either 11. Bg2 or 11. Bh3 with advantage to White.

9. Nf3

Now, however, 9. Bd3 c4! – with tempo – would be well-timed, e.g. 10. Be2 Bd7 11. Nh3 0-0-0 12.Nf4 Rhg8 13.Bg4 Ng6 14. Nh5 Rdf8! and eventually ...f6.

Also, 9. c4? Qc7 gives Black great center counterplay.

Decisions

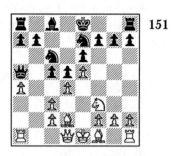

151

9. ...   Bd7

Again 9... c4? is premature because of 10. Ng5 and if 10... h6 then 11. Nh3 Bd7 12. Nf4 and Nh5.

Or 10. g3 Bd7 11. Bh3 0-0-0 12. 0-0 h6 13. Nh4.

10. Be2

On 10. c4? Qc7 Black stands well (11. cxd5 exd5 12. dxc5 0-0 13. Be2 Nxe5).

10. ...   c4

For many years this was the main line but the flexible 10... f6! was found to be better.

Then 11. c4 Qc7 12. exf6 gxf6 13. cxd5 Nxd5 is highly double-edged and can easily turn in Black's

favor after 14. c4 Nde7.

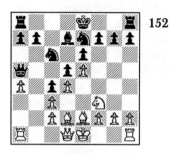

152

11. Ng5!

And White is better after 11... 0-0 12. 0-0 f6 13. exf6 Rxf6 14. Bg4 or 11... h6 12. Nh3 0-0-0 13. Nf4.

Pat: Are there any special cases of commiting moves? You know, that come up an awful lot – and are usually mistakes.

Noah: Sure. There's one group I call "safety first" moves.

Pat: Safety first?

Noah: Yes, by playing them you avoid anxiety – at the risk of making what may turn out to be a wasted move.

Pat: I'm sure you have an example that will make this clear to me.

Noah: The simplest is when White plays h3 to prevent a ...Bg4 pin.

Pat: Is that good or bad?

Noah: It's a matter of timing. If White plays h3 on the third or fourth move it's cowardly and wasteful. But on the ninth move of a main line Ruy, it makes excellent sense.

The main line of the Lopez goes 1. e4 e5 2. Nf3 Nc6 3. Bb5 a6 4. Ba4 Nf6 5. 0-0 Be7 6. Re1 b5 7. Bb3 d6 8. c3 0-0 9. h3! because White is finally ready to play 10. d4 – and 9. d4 would have allowed a good 9... Bg4!.

Pat: What about playing h3 somewhere in between move three and move nine? Isn't it just a matter of taste then?

Noah: That depends on how comfortable you are with tactics. In some positions, a safety-first move can be, as the annotators say, "inaccurate."

It's like when you castle kingside and play f4. Throwing in Kh1 may turn out to be wasteful.

But at the same time the move can be practical – because it saves a lot of clock time when you don't have to worry about checks on the a7-g1 diagonal.

Pat: So far I'm with you.

Noah: But in a sharper position a wasted tempo will cost you a lot more than in a quieter one.

That's the case in Diagram 153, the old main line of the Richter-Rauzer, where White can toss in safety-first moves such as Kb1 or a3 at any point.

Pat: I always play a3 in positions like that. Then I don't have to worry about ...b5-b4 or ...Nb4 or even some business with ...Qa5 and an Exchange sack on c3.

Noah: But Black isn't threatening any of those things in the diagram – and those safety first moves turn out to be just wastes of time in what is really a sharp position.

1. e4	c5
2. Nf3	Nc6
3. d4	cxd4
4. Nxd4	Nf6
5. Nc3	d6
6. Bg5	e6
7. Qd2	a6
8. 0-0-0	Bd7
9. f4	Be7

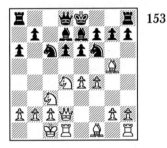

153

After either 10. Kb1 or 10. a3 Black seizes the intiative with 10... Nxd4. For example:

10. Kb1	Nxd4
11. Qxd4	Bc6

Black has excellent chances (12. e5 dxe5 13. Qxe5 Qb8!).

Better was 10. Nf3, which pre-pares both e5 and the positional threat of Bxf6 (since ...Bxf6 allows Qxd6).

Pat: How do I know for sure whether a move is a time waster or not?
Noah: Usually you don't know any-thing for sure about a chess game

"Moves with the rook's pawn to stop B (or N)-g5 are, in the opening, nearly always to be condemned."
– the dogmatic Dr. Tarrarsch

until the post-mortem.

But if there's a specific, tactical reason, then you're probably on solid ground to seek safety first. Diagram 154 comes to mind.
Pat: Another Sicilian.
Noah: Naturally. The Sicilian De-fense leads the league in safety-first precautions.

Here White shows he's very con-scious about timing because he wants to play f4 without spending a tempo on Be3.
Pat: I thought lost tempi don't count.
Noah: Don't necessarily count. But they do count in dynamic situa-tions such as this. The million-dol-lar question is whether White needs to play Kh1 before advancing his f-pawn.
Pat: And the answer is....
Noah: The answer is determined by tactics: 9. Kh1 is more accurate than 9. f4 because the ♟ move allows Black to start his queenside attack with 9... b5!.

It turns out that 9. Kh1 costs Black

a tempo, not White, because he then needs ...a6 or ...Rb8 to pre-pare ...b5.

1. e4	c5
2. Nf3	d6
3. d4	cxd4
4. Nxd4	Nf6
5. Nc3	g6
6. Be2	Bg7
7. Nb3	0-0
8. 0-0	Nc6

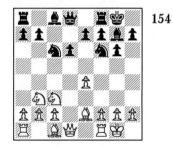

154

9. f4

After 9. Kh1 Black needs counterplay from something like 9... a6 10. f4 b5 with play as in the main line. But White then has added a useful move – Kh1 – and Black has added a fairly useless one: ...a6.

    9. ...   b5!

The tactical justification is 10. Nxb5 Nxe4 or 10. Bxb5 Qb6† 11. Kh1 Nxe4! 12. Nxe4 Qxb5.

    10. Bf3

This meets the threat to the e-pawn of 10... b4.

    10. ...   b4!
    11. Nd5   Nxd5
    12. exd5   Na5

155

White's play along the e-file and potential use of c6 is balanced by Black's play along the c-file and ...Nc4.

"Just as the position reached its most critical point, just when decisive action was required, just when White should be thinking about playing e5 or f5, if not Nd5 or Nf5, Nxb5 or Nxe6, I would produce – wait for it – a3, or perhaps on a good day Kb1."
– GM Joe Gallagher, explaining his poor experiences on the White side of a Najdorf Sicilian

Pat: What's the story in 1. d4?

Noah: In the closed openings, there are fewer tactical reasons for safety-first moves so you have to think in more general terms.

For example, if you don't like being surprised by a check in an open English or some Queen's Indian line, you might take time out for a3.

Pat: That must be what's going on in

Diagram 156.

Noah: Exactly. This is from a symmetrical English in which Black often plays ...Bb4. There are two quite good lines in which White gets a fine game with a3.

    1. c4   c5
    2. Nf3   Nf6
    3. Nc3   Nc6
    4. d4   cxd4
    5. Nxd4

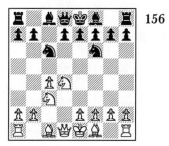

156

Here 5... Qb6 6. Nb3 e6 and now 7. a3 is good.

    5. ...   e6
    6. a3

This stops 6... Bb4 and enables

White to exert extra pressure on the center with e4 or Bg5.

For example, 6... Be7 7. e4 or 6... Bc5 7. Nb3 Be7 8. e4 give White a small pull.

6. ...   d5

Black tries to exploit White's loss of time.

7. Bg5

White's pressure on d5 cannot be balanced by ...Bb4 or ...Qa5 now and he has a fine game. Also good is 7. cxd5 exd5 8. Bg5.

Pat: There must be some safety-first moves in 1. d4 openings that are more likely to be wastes than others.

Noah: Sure. At the top of the list of suspects is pushing your a-♙ two squares to prevent your opponent from advancing his b-♙ two squares.

This can be even worse than a loss of time because you're also weakening your ♙-structure and giving up control of a key square or

---

A3!?

The **Petrosian Variation** of the **Queen's Indian Defense,** with an early a3, was introduced to GM chess when Sultan Khan used it to beat José Capablanca at Hastings 1930-31: 1. Nf3 Nf6 2. d4 b6 3. c4 Bb7 4. Nc3 e6 5. a3 and then 5... d5 6. cxd5 exd5 7. Bg5 with a nice version of the **QGD,** by transposition.

But Benjamin Blumenfeld, the leading Soviet expert on openings, criticized 5. a3 for "losing time, since White does not develop his pieces and does not make way for them either."

---

two. In Queen's Gambit Accepted positions White is usually better off waiting for ...b5 – because then a4! is stronger. Take a look at Diagram 157.

Pat: Looks a little like the Janowsky position.

Noah: But it's not the same, since 2... dxc4 is a lot different from 2... e6. This position usually leads to a normal line of the QGA by transposition.

Pat: Transposition again. So what's the point?

Noah: Two points. The first is the minor finesse of 3... a6 ruling out Qa4† as a way of regaining the gambit ♙. That's a common theme in the QGA.

Pat: You mean 4. Qa4†? doesn't work here because of 4... b5!.

Noah: Yes. The second point is that 3... a6 is a psychological weapon. It seems to threaten to protect the c4-♙ with ...b5. And that panics some players into the knee-jerk reaction of 4. a4 – a bad move.

Pat: But if Black can spend a tempo on his a-♙ at move three why can't White do the same at move four?

Noah: Because there's a hidden cost. After 4. a4 Nf6 it turns out that Black's ♙ move is much more useful than White's.

1. d4	d5
2. c4	dxc4
3. Nf3	a6

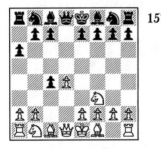

157

More common is 3... Nf6 4. e3 e6 5. Bxc4 c5 and ...a6 – reaching the same position that could now come about via 3... a6 4. e3 e6 5. Bxc4 Nf6.

But after 3... a6 Black has another option, meeting 4. e3 with 4... b5, holding onto the gambit pawn. So, some White players will answer:

4. a4?!   **Nf6**
5. e3

Similar is 5. Nc3 Nc6! and White has problems regaining the ♟.

For example 6. d5 Na5 (since there's no 7. Qa4†), or 6. e4 Bg4 or 6. e3 Na5 7. Ne5 Be6 and Black keeps his ♟ safely.

5. ...   **Bg4**
6. Bxc4   **e6**
7. Nc3   **Nc6!**

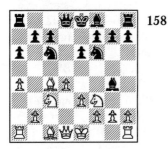

Black can attack the center with ...e5 and not fear Bb5 (or Qb3

which can be met by ...Bxf3 and ...Na5).

Pat: What should White do after 3... a6 ? I mean he can't let Black just walk all over the queenside.
Noah: White should consider what happens if he just ignores Black's alleged "threat" – and responds with a4 after ...b5. You'll see that happen in Diagram 159.

1. d4   **d5**
2. c4   **dxc4**
3. Nf3   **a6**
4. e3   **b5**
5. a4!

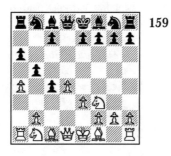

And with b3 White favorably collapses the Black queenside. For example:

5. ...   **Bb7**
6. b3!   **cxb3**
7. axb5   **axb5**
8. Bxb5†   **c6**
9. Rxa8

White is better after 10. Bc4.

Pat: How often does it turn out that a4 is better after ...b5 rather than before?
Noah: An awful lot in the closed openings, such as the QGD, the King's Indian and the Benoni. Another case is Diagram 160.
Pat: I think I get this one. White has a really nice game after he plants his ♞ on c4. But that costs him more time than 5. a4 would have.
Noah: True, but in a closed position, time doesn't count as much as control of squares. And White has a lot of squares after 14. a5.
Pat: Yeah, Black looks like he's in

real trouble on the queenside.
Noah: It's the old story. Black paid the price of learning that ♟s can't move backward.
Pat: So this ...b5/a4 business should be like, uh, an automatic reaction.
Noah: Almost automatic. It's one of a small family of moves by your opponent that should trigger Pavlov-like reactions.
Pat: Pavlov, you mean like the drooling dogs?
Noah: The same. When you see ...b5, you should start salivating about playing a4.

It isn't always the right reply but it should be the first thing you think about.

Jakovic-Rashkovsky
Ekaterinburg 1997

1. d4   **c5**
2. d5   **e5**
3. e4   **d6**
4. Nc3   **a6**

Here 5. a4 Be7 and ...Bg5xc1 has been known to give Black good play on the dark squares (6. Nf3 Bg4 7. h3 Bxf3 8. Qxf3 Bg5).

5. Nf3	**b5**
6. a4!	**b4**
7. Nb1!	

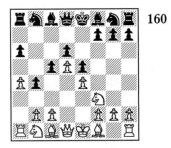

160

This is the only way for the ♘ to reach its best outpost, c4.

7. ...	**Nf6**
8. Nbd2	**g6**
9. Bd3	**Bg7**
10. Nc4	**0-0**
11. Bg5	**h6**
12. Bh4	**Qc7**
13. Bxf6!	

This avoids ...Nh5-f4 and leaves Black with a bad ♗.

13. ...	**Bxf6**

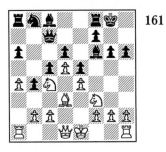

161

14. a5

And after 14... Bg7 15. 0-0 Nd7 16. c3 Rb8 17. Qa4 White had a powerful bind on the queenside.

Pat: Is there anything else that's supposed to make me drool?

Noah: Lots. What do you make of Diagram 162?

Pat: Not much. White's made one of those funny moves with his a-♙ that the GMs give exclamation points to themselves for – and nobody else understands.

And Black then put his ♘ on h6 for no apparent reason.

Noah: There is a reason, at least for

...Nh6. The ♘ is going to f5 and perhaps then to d4.

But the ♘ move also works like the bell that Professor Pavlov rang for his laboratory dogs.

Pat: Why is 6. h4 so strong?

Noah: It's strong when you can open the h-file like that. But usually White can't get his ♙ to the fifth rank – because Black can meet h4 with ...h5.

Or he can play ...h6 and answer h5 with ...g5.

Pat: In the end White doesn't open the h-file at all.

Noah: That's because h6! turned out to be even stronger than hxg6. White's conditioned reflex paid off.

Hodgson-Arkell
Isle of Man 1996

1. c4	**c5**
2. Nc3	**Nc6**
3. g3	**g6**
4. Bg2	**Bg7**
5. a3	**Nh6**

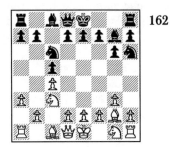

162

6. h4!	**Nf5**
7. h5	**b6**
8. d3	**Bb7**
9. h6!	

Now 9... Bxc3† may be the best of a bad lot of choices since 9... Be5 10. g4! Nfd4 11. f4 Bc7 12. e3 Ne6 13. Nd5 leaves Black's minor pieces in a mess.

9. ...	**Bf8**
10. b4!	

White plans Bb2 and Ne4.

10. ...	**Qc8**
11. Ne4	**cxb4**
12. axb4	**Nxb4**
13. Bb2	**f6**

Decisions

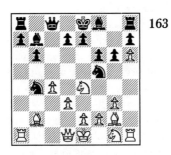

163

14. g4   Nxh6
15. g5!
With a murderous attack.

Pat: I always wondered how masters seem to know just when to push their h-♙.

Noah: It's something to think about whenever your opponent's f-♗ is fianchettoed. But another time you should think of it is when you can attack a ♘ on the sixth rank with tempo.

You see that working nicely for Black in Diagram 164.

Pat: And I see the results in Diagram 165. Black's got the better pieces in

the center. But I don't understand why it got so good for him so fast?

Noah: Pushing the h-♙ to h4 was part of a strategy of controlling the dark-squares, along with ...e5. White just made it more successful by allowing ...h4 to be played with tempo.

Dautov-Hickl
Nussloch 1996

1.	d4	d6
2.	e4	g6
3.	Nc3	Bg7
4.	Nge2	Nd7
5.	Be3	c6
6.	a4	Ngf6
7.	Ng3	

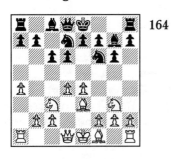

164

7. ...   h5

Now 8. Be2 h4 9. Nf1 e5 10. Nd2 Ng4! 11. Bxg4 exd4 gives Black good play on the dark squares.

For example, 12. Nc4 dxe3 13. Nxd6† Ke7 14. fxe3 Be5∞

8.	f3	h4
9.	Nge2	e5
10.	Qd2	Qc7
11.	dxe5	dxe5
12.	Nc1	Nf8

Black's ♘ is headed to f4 or d4 via e6.

13.	Nb3	Be6
14.	Nc5	N6d7!
15.	Nxe6	Nxe6
16.	Bc4	Nd4

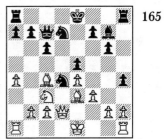

165

Lautier-Hall
Harplinge 1998

1.	e4	c5
2.	Nf3	Nc6
3.	d4	cxd4
4.	Nxd4	e6
5.	Nc3	d6
6.	g4	a6
7.	Be3	Nge7
8.	f4	b5
9.	Nb3	Bb7
10.	Qe2	Na5
11.	Nxa5	Qxa5
12.	Bg2	

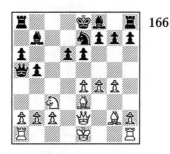

166

12. ...   b4
13. Nd1   d5!

Now 14. e5 h5! 15. h3 hxg4 16.

OTHER PAVLOVIAN REACTIONS

After White pushes his f-♙ in a typical opening, Black should think of ...c5, to attack the d4-♙ and open the c5-g1 diagonal.

Black should consider challenging any White ♙ advance on the queenside. For example, c5 might provoke ...b6. And on b4 Black should consider ...a5.

For example, 1. e4 c6 2. d4 d5 3. exd5 cxd5 4. c4 Nf6 5. Nc3 e6 6. Nf3 Be7 7. c5 and now 7... 0-0 8 Bd3 b6! 8. b4 a5!.

After White plays Bf4 or Bg5 in a queenside opening, Black should look at pushing his c-♙ because ...Qb6 or ...Qa5† can be strong. For example, 1. d4 d5 2. Bg5 and now 2...h6 3. Bh4 c6 4. e3 Qb6! (5. Qc1 e5 6. dxe5?? Qb4† and 7... Qxh4).

After g4 in a Sicilian, Black should examine ...d5 even at the price of a ♙-sacrifice. For example, see Lautier-Hall, Diagram 166.

Where are my chess dogs?

166

hxg4 Rxh1† 17. Bxh1 Nc6 is fine for Black.

14. Nf2	dxe4
15. Bxe4	Bxe4
16. Nxe4	Nd5!

And Black stood very well.

Pat: That's a lot of reactions I'm supposed to know. And they're all ♙ moves.

Noah: That shouldn't be surprising. The opening is filled with sly ♙ moves and counter-moves.

And it's particularly difficult because you often have to live with a ♙-structure that you don't want to change.

Pat: Because it's a favorable center for you.

Noah: Not always. There are many typical centers in which neither player is eager to change. I call them *zugzwang* centers.

Pat: *Zugzwang?* In the opening?

Noah: Well, it's not a real *zugzwang*. That only happens when a player is at a disadvantage because it's his turn to move.

What I mean is a situation with a fluid ♙ center which could be changed by a capture or advance. But neither player wants to advance or capture.

Pat: Why not?

Noah: Because the changes are usually unfavorable for the player who makes them. So they leave the center undisturbed for several moves – an extended kind of *zugzwang*.

Check out the various options in Diagram 167.

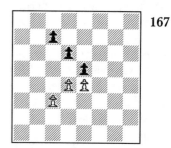

167

This is a typical ♙-structure of the *Ruy Lopez*. For example, it comes about from 1. e4 e5 2. Nf3 Nc6 3.

Decisions

Bb5 a6 4. Ba4 Nf6 5. 0-0 Be7 6. Re1 b5 7. Bb3 d6 8. c3 0-0 9. d4.

And from 1. e4 e5 2. Nf3 Nc6 3. Bb5 a6 4. Ba4 d6 5. c3 Bd7 6. d4.

It also arises in the *Giuoco Piano* – 1. e4 e5 2. Nf3 Nc6 3. Bc4 Bc5 4. c3 Bb6 5. d4 Qe7 and ...d6.

And in related 1. e4 e5 openings such as the *Ponziani:* 1. e4 e5 2. Nf3 Nc6 3. c3 Nf6 4. d4 d6.

It even appears in *Indian* defenses: 1. e4 g6 2. d4 Bg7 3. Nf3 d6 4. c3 Nf6 5. Bd3 0-0 6. 0-0 Nbd7 or 6... Nc6 followed by 7... e5.

Pat: Well, White can take on e5 or push to d5.

Noah: But he should be reluctant to play either one. And you should be able to tell me why.

Pat: I should? Well, I guess after dxe5 and ...dxe5 Black's diagonal is opened from f8 out to a3. That's gotta be good for his dark-squared ♗ and it also gives him c5 for a ♘.

Noah: It even releases tension in the center that almost always favors White. What about d4-d5?

Pat: That also gives away c5 and it reduces tension. But it cramps Black a bit.

Noah: What all of this means is that White doesn't want to change this center unless he has a good reason, such as exploiting the open d-file after dxe5. The same is true for Black and his options.

Pat: You mean, ...exd4 is bad because White rules after cxd4.

Noah: Also, Black can change the center with ...c5, to put pressure on d4 – but that surrenders ♟ control of d5.

And ...d5 leads to a symmetrical position that might blow up in Black's face for tactical reasons.

Pat: If all the ♟ moves are bad, the center would never change.

Noah: But it always does – eventually. Black often plays ...exd4 in order to pressure e4 with ...Re8!.

As for ...d5 by Black... well, let's take a look at an example with colors reversed, in Diagram 168.

Pat: Maybe I'm getting the hang of this colors reversed thing. Black has the same ♟-structure that White did in 167.

Noah: And both players have the same kinds of options that we saw then. Except that this time it's Black who can open the d-file, with ...dxe4. But after the reply, dxe4, White's B/f1 becomes alive and he gets c4 for his pieces.

What's especially interesting in this position is the possibility of d4 by White.

Pat: That has to blow the center completely away.

Noah: And blowing the center away usually benefits the player with the better placed pieces. It doesn't work for White after 4... Bd6 – but it does after 4... Nd7 ?

1. e4	c6
2. d3	d5
3. Nd2	e5
4. Ngf3	

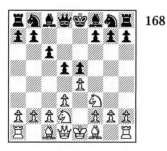

168

4. ...   Nd7?

Better is the solid 4... Bd6, which leads to a normal center *zugzwang* after 5. g3 Nf6 6. Bg2 0-0.

5. d4!

Now 5... exd4 6. exd5! cxd5 7. Nxd4 is a big edge for White because Black's N/d7 is misplaced.

For example, 7... Ngf6 8. Nf5! Qb6 9. Qe2† Qe6 10. Nb3 Qxe2† 11. Bxe2 and Nbd4 with a great endgame for White.

5. ...	dxe4
6. Nxe4	exd4
7. Qxd4	

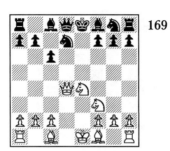

169

With a huge spatial edge for White (e.g. 7... Ngf6 8. Bg5 Be7 9. 0-0-0 as in a famous Tal brilliancy).

Pat: So far this *zugzwang* center makes a little sense. But what if you're not getting great piece play like White did in Diagram 169. Why would you change the center then?

Noah: One good reason is to avoid getting bad piece play. A case in point is Diagram 170. It comes from a traditional French Defense center, which is a sort of *semi-zugzwang*.

After Black's second move White doesn't want to play exd5 because that would liberate Black's B/c8

after ...exd5. And Black doesn't like ...dxe4 from move two on because it would leave White with the superior center.

Pat: This position is a little different from the usual French, isn't it? I mean, White doesn't usually exchange on c5.

Noah: Sometimes he does it to eliminate the pressure on d4. But it comes at the expense of developing Black's B/f8 on an excellent square, c5.

Kholmov-Kiriakov
Perm 1996

1. e4	e6
2. d4	d5
3. Nd2	a6
4. Ngf3	c5
5. dxc5	Bxc5
6. Bd3	Nf6
7. 0-0	Nc6
8. a3	0-0
9. b4	

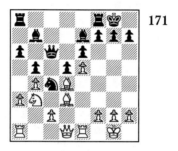

170

9. ...　　　　Be7?

This was the time to liquidate the center with 9... dxe4. Then 10. bxc5 exd3 is fine for Black.

So the key line is 10. Nxe4 Be7! 11. Bb2 with a minimal edge for White.

10. e5!	Nd7
11. Bb2	Qc7
12. Re1	

White has converted the center to a more permanent – and favorable – one. Here, for example, 12... f6 13. exf6 Nxf6 14. c4! favors him.

12. ...	b5
13. Nb3	Nb6
14. Nfd4!	Nc4

Or 14... Nxe5 15. Nxb5! axb5 16. Bxe5 with a big edge.

15. Nxc6	Qxc6
16. Bd4	Bb7

171

17. Qh5

And White soon had a winning attack (17... g6 18. Qg4 Rfc8 19. h4! a5 20. h5).

Pat: That square wasn't enough to save him.

Noah: No, Black missed his opportunity to liquidate with ...dxe4. After 10. e5! White had no center tension to worry about and his attack played itself.

Pat: Why is center tension so important?

Noah: Because it's often the only source of counterplay a defender has. As Diagram 172 shows.

Pat: This is sort of what I had in mind. Why isn't Black better off when he at least has a ♟ on the fourth rank, after 7... d5, than when it's only on the third?

Noah: Because on the third rank there was the chance for ...dxe5, with or without ...c5. Once that possibility of dissolving the center disappeared, White's space edge couldn't be contested and he built up his forces at his leisure.

Karpov-Torre
Leningrad 1973

1. e4	Nf6
2. e5	Nd5
3. d4	d6
4. Nf3	g6
5. Bc4	Nb6
6. Bb3	Bg7
7. Ng5	

172

7. ...	d5?

White now has a free hand and continued:

8. f4!	Nc6
9. c3	f6
10. Nf3!	Bf5
11. 0-0	Qd7
12. Nbd2	

Black can't break the ♟ chain and eventually the advantage in space told:

12. ...	fxe5
13. fxe5	0-0
14. Rf2!	Na5
15. Bc2	Bxc2
16. Qxc2	Qf5?
17. Qd1	e6

18. Nf1	

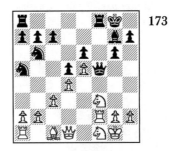

173

18. ...	c5

Too late. The game ended with 19. h3 cxd4 20. cxd4 Nc6 21. b3 Nd7 22. Ba3! Rf7 23. g4! Qe4 24. Ng5 Resigns.

Pat: What's the story with 1. d4 centers? Any *zugzwangs* there?

Noah: Many. A typical one is Diagram 174, a standard position early in the Queen's Gambit Accepted.

Pat: Even I've seen this one. Everybody has. But where's the *zugzwang?*

Noah: In the tension between the ♟s at d4 and c5. Count up all the ways that can change.

Pat: Okay, the obvious way is if White plays dxc5.

Noah: But that's just a bad liquidation if played at move six or seven – and it offers nothing to White at move eight.

Pat: Then there's Black playing ...cxd4.

Noah: And that's usually unfavorable to him because it opens the diagonal for White's B/c1, which can find a nice square at g5.

Any other ways the center can change?

Pat: I suppose Black can reduce the tension by playing ...c4 instead of ...cxd4. He needs to play ...b5 first.

Noah: And that's not a terrible idea because after ...b5 and ...c4 Black has a queenside majority.

But by eliminating the tension in the center Black is vulnerable to e4 or d5 advances by White.

Pat: I wanted to say that d5 was the fourth way to end the tension. It really busts up the center.

Noah: But it only works in positions

such as Diagram 176.

1.	d4	d5
2.	c4	dxc4
3.	Nf3	Nf6
4.	e3	e6
5.	Bxc4	c5

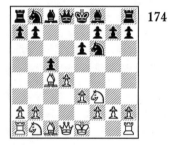

174

Now 6. dxc5? gives up any hope of advantage (6... Qxd1† 7. Kxd1 Bxc5).

6. 0-0   a6

Steinitz liked to play 6... cxd4 7. exd4 Be7 but White has a clear edge after 8. Qe2 0-0 9. Nc3.

For example, 9... Nbd7 10. Rd1 Nb6 11. Bb3 Nbd5 12. Bg5 Qa5 13 Rac1 and Ne5.

7. Qe2

Again 7. dxc5 is painless to Black (7... Qxd1 8. Rxd1 Bxc5).

7. ...   Nc6

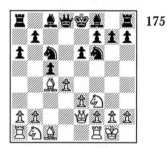

175

White is too strong in the center after 7... b5 8. Bb3 c4 9. Bc2 Bb7 10. e4.

8. Nc3!

Again 8. dxc5 leads nowhere because of 8... Bxc5. For example, 9. a3 0-0 10. b4 Bd6 11. Bb2 e5.

8. ...   Qc7

And here 8... cxd4 9. exd4 (or 9. Rd1) will lead to another White edge if Black doesn't grab the ♙ (9... Be7 10. Rd1 Nb4 11. Bg5).

On 9... Nxd4 10. Nxd4 Qxd4

White has compensation with 11. Rd1 Qb6 12. Be3 Qc7 13. Rac1.

9. d5!

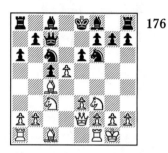

176

White gets an excellent game now because he gains the use of the d-file and b2-g7 diagonal.

White could also have timed the dxc5 exchange accurately with 9. Bd3 Be7 10. dxc5! and then 10... Bxc5 11. Ne4 Be7 12. b3 with advantage.

9. ...   exd5
10. Nxd5   Nxd5
11. Bxd5

With advantage to White. e.g. 11...Bd6 12. b3 0-0 13. Bb2 Bg4 14. h3 Bh5 15. Rfd1 Rfe8 16. Rd2 and

17. Rad1.

Pat: But once one of these *zugzwang* centers is changed I don't have to worry about it, right?

Noah: Wrong. Sometimes they occur more than once a game. Look at Diagram 177.

Pat: There's more of that funny business with Black checking at b4 and then retreating the ♗.

Noah: But it didn't matter because White realized his ♗ was misplaced at d2 and gave back the extra tempo at move nine.

I'm more interested in the diagram. What about it occurs to you?

Pat: I guess you could call that a *zugzwang*. White probably shouldn't take on d5. And Black shouldn't be in a rush to play ...dxc4.

Noah: And there's a second *zugzwang* at the 18th move. Normally, e4 in such a center would be dubious because it leaves White with an isolated d-♙ after ...dxe4.

But in Diagram 178 it's White's

best resource – and it ended up giving him the upper hand.

Atalik-Belyavsky
Yugoslavia 1998

1. d4	Nf6
2. c4	e6
3. g3	Bb4†
4. Bd2	Be7
5. Bg2	d5
6. Nf3	c6
7. Qc2	0-0
8. 0-0	Nbd7
9. Bf4	b6
10. Rd1	Ba6

177

11. cxd5?

White should preserve the ten-sion with 11. b3!. Then Black should be wary of ...dxc4, even if it wins a ♟, because it gives up the center.

For example, 11... Rc8 12. Nc3 dxc4 13. e4! with advantage to White.

11. ...	cxd5
12. Nc3	b5!

Black, who can attack on the queenside and c-file, is better.

But he fails to secure his edge with ...Rc8 in the next few moves.

13. a3	Qb6?!
14. Ne5	Nxe5
15. Bxe5	Bb7?!
16. Qd3	Bc6
17. Rac1	a5?!

Better was 13... Rc8 – or later 15... Rac8, or 16... a6/17... Rac8 or, finally 17... Rac8 in place of 17... a5. Now White has good reason to open the center.

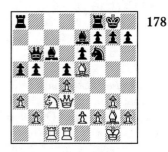

178

18. e4!

Now 18... dxe4 19. Nxe4 Nxe4 20. Bxe4 Bxe4 21. Qxe4 Rac8 22. d5! favors White's ♖s.

18. ...	b4
19. exd5!	

Here 19... exd5 20. Bxf6 Bxf6 21. Nxd5 Bxd5 22. Bxd5 costs Black a pawn. Also poor are the complications of 19... bxc3 20. dxc6 cxb2 21. Rc3.

In the game White exploited the queenside after 19... Nxd5 20. Nxd5 Bxd5 21. Bxd5 exd5 22. a4!.

Pat: Do you ever have one of these positions when nobody does any-

thing? I mean where the two guys just sit there and stare at one an-other.

Noah: Not for long. But it did happen for a while in the Battle of the Tempo games during the 1920s and '30s.

Pat: Battle of the Tempo?

Noah: That was something in the Queen's Gambit Declined that the masters really got worked up over.

It goes this way: Black wants to ease his game in Diagram 179 with ...dxc4, followed by ...Nd5. So White doesn't want to hand him an extra tempo by playing Bd3, since he'd like to wait for ...dxc4 and then recapture with a B/f1, saving a move.

Pat: But White has to develop the ♗ sometime. After all, he needs to castle and connect ♖s.

Noah: True. But White has constructive moves he can make before Bd3, such as Rc1 and Qc2.

He "wins the battle" if Black plays ...dxc4 before Black runs out of his constructive moves, such as ...c6 and ...a6.

Pat: I'm glad I wasn't around in the old days to worry about stuff like that.

1.	d4	d5
2.	c4	e6
3.	Nc3	Nf6
4.	Bg5	Nbd7
5.	e3	Be7
6.	Nf3	0-0

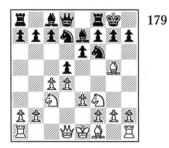
179

Now 7. Bd3 enables Black to simplify with tempo – 7... dxc4 8. Bxc4 c5. Dozens of games have shown White has a slight but significant edge after 9. 0-0 a6 and

now 10. a4 cxd4 11. cxd4.

7. Rc1

A good alternative is 7. Qc2 and then 7... c6 8. Rd1 Re8 9. a3.

7. ...   c6

Other useful passes include 7... a6 but not 7... c5, which gives White an edge with 8. dxc5! Qa5 9. a3 dxc4 (9... Bxc5?? 10. b4 or 9... Qxc5 10. cxd5 Nxd5?? 11. Nxd5 wins material) 10. Bxc4 Qxc5 11. Qe2.

8. Qc2

White also passes. The most popular line is 8. Bd3 after which 8... dxc4! 9. Bxc4 Nd5! 10. Bxe7 Qxe7 frees Black's game.

8. ...   dxc4?

Black gives up the fight too easily. Better are 8... a6 or the simplifying 8... Ne4.

9.	Bxc4	Nd5
10.	Bxe7	Qxe7
11.	Ne4	

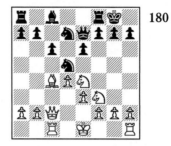
180

White has one more move – Qc2– than he would have in the 8. Bd3 dxc4 line. He stands better because of that move, e.g. 11... N5f6 12. Ng3 e5 13. 0-0 exd4 14. Nf5 Qd8 15. N3xd4.

Noah: Well, you may have to face something similar because there's a modern version of the battle, in Diagram 181.

Pat: But there's no tempo to fight over because White's already developed his B/f1.

Noah: Right. This one is all about ♟-structure. Do you see the *zugzwang?*

Pat: I see some of it. I see that White doesn't want to exchange on d5 because Black solves a lot of his problem after cxd5 and ...exd5.

Noah: Correct. Black's B/c8 is freed and he gets the use of the e-file, which is a lot more useful to him than the c-file is to White.

Pat: And I guess Black doesn't want to play ...c5 or ...e5 because he ends up with an isolated d-♟.

Noah: There's more. The best idea for Black in these positions is usually ...dxc4 followed by ...e5. In that way he liberates his pieces yet doesn't get the isolated d-♟ he would if he'd played ...e5 alone.

Pat: But after Bxc4 White has a lot of junk on the light squares, like Ng5, threatening Bxf7†.

Noah: So Black passes in the diagram. He knows that eventually he's probably going to play ...dxc4. But he tries to find useful moves to insert before "eventually" becomes "now."

Pat: And White?

Decisions

Noah: White tries to do the same. So you see pass after pass until Diagram 182, when Black has no useful passes left. Or at least no passes as useful as the move White was ready to make, Bb2.

Karpov-Illescas
Wijk aan Zee 1993

1. d4   d5
2. c4   c6
3. Nf3   Nf6
4. Nc3   e6
5. e3   Nbd7
6. Qc2   Bd6
7. Be2   0-0
8. 0-0

Here 8... e5 9. cxd5 cxd5 gives White chances to gain an edge with 10. Nb5 followed by 11. dxe5 and Rd1.

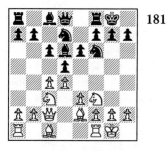

181

And 8... dxc4 9. Bxc4 e5 is thematic but White has a slight edge after, for example, 10. h3 Qc7 11. Bd2 and then 11... Re8 12. Ng5! Re7 13. Rac1.

8. ...   Qe7

A pass, which prepares a later ...dxc4 and ...e5.

Black stands well after 9. e4 Nxe4 10. Nxe4 dxe4 11. Qxe4 e5 – and after 12. dxe5 Nxe5 he's better (13. Nxe5 Qxe5! with an endgame edge or 13. Be3 Bg4!).

9. Rd1

Pass. White wants to pound d5 after ...e5/dxe5.

9. ...   Re8

Another pass. The ♖ will be well-placed after ...dxc4 and ...e5.

10. h3

This useful move will keep pieces off g4 and protect against ...Bxh2† after ...dxc4/...e5-e4.

10. ...   h6

So that ...dxc4/Bxc4/ and ...e5 will not allow Ng5!, attacking f7.

11. a3

Taking some sting out of ...dxc4/ Bxc4 and ...b5. Now 11... dxc4 12. Bxc4 e5 invites 13. Nh4 with an edge. For example, 13... Nb6 14. Ng6! Qc7 15. Nxe5.

11. ...   a6

A fourth Black pass that prepares ...dxc4/Bxc4 and then ...b5 followed by ...c5.

Now 12. e4 dxe4 13. Nxe4 Nxe4 14. Qxe4 allows Black to equalize with 14... e5!.

12. b3

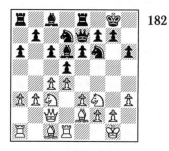

182

A fourth White pass, preparing Bb2.

12. ...   dxc4

Black blinks first. Now 13. Bxc4 b5! 14. Bf1 e5 is fine for Black but 13. bxc4! e5 14. Nh4 Nf8 15. Nf5 favors White slightly.

Pat: And what's the story in hypermodern openings, like 1. Nf3 and 1. c4?

Noah: In those openings there are even fewer ♟ exchanges in the opening than after 1. e4 or 1. d4.

And that's for a good reason – the exchanges are premature more often than not. Take a gander at Diagram 183.

Pat: These positions always seem like a mystery to me.

Noah: They shouldn't be – if you reason them out with logic. Once again White doesn't want to play cxd5 because after ...exd5 Black's B/c8 becomes alive.

Pat: Black probably also gets more out of the e-file after ...exd5 than White will get from the c-file after cxd5.

Noah: And there's not much else White wants to do in the center. He could play d4 at any point but he wants to retain the option of d3. And playing e4 in some fashion only creates a big hole at d4.

Pat: That much I can understand. But what's the deal with Black?

Noah: Black has two basic options. He can play ...c5 and try for ...d4. But that can be risky because White can attack a pawn at d4 with three minor pieces, and that's usually two more than Black has to defend it.

Pat: The other option has to be ...dxc4. Why is that bad? After all, Black gets a great d-file for his ♖s.

Noah: It's bad because White can take over the center by putting ♙s at d3 and f4, and in the absence of center tension he can begin a strong kingside attack.

Averbakh-Spassky
Soviet Championship 1955

1.	c4	Nf6
2.	Nf3	e6
3.	Nc3	d5
4.	e3	Be7
5.	b3	0-0
6.	Bb2	

183

6.	...	dxc4?
7.	bxc4	c5
8.	Be2	Nc6
9.	0-0	b6
10.	d3!	

Not 10. d4? which gives Black counterplay after 10... cxd4.

10.	...	Bb7
11.	Ne1	Qc7
12.	f4!	Rfd8
13.	Bf3	Rd7

184

And now 14. g4! would have given White a strong game.

Pat: And Black's ♖s don't mean much then.

Noah: But again this is a matter of

"The art of treating the opening stage of the game correctly and without error is basically the art of using time efficiently."
– Svetozar Gligoric

timing. In Diagram 185 Black makes the same ...dxc4 capture – but at a moment when he is well developed and White can't begin a kingside attack.

Romanovsky-Goglidze
Moscow 1935

1. Nf3	d5
2. b3	Nf6
3. Bb2	e6
4. c4	Be7
5. e3	0-0
6. Be2	c5
7. 0-0	Nc6
8. d3	b6
9. Nbd2	Bb7
10. Re1?	

The ♖ does nothing here. Better was 10. Rc1 and even Rc2/Qa1.

10. ...	Rc8
11. Nf1	Rc7!
12. a3	

185

12. ...   dxc4!

Now 13. dxc4 Qxd1 and 14... Na5! would leave White's queenside pawns weak.

13. bxc4	Nd7
14. Ng3	Bf6
15. Bxf6	Nxf6
16. Qc2	Rd7

And Black was better.

Pat: Now I'm beginning to think that every time I touch a ♙ I'm going to make a mistake.

Noah: Nobody ever said chess was going to be easy. Decision-making is always hard. and you make the first decisions in the opening.

But if you appreciate what the Pavlovion reactions are and recognize what a safety-first move looks like...

Pat: ... and how to keep my options open and know what a *zugzwang* center is, and...

Noah: Then you'll understand how good opening decisions are made. But that's enough for one day.

Tomorrow I want to talk more about the single most important moment in the opening – or, perhaps, in the entire game.

"You played a match for the world championship – so you should understand the position better."
– **Viktor Korchnoi to Nigel Short after Short played ...dxc4? in their game from Gröningen 1996 (1. Nf3 d5 2. b3 c5 3. e3 Nf6 4. Bb2 e6 5. c4 dxc4? and 6. bxc4 Be7 7. Be2 0-0 8. Qc2! Nc6 9. a3 Re8 10. 0-0 b6 11. Nc3 Bb7 12. Ng5! h6 13. Nh3 Qd7 14. f4.). But Black won.**

A Winner

GM Soltis has been around the chess scene for a long time—from his days when he knew Fischer to his annual Bermuda tournaments, as well as his articles in the *New York Post.*

Andy has won his share of tournaments but the one which sticks in my mind is his co-win (with IM Bill Martz) of the U.S. Open in 1982, when Chessco (the retail arm of Thinkers' Press) was the vendor of record at this event.

In which Pat discovers Capablanca's Rule as well as Blumenfeld's and what it takes to survive a new move.

Chapter Seven:

DE-BOOKED

Pat: Okay, you knew I'd be back today.

What's this "most important moment" you advertised?

Noah: It happens when you discover you're no longer in a book position, or at least not in your book.

It's the first time in the game when you're truly on your own. That can have a huge impact on you emotionally.

Pat: You got that right.

I'm usually zipping along in the first five or ten moves and then – Wham!

The board suddenly looks like something out of a bad video game.

Noah: What do you usually do then?

Pat: I think about what a dweeb I am for forgetting the right move.

Then I play something quickly to show it didn't bother me.

Noah: And then you get crushed.

Pat: And then I get crushed.

Noah: No wonder. It's almost always a mistake to move fast after

you're surprised.

That's what did Black in in Diagram 186.

Pat: What do you call that opening?

Noah: Take your pick.

It's almost a Trompowsky and more than a "Queen Pawn's Game."

Probably the closest is "Albin Counter Gambit – with colors reversed."

Pat: When did this leave book?

Noah: Around 6. Qd2 – and you can figure out why that move makes sense.

Pat: Because of analogy?

Noah: Of course.

In the normal Albin it's Black who sacrifices a ♙ and then plays ...Qd7 and ...Bh3 – the mirror image of what White does there.

Pat: And Black played 6... g6, just like what White does in a normal Albin.

So where did he go wrong?

Noah: He went wrong by moving quickly.

In fact he only took nine minutes

for the entire game.

I. Sokolov-Oll
Pärnu 1996

1.	d4	d5
2.	Bg5	c5

A better way to exploit the ♗'s absence from c1 is 2... h6 (deflecting the ♗ to a lesser diagonal) 3. Bh4 c6 and 4... Qb6.

3.	e4!?	dxe4
4.	d5	Nd7
5.	Nc3	Ngf6
6.	Qd2	

In previous games White played 6. Qe2.

6. ...   g6

7.	0-0-0	Bg7
8.	Bh6	Bxh6?

Black can defend better with another idea from the Albin, the simple 8... 0-0.

Then 9. Bxg7 Kxg7 10. h4 h5! or 9. h4 Bxh6! 10. Qxh6 Ng4 11. Qf4 Ndf6 and 11... Qd6.

9. Qxh6   a6

Otherwise Black has problems meeting Nb5/d6, e.g. 9... Qc7 10. d6 exd6 11. Nb5 or 9... Ne5 10. Bb5† Bd7 11. d6 e6 12. Nh3.

10.	Nh3	Qc7
11.	d6!	exd6

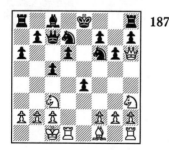

12. Ng5

Black has no adequate answer

to the threats of Bc4xf7† and Ngxe4xd6†.

He lost soon after 12... d5 13. Nxd5 Nxd5 14. Rxd5 Qf4† 15. Kb1 Nf6? 16. Rd8†! Kxd8 17. Nxf7† and 18. Qxf4.

Pat: It shows. He must have missed something big.

Noah: It wasn't just miscalculation.

You don't lose a game like that unless you've also made some huge error in attitude.

Pat: Attitude?

Noah: Sure, in this case a snap judgment, such as thinking to yourself, "What a stupid move he just made!"

This is often fatal when your opponent plays some "obviously" bad move, as in Diagram 188.

Pat: You're right. I was ready to say "What a lame move."

Noah: But 2. h4 has some good points to it.

It allows White to meet 2... g6 with 3. h5!, for example.

Pat: Okay, but 4. g4 must be going too far.

Noah: Only a bit.

What burned Black was that he started playing as if White had made a horrendous error that he should be able to exploit.

And the way to do that seemed to be ...h6xg5.

Depasquale-Kavian
Asian Team Championship 1992

| 1. d4 | d6 |
| 2. h4!? | |

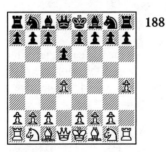

188

Bizarre – but that's not the same as bad.

| 2. ... | c6 |

The beginning of a passive policy. Black does better with 2... e5 or 2... Nf6 – or even 2... d5 when White's 2. h4 is irrelevent and potentially a liability.

3. Nc3	Nd7
4. g4	e5
5. e4	Be7
6. g5!	

A good space-gainer that stops ....Nf6. Black tries to refute it – and fatally underestimates it.

6. ...	h6
7. dxe5	dxe5
8. Qf3!	

189

| 8. ... | hxg5?? |
| 9. Bc4 | 1-0 |

Black is lost on 9... Nh6 10. hxg5 or 9... Bf6 10. hxg5 Rxh1 11. Qxh1 Bxg5 12. Qh5 (and also 11... Be7 12. Qh5! g6 13. Qh7).

Noah: The other foolhardy bit of gamesmanship is to simply ignore whatever opportunity a new position presents.

"A new move by the opponent is first of all a blow to your nerves."
– Artur Yusupov

Pat: What opportunity?

Noah: Every new position has its plusses and minuses – and that means there's usually a way to exploit the minuses.

Maybe Diagram 190 will make this clear.

Pat: Clearer but not clear.

Noah: Well, here's the backstory – Black came up with a spur-of-the-moment TN when he chose his 12th and 13th moves.

Pat: I'm with you so far.

Noah: Now, from Black's point of view the benefit of the ♗-trade and ...Qb6 is simple.

Pat: Sure, if he gets to swap ♛s he's not gonna get mated in the middlegame.

Noah: As Black so often does in the Dragon.

But there are also a few minuses to 13... Qb6 to go with this plus.

Pat: You mean because Black loses a ♙.

Noah: I said minuses, plural.

One of the minuses is that Black's

♙s and dark-squares are weak after 12... Bxd4. White can exploit that with 14. Na4.

Pat: Yeah, but he wanted more.

Noah: That's why he grabbed a ♙. But that was "incredibly risky," as Black said afterwards.

I. Gurevich-Rogers

London 1992

1. e4	c5
2. Nf3	d6
3. d4	cxd4
4. Nxd4	Nf6
5. Nc3	g6
6. Be3	Bg7
7. f3	Nc6
8. Qd2	0-0
9. 0-0-0	d5
10. exd5	Nxd5
11. Nxc6	bxc6

Many tests over the years indicate Black has good practical chances after 12. Nxd5 cxd5 13. Qxd5 Qc7 (14. Qc5 Qb7).

12. Bd4	Bxd4
13. Qxd4	Qb6

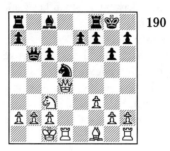

190

White can get a slight edge with 14. Na4 because of endgames such as 14... Qxd4 15. Rxd4 and 14... Qa5 15. b3 Rb8 16. Qc5 (16... Qc7? 17. Rxd5).

14. Nxd5	**cxd5**
15. Qxd5?!	

The practical choice for White was between the endgame of 15. Qxb6 or the solid middlegame of 15. Qe5.

15. ...	**Be6**
16. Qd4	

Or 16. Qb5 Qc7 17. Qa4 a5 with ...Rab8-b4 coming up.

16. ...	**Qa5**

Both 17... Qxa2 and 17... Rfd8

are threatened.

17. a3	**Rfd8**
18. Qb4	**Qg5†**
19. Rd2	**a5!**

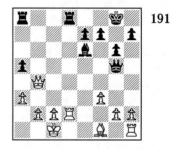

191

Black has a terrific initiative and eventually won.

Pat: What do GMs think about when their opponents spring something new?

Noah: The first thing they do – whether by design or by instinct – is the same as what B-players do.

They try to figure out the point of the other guy's move.

Pat: Like "What's his idea?"

Noah: Right. That idea might be

the beginning of a deep plan.

Or it might be something tactical and transparent, as in Diagram 192.

Pat: Transparent in a Candidates match?

Noah: Maybe not transparent to everyone.

But when White played 14. dxc5 some sort of tactical alarm went off in Black's head.

Pat: Why?

Noah: Because it's just anti-positional to ruin your center like that.

So Black knew there had to be something that justified 14. dxc5.

Once he found it, he saw a good reply that gave him compensation for a ♟.

Pat: Enough comp?

Noah: Enough to give Black a bit of an advantage. Eventually he won.

Kasparov-Korchnoi
Candidates match 1983

1. **d4**	**Nf6**
2. **c4**	**e6**
3. **Nf3**	**b6**

4. **Nc3**	**Bb7**
5. **a3**	**d5**
6. **cxd5**	**Nxd5**
7. **e3**	**g6**
8. **Bb5†**	

A minor finesse which temporarily closes Black's diagonal, compared with 8. Bb3.

8. **...**	**c6**
9. **Bd3**	**Bg7**
10. **e4**	**Nxc3**
11. **bxc3**	**c5**
12. **Bg5**	**Qd6**
13. **e5**	**Qd7**

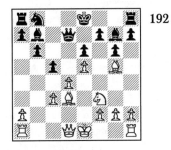

192

14. dxc5?
White had a pefectly good game with 14. 0-0.

14. **...**	**0-0!**

On 14... bxc5 there is 15. Bb5 (15... Qxb5?? 16. Qd8#; 15... Nc6 16. Qxd7† Kxd7 17. 0-0 with advantage in the ending) or just 15. Qe2 followed by a strong Rd1.

15. **cxb6**	**axb6**
16. **0-0**	**Qc7**

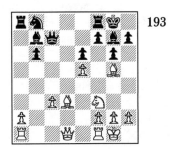

193

Black stood slightly better because of White's bad ♟s (17. Bb5 Bxe5 or 17. Bf4 Nd7).

Pat: How else should I act when I'm hit with a new move?

Noah: You already know a basic guideline when treading in unknown waters –

USE YOUR COMMON SENSE

Pat: Like I had any.

Noah: It's easy to find some.

José Capablanca was just recommending common sense when he formulated his rule.

CAPABLANCA'S RULE:
When you face an unfamiliar opening move you should develop the rest of your pieces quickly, place them on protected squares and safeguard your ♔.

Pat: Sounds too easy.

Noah: It is – that's why GMs violate it so frequently.

Safe, developing moves are often *second-best* moves – moves that fail to achieve an advantage for White or to gain complete equality as Black.

Paul Keres invented the Keres Variation of the Sicilian (6. g4 after 1. e4 c5 2. Nf3 d6 3. d4 cxd4 4. Nxd4 Nf6 5. Nc3 e6) over the board at Salzburg 1943.
His opponent, Efim Bogolyubov, replied with the faulty 6... Nc6 7. g5 Nxd4? 8. Qxd4 Nd7 9. Be3 and lost.

But Capa's Rule is still a good policy for non-GMs because it will keep you alive until you reach a middlegame where you make a real fight of it – as we'll see next.

Pat: You mean Diagram 194 is all about common sense?

Noah: Pretty much, starting with White's first move out of book.

After 5... e5 he correctly concluded he had to take on e5 and that the N/c6 was more valuable than the ♗.

So on general principles 6. Bxe5 should be better than 6. dxe5.

Pat: But he must have analyzed both.

Noah: Naturally, that's what GMs do.

White also followed basic principles at moves 8 and 9 – and dodged a bullet.

Pat: You mean, by not trying to mess up Black's development with 8. Qa4†.

Noah: Yes, Black seemed happy with his position as White consid-

ered his eighth move

So, White concluded, there must be a trap after the ♛-check.

And when he looked for it, he found it.

Pat: Seems GMs always have a general principle to justify their move – when the move works.

Like White moving towards the center at move 9, rather than away from it.

Noah: It's also a matter of simple tactics.

From e4 the ♞ can retreat to d2 to answer checks.

A move later White again followed Capa's Rule: Get your pieces out.

Pat: But you said this leads to second-best moves now and then.

Noah: As a practical matter, being alive now is better than trying to refute your opponent's play then.

White might have been right in thinking that 10. Qxd4 was the best move – objectively.

But over the board, 10. Rb1 is the

move – practically.

Yusupov-Timman
Linares 1989
1. d4   d5
2. c4   c6
3. cxd5

White didn't like 3. Nc3 dxc4 so he chose the earliest opportunity for cxd5.

But in later GM games, he adopted a different move order (3. Nc3 and if 3... Nf6 then 4. cxd5) to avoid what ensues.

3. ...   cxd5
4. Nc3   Nc6
5. Bf4   e5!?

A surprise for White.

6. Bxe5!

Better than 6. dxe5? d4.

6. ...   Nxe5
7. dxe5   d4

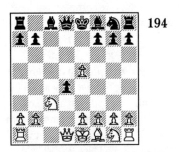

194

Here 8. Qa4† looks good at first (8... Bd7? 9. Qxd4; 8... Qd7 9. Nb5).

But Black has 8... b5!.

Then White loses after 9. Qxb5† Bd7 and is in trouble after 9. Nxb5 Bd7, threatening 10... a6 (10. Qb3 Qa5†).

8. Ne4!   Qb6
9. Nf3!

Not 9. Nd6†? Bxd6 10. exd6 Qxb2, which favors Black.

9. ...   Qxb2
10. Rb1

The risk not taken: 10. Qxd4 Bb4† 11. Kd1 Qa3.

The text is semi-forcing and prepares 11. e3 or 11. Nxd4.

10. ...   Bb4†!
11. Ned2   Bxd2†
12. Nxd2   Qxa2

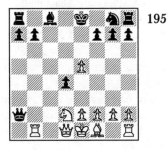

195

13. e3!

And White stood well after 13... dxe3 14. fxe3 Be6 (14... Ne7 15. Bc4! clearly favors White) 15. Rxb7 Rd8 16 Qc1 g6 17 Qc3.

Pat: But there must be plenty of times when the logical move, the common sense move will get you slaughtered.

Believe me, I know.

Noah: Of course, because tactics trumps logic – and general prin-

ciples.

That's why you should always check out the tactics as well – and in the end, apply the guideline of Russian master Benjamin Blumenfeld.

BLUMENFELD'S RULE:
When you stop calculation,
look at the position with the
eyes of a beginner.

Pat: You mean like asking "Did I leave my ♛ hanging?"

Noah: Or "Is there a strong check?" "Is there a fork?" And so on.

Blumenfeld's Rule is worth remembering in any position – but particularly in those first stumbling moves after you get out of book.

Pat: I know what you mean by stumbling.

But when it happens to me I can't tell whether it's because my opponent played a new move or I just forgot the book?

Noah: Good point. There is a dif-

ference between the two, and it has a big psychological impact.

Pat: Sure is. I know I feel much better if I know it's not my fault that the position looks bizarro.

Noah: But you should know that even top GMs – who prepare everything in their arsenal – forget their analysis from time to time.

Yet that doesn't mean they have to suffer for it, as the next example shows.

Korchnoi-Short
Madrid 1995

1. d4	**Nf6**
2. c4	**e6**
3. Nc3	**Bb4**
4. e3	**b6**
5. Ne2	**Ba6**
6. Ng3	**c5?!**
7. d5	

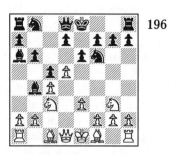

196

Short had forgotten his analysis here – book is 6... Bxc3†, 6... 0-0 or the Pavlovian 6... h5.

So he began to improvise using common sense.

7. ...   0-0

Inexact because White can establish a strong center now.

But considering the circumstances – quite good.

After 7... exd5 8. cxd5 Bxf1 9. Kxf1 0-0 10. e4 White has a great game.

8. e4   Re8

So that 9. e5? is met by 9... exd5.

9. f3   d6

10. Be2

White has an edge but a relatively slight one.

In fact, Black got a bad game only after he sacrificed a ♟ with 10... exd5 11. cxd5 Bxe2 12. Nxe2 b5 13. 0-0 a6 14. a4 Nbd7? 15. axb5 (better 14... Bxc3 15. bxc3 Nbd7 or 14... bxa4).

Noah: Knowing that a position is truly new is a weapon you can use.

It gives you a reason to figure out what's wrong with your opponent's play, as in the next example.

Pat: Walk me through this one slowly.

Noah: All right. Imagine that you're White.

You can be reasonably sure that your first five moves were perfectly sound.

Pat: Because they must've been played a gazillion times before.

Noah: Correct. But the position starts looking new to you after 5... Bxf3.

Pat: It sure does. Is it book?

Noah: A rare book, but book nonetheless.

In any event, logic tells you that 6. Qxf3 must be the right move.

That leaves you at Diagram 197 – saying to yourself "How come nobody's ever played 6... Nc6 before?"

Pat: You mean, there's gotta be a reason.

Noah: And there is – 7. d5!, which virtually refutes Black's sixth move.

Pat: But White didn't look for a refutation.

Noah: No, he treated the position like just another odd-looking King's Indian – and in a sharp opening like the King's Indian that's highly risky.

Pat: Funny how White can end up with the worst of it by making routine moves.

1. d4	Nf6
2. c4	g6
3. Nc3	d6
4. Nf3	Bg4

Much more common is 4... Bg7 and then 5. e4 0-0.

5. e4   Bxf3

6. Qxf3   Nc6

The usual move in this rare line is 6... Nfd7, followed by attacking d4 with ...Bg7, ...Nc6 and ...e5.

Then White can defend d4 with 7. Qd1 – and avoid an old trap (7. Bd3 Bg7 8. Be3 Nc6 9. Ne2? Nde5! 10. dxe5 Nxe5, winning a ♟).

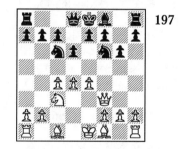

197

7. Qd1?

Much better is 7. d5! since 7... Ne5 8. Qe2 poses a major positional threat of 9. f4 and 10. e5.

Black is worse after 7... Nd4 8. Qd1 c5 9. dxc6 or 7... Nb8.

7. ...	Bg7
8. Be3	

White misses a second chance for 8. d5.

8. ...	0-0
9. Be2	e5!

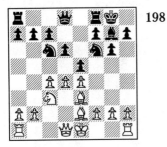

198

Black is at least equal (10. dxe5 dxe5 and ... Nd4).

10. d5	Nd4!

And White is worse if he accepts the offered ♙ (11. Bxd4 exd4 12. Qxd4 Re8 13. Qd3 Nd7 14. f3 f5! 15. 0-0 Nc5 16. Qc2 fxe4 17. fxe4 Qg5!).

Noah: That's what I meant about the loopholes to Capa's Rule.

The sharper the position, the less that common sense makes sense.

But in general it's a good compass – even when you leave book early.

Pat: How so?

Noah: Well, if you haven't blundered, it's unlikely that a position that seems new to you can be that dangerous.

After all, no new move is going to refute the Ruy Lopez.

Pat: But what if it looks strong?

Noah: Then you probably haven't examined the board hard enough to find a refutation. That's what Black was thinking in the next example.

Pat: I don't know anything about these lines that are half English and half... what?

Noah: Half Gruenfeld. But the name doesn't matter.

The point here is that after White's sixth move Black had good reason to think the position was either original or very rarely played.

Pat: Seems reasonable.

Noah: And just by rechecking his scoresheet he could see that he couldn't have blundered in his first five moves – and that he didn't have much choice at moves six and seven.

Yet when he considered the normal moves in the diagram, they all led to positions in White's favor.

Pat: White's favor, big time.

Noah: Furthermore logic told Black he couldn't have a bad game if he hadn't done anything wrong.

That meant there had to be a good, abnormal move in Diagram 199.

Strange positions often demand strange moves.

Pat: How strange is strange?

Noah: Well, you have to agree 8... Nxe2! is not the type of move you meet every day – or month.

Nesterov-Yandemirov
Beskidy 1991

1. Nf3	Nf6
2. c4	g6
3. Nc3	d5
4. cxd5	Nxd5
5. Qa4†	Bd7
6. Qe4	

Several other moves had been tried, including 6. Qb3, 6. Qd4 and 6. Qh4.

6. ...	Bc6

On 6... Nxc3 7. dxc3 Nc6 8. Bg5 or 7... Bc6 8. Qe5 White has a promising game.

7. Nd4	

To punish Black's last move. On 7. Qe5 f6 Black is a little weakened but otherwise okay.

7. ...	Nxc3
8. Qe5	

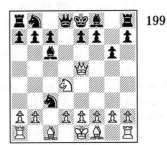

199

Now 8... f6 9. Nxc6! Nxc6 10. Qxc3 is excellent for White – as is 9... fxe5 10. Nxd8.

8. ...   Nxe2!!

But here 9. Qxh8 Qxd4! 10. Qxd4 Nxd4 or 10. Qxh7 Nxc1 favors Black.

9. Nxc6   Nxc6
10. Qxh8   Ned4
11. Kd1   Qd5

Black has huge compensation and ample threats, including ...Nb4xa2.

The rest was: 12. Qxh7 Nb4 13. b3 Qf5! 14. Bc4 Qc2† 15. Ke1 Nd3† White resigns.

Noah: But offbeat ideas in the opening are more often akin to what happens in Diagram 200.
Pat: Seems like both guys broke rules before that.
Noah: Yes, I know Black is not supposed to block his c-♟ with moves like 3... Nc6.

Yet he can transpose that way into quite a reasonable Nimzo-Indian,

The youngest player to create a Theoretical Novelty was 13-year-old José Capablanca, in his 1901 match with Cuban Champion Juan Corzo. After 1. e4 e5 2. Nc3 Nc6 3. f4 exf4 4. Nf3 g5 5. h4 g4 6. Ng5 h6 7. Nxf7 Kxf7 8. d4, then a main line, Capa came up 8... d5! over the board, improving on 8... f3 and 8... d6 – and establishing a won game in a matter of minutes.

with Nc3 and ... Bb4.
Pat: So White stops that with 4. a3. And his N/b1 goes to d2 to safeguard the c-♟.
Noah: But think about that in general terms for a second – without looking at the board.
Pat (looking up)**:** Think about what?
Noah: Does it make sense that your opponent can benefit from moves like 4. a3 and 5. Nbd2 – regardless of the opening – while you've made solid, more constructive moves?
Pat: You mean there must be a way to exploit it – like 5... g5!.
Noah: You weren't supposed to look at the board.

But you're right. Unusually passive play by White is bound to permit unusually aggressive play by Black.

1. d4   Nf6
2. c4   e6
3. Nf3   Nc6
4. a3

On 4. Nc3 Bb4 Black reaches a Nimzo-Indian, e.g. 5. Qc2 d6 and ... e5 or 5. a3 Bxc3† 6. bxc3 d6. Also good may be 4... d5 and then 5. Bg5 Bb4.

4. ...   d5
5. Nbd2

This avoids 5. Nc3 dxc4 6. e4 Na5, for example.

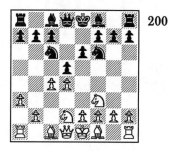

200

5. ...   g5!

This threatens 6... g4, winning the d-♟.

On 6. h3, another passive move, Black is in splendid shape after 6... Bg7.

6. Nxg5   Nxd4
7. e3   Nf5

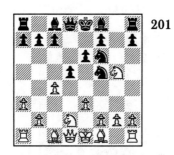

201

With fine play for Black.

Pat: So the moral is... what? That active play always beats passive?

Noah: Not quite.

GMs often encounter new positions that are characterized by very conservative enemy setups – setups that aren't easily refuted.

Pat: You mean when the other guy's pieces don't move past the third.

Noah: Yes. That's too far away for you to exploit with a frontal attack – and you can easily overextend yourself trying to do so.

Pat: You must be leading up to Diagram 203.

Noah: Where else?

Here we see Black's using two rare moves, ...e6 and ...Nce7, in trying out a new system of development.

Pat: New system maybe.

But there's no threat, no attack, who cares?

Noah: White does because that means Black is passive yet solid.

White should adopt a policy of watching and waiting.

Pat: With common sense moves, right?

Noah: Right. He avoids temptation – such as 11. e5? – and has free rein to improve his position slowly.

After all White can use five ranks and Black is restricted to three.

You do the math.

Pat: Five beat three.

Noah: It usually does – unless you miss something tactical.

In this case, Black has to reveal his intentions eventually – and then White is perfectly set for action, in Diagram 203.

Dolmatov-Azmaiparashvili
Elenite 1995

1. e4	d6
2. d4	g6
3. Nc3	Bg7
4. f4	Nc6
5. Be3	e6

Odd but not easily refuted.

| 6. Nf3 | Nce7 |

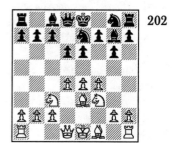

202

| 7. Bd3 | b6 |
| 8. Qe2 | |

Black's formation reveals itself slowly, e.g. 8. h3 Bb7 9. Qd2 Nf6 10. 0-0-0 0-0 11. Rhe1 c5 with, among other ideas, ...c4!

| 8. ... | Nf6 |
| 9. 0-0 | Bb7 |

Now it becomes a bit clearer: Black stops d5 and can meet e5 with ...Nfd5.

10. Rad1!

Despite the ♟s in the way, this ♖ should line up against the ♛.

| 10. ... | 0-0 |

11. Bc1!

Premature is 11. e5? Nfd5 12. Nxd5 Nxd5 followed by either 13... Nxe3 or (after 13. Bc1) 13... Nb4 (and 14. Bc4 d5 15. Bb3? Ba6).

| 11. ... | Qc8 |

This gets the ♛ off the potentially hot file – but also removes protection of the N/e7.

12. e5!

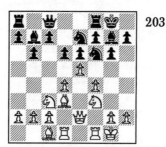

203

Now 12... Nfd5 13. Nxd5 Nxd5

"All this preparation, and all this talk about theoretical novelties, it's all nonsense. You know your theory, and if the opponent makes a surprising move you just start thinking and find the right answer."
– Svetozar Gligoric

can now be met by 14. c4 Ne7 15. b3 or 14... Nb4 15. Bb1 and 16. a3 with a huge edge in space for White.

Even worse is 13... exd5 14. exd6!.

In the game Black had poor play after 12... Ne8 13. Ne4.

Pat: That was easy enough, I guess.
Noah: Then let me show you something from another Modern Defense that's a bit trickier, Diagram 204.
Pat: Hmm. Looks like some position I should know.

But maybe not. Isn't Black supposed to be playing ... Nf6 ?
Noah: He usually does – that's the pure King's Indian.

But you can guess that this isn't an entirely new position.
Pat: It must be in the books somewhere.
Noah: Right, so let's go through the drill.

First question – What's the point of Black's last move?

Pat: Either to play ...b5 in some way or to get the ♛ out to a5 or b6.
Noah: You were closer the second time. Ideally, Black wants to attack d4 with ... Qb6.

Or, in some cases, to pressure e4 with ...Qa5 and ...Nf6.
Pat: How does it help me to know that?
Noah: It should tell you that 5. f4 is going to be dubious because of 5... Qb6!.

But it should also tell you how to take advantage of the drawbacks of 4... c6.
Pat: Give me a hint.
Noah: When Black puts his ♟ on c6 it means he can't develop a ♞ there. So...
Pat: So White doesn't have to worry about an attack on d4 with ...Bg4 and ...Nc6.

That means Nf3 works well.

1. d4	g6
2. c4	Bg7
3. Nc3	d6

4. e4	c6

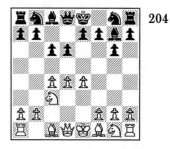

204

Among the good alternatives was 5. Nf3, and then 5... Bg4 6. Be3 Nd7 7. Be2, so that White can meet 7... Ngf6 favorably with 8. e5!.

On 7... Bxf3 8. Bxf3 Ngf6 9. 0-0 he has a small but secure superiority.

5. f4?!

This would have been the most challenging reply to 4... Nd7 – but is one of the weakest to 4... c6.

5. ... Qb6!

Now if White defends the d-pawn with 6. e5 Black exploits the f5 hole with 6... Nh6 followed by ...Bg4 and/or ...Nf5.

6. Nf3   Bg4

White's center is breached by the 7... Bxf3 threat since 7. Be3? Qxb2 can't be played.

7. d5   Nf6

205

With a great game for Black who can control two good dark-square diagonals.

For example, 8. h3 Bxf3 9. Qxf3 Na6 10. Rb1 Nd7! (stops 11. Be3 Bxc3†) 11. Bd2 Ndc5.

Noah: Correct. Sometimes you can tell almost as soon as you sit down that your opponent is going to try something flaky, such as in Diagram 206.

Pat: What do I do then?

Noah: It often depends on how much you want to punish him.

Remember what I said a while ago about figuring out how much of an advantage to aim for?

Pat: Right – You go for the edge you deserve.

Noah: Well, by the second move Black knows something strange is happening.

And two moves later he should realize White's goal is to enjoy a nice diagonal from g2 to b7.

White will get that if he's allowed to regain the ♙ – and he may also have a promising gambit if Black tries to hold it with 4... f5.

Pat: I don't like 4... Nf6 any better.

Noah: No, but when Black realizes he'd be slightly worse after 5. Nxe4, he has reason to believe there must be something better.

White's second and fourth moves just can't be that strong.

Pat: But that's not a reply that would occur to me, I mean 4... Bd7 ?

1. e4   e6
2. g3

Dubious – if Black is alert.

2. ...   d5

Now 3. exd5 exd5 would leave a White's B/g2 "biting on granite."

3. Bg2   dxe4
4. Nc3

Black meets 4. Bxe4 with 4... Nf6 5. Bg2 Nc6 and ...e5 with excellent center play and development.

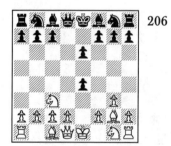

206

White is ready to offer a gambit: 4... f5 5. f3 exf3 6. Nxf3.

After 4... Nf6 5. Nxe4 Black is slightly worse (5... Nxe4 6. Bxe4 Nd7 7. Ne2 Nf6 8. Bg2 e5 9. 0-0 c6 10. d4!).

4. ...   Bd7!

This prepares to keep the extra ♙ with 5... Bc6 and 6... Nf6 or trade off White's ♗ after 5. Bxe4 Bc6.

5. Nxe4?

Consistent but...

5. ...   Bc6

White has no good reply to 6... f5 except the clumsy 6. f3.

Noah: Perhaps ugly – but whose position looks uglier after 5. Nxe4 Bc6 6. f3 ?

The point is – Unless a new or unfamiliar move refutes your opening outright there are bound to be some negative points to it.

Let me repeat – every move, short of checkmate, has plusses and minuses.

Which brings up Diagram 207.

Pat: What's the deal with 10. d4 ? It seems pretty normal.

Noah: Okay, then, what's the point of it?

Pat: To win the e-♟.

Surround it and kill it.

Noah: That's right, with Qd3 and Bxe3.

But there's a reason why 10. d3 was the book move.

Pat: I get it. White can't control c4 any more.

Noah: And that's really all Black needed to know.

With relatively simple moves such as ...Na5 and ...Bb7 he took control of key squares.

Pat: Yeah, but White still managed to win the e-♟.

Noah: And Black won a ♟ right back – with excellent piece play. All because he spotted the drawback that he knew had to be there.

H. Olafsson-Naumkin
Belgrade 1988

1. c4	e5
2. Nc3	Nf6
3. Nf3	Nc6
4. g3	Bb4
5. Bg2	0-0

6. 0-0	e4
7. Ng5	Bxc3
8. bxc3	Re8
9. f3!	e3!

This became instant theory after a *1987 Kasparov-Karpov world championship* game that went 10. d3 d5 11. Qb3 Na5 12. Qa3 c6.

If instead 10. dxe3 then 10... h6 11. Nh3 b6! and ...Ba6 eventually regains the ♟ favorably.

10. d4

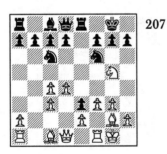

207

10. ...   **Na5!**

Black is in no hurry to dissolve his only target (not 10... d5?).

Now 11. Qa4 b6 prepares ...Ba6.

11. Qd3   **b6**

Here 12. Bxe3 Ba6 13. Rfe1 Nxc4 14. Bf2 is best.

12. c5?   **Bb7**

13. Bxe3

The only consistent move.

13. ...   **Qe7**

14. Bf4

Now 14. Kf2?? loses to 14... Ba6! 15. Qxa6 Qxe3†.

14. ...   **Qxe2**

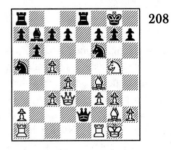

208

And Black assures himself of either:

(a) a superior endgame (15. Qxe2 Rxe2 16. Bxc7 Nd5!) or,

(b) an excellent middlegame (15. Qf5 h6 16. Ne4 Nxe4 17. Rae1 Nxg3!).

"Even though unlimited time is available for preparation before a competition, it often happens that the chess player sees less then, than under the tension produced by the time limit."
– Laszlo Szabo

He eventually won.

Pat: You don't mean that there has to be a drawback in every new position?

Noah: Not as a hard and fast rule.

But when your opponent moves a developed piece – and thereby create new possibilities for it, protects new squares, and so on – there's a down side.

Pat: You mean he has to be releasing protection of other squares and shedding some options.

Noah: Exactly. Let's do the next example together.

Maybe it'll sink in.

Pat: I'm with you.

Noah: Okay. The first thing you should notice is that we're in a fairly sharp line of the QGD.

Pat: I like White. He can attack on the kingside or pressure d5 – both.

Noah: But it's Black's ninth move that makes matters particularly interesting.

Tell me what's good about it.

Pat: Isn't that obvious? Development.

Black's gotta get the B/c8 off the first rank fast so he can connect ♖s.

Then he gets his R/a8 lined up against the ♔ and ♕ at c8.

Noah: So, 9... Nb6 is the perfect chess move?

Pat: Nothing's perfect.

Noah: Therefore...

Pat: There must be something wrong with it.

But the only thing I can see is that it disconnects Black's ♘s and removes protection of e5.

Noah: And it also weakens the kingside a bit.

White can exploit that by threatening Bxh7† – which prompts Black to defend with ...h6.

Pat: Even I can tell that looks like a lemon.

Then White can open the kingside with g4-g5.

Noah: And, as the annotators say, the attack plays itself.

Vyzhmanavin-Ruban
Sochi 1989

1. d4	**Nf6**
2. c4	**e6**
3. Nf3	**d5**
4. Nc3	**Nbd7**
5. Bg5	**Be7**
6. e3	**0-0**
7. Qc2	**c5**
8. 0-0-0	**Qa5**
9. h4	**Nb6**

Preparing 10... Bd7 and ...Rac8. Better, 9... cxd4 10. Nxd4 Bb4.

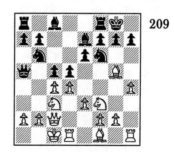

209

Now 10. cxd5 exd5 11. dxc5 Qxc5 12. Nd4 is a typical way of exploiting an isolated d-♟.

But after 12... Bd7 and ...Rfc8

Black has queenside counterplay.

10. Bd3!   h6?

This meets the threat of 11. Bxh7† (or 11. Bxf6 Bxf6 12. Bxh7†). But Black should have tried instead for complications (10... cxd4 or 10... Nxc4).

11. Bxf6   Bxf6

12. g4!

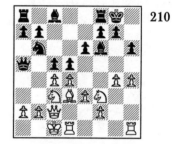

210

White had a winning attack soon after 12... cxd4 13. exd4 dxc4 14. Bh7† Kh8 15. g5 Be7 16. gxh6 gxh6 (16... g6 17. Bxg6! and Ne5) 17. Rdg1.

Pat: I'll bet you're making this stuff up as you go along.

Noah: Well, GMs do make a living by oversimplifying things.

So let me remind you of something we talked about when we first discussed Opening-Think.

Pat: And that is?

Noah: That you also have to keep a sense of reality about what you get out of the opening.

Pat: I always try to keep it real.

Noah: I'm serious. There are times

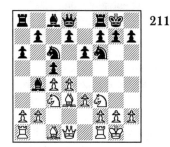

"A ♘ is always bad on b6."
– Siegbert Tarrasch

when you can punish an unfamiliar move – and there are times when it's asking too much.

And that brings up Diagram 211.

Pat: Black's fourth move can't be any good.

Noah: You're right that it has limited value.

But that doesn't mean it can be crushed – any more than 1. d4 d6 2. h4 can be, as we saw earlier today.

Pat: Okay, but here the point was to play ...b5 – and White didn't let him.

Noah: He would have after 5. Ne2 b5.

Or later on, if White had played d5 at some point, then ...b5 makes it a kind of Benko Gambit.

Pat: But none of this happened.

Noah: No. White played solidly and by the diagram he could have achieved a clear edge with simple moves – as if he was saying "What's ...a6 got to do with this position?"

Pat: Just like that Janowsky QGD from the other day.

Noah: Quite right. But even the more ambitious 8. d5 was good – if White had supported it with 9. e4.

Pat: So what went wrong?

Noah: He tried for *too* much with 9. d6, a move that looks positionally crushing.

The trouble is – it ended up justifying ...a6 after all.

Speelman-Short
London 1980

1. d4	Nf6
2. c4	e6
3. Nc3	Bb4
4. e3	a6

Black has experimented with almost every reasonable fourth move – including 4... 0-0, 4... c5, 4.... b6, 4... Nc6, 4... d5, 4... d6 and 4... c6 – but rarely with this.

5. Nf3	c5
6. Bd3	0-0
7. 0-0	Nc6

Simple, good moves – developing and castling.

8. d5

White has a modest edge after 8. Qe2.

8. ...   Ne7

Not 8... exd5 9. cxd5 Bxc3 10. bxc3 Nxd5 because 11. Bxh7† – and 12. Qxd5 favors White.

9. d6?

But here 9. e4 gives White a clearly superior game.

9. ...   Ng6

10. Ne2

White's idea is to embarrass the ♗ by attacking it with the b-♙, e.g. 10... b6 11. a3 Ba5 12. Rb1 and b4.

10. ...   b5!

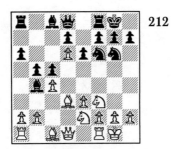

212

Black stood well after 11. a3 Ba5 12. b4 Bb6! 13. cxb5 axb5 14. Bb2 c4.

If White had accepted the ♙ with 12. cxb5 Qb6 Black gets excellent Benko-play (13. bxa6 Bxa6 14. Bxa6 Rxa6) and wins the d-♙.

Pat: Is doing the right thing always this confusing?

Noah: Yes – and no.

Pat: Thanks a lot.

Noah: I feel your pain.

But maybe it will be more understandable tomorrow.

Pat: Tomorrow?

Noah: Tomorrow we'll go further into the crucial principle of the opening – and the middlegame as well.

The Caricatures

The two "Grandmaster Secrets" books produced so far have inspired a large number of caricatures. To produce so many requires a lot of time, patience, pictorial resources, and capital outlay.

You are in luck, some of these caricatures are available for purchase at a rather attractive price, fifty to seventy five dollars. If you are interested in a particular personality, send us a self-addressed and stamped envelope and we will send you a list of what is available.

We regret to inform that these are for personal admiration and framing and may not be used in articles, for chess publications, etc. The copyright to the art is owned by Thinkers' Press.

We have several to thank for helping us locate pictures to work from including Phil Millette.

In which Noah explains that when openings are off balance, opportunities must be taken and windows shut fast.

Chapter Eight:

GIVE
AND
TAKE

Pat: Today's the day you're going to make everything in the opening make sense, right?

Noah: I hope to – beginning with this simple principle:

TAKE WHAT HE GIVES YOU

Pat: Which means?

Noah: Which means that the nature of the opening is a dynamic imbalance, in which your opponent has to give you something – and you must know how to take it.

Pat: Imbalance?

Noah: Sure. In a typical modern opening one player accepts disadvantages – such as loss of time.

Or trading a ♗ for a ♘ – or messed up ♙s.

Pat: But why?

Noah: He does it in order to obtain other advantages, such as a centralized ♘, or a queenside ♙-majority, or a kingside attack.

Trying to exploit the other player's minuses is the easiest way you can come up with your own TNs.

Pat: In my dreams.

Noah: No, seriously, there are strong new opening ideas out there for anyone to discover just by taking what the position offers.

A good case in point is the Caro-Kann in Diagram 213.

Pat: I never understand closed positions like that.

Noah: Humor me here. I'm just trying to make a point.

For decades good players followed bad strategy in the Advanced Variation Caro because they didn't take what Black is giving.

Pat: Which is?

Noah: I'll get to that in a second but I want to start by asking what's good about White's position?

Pat: Space. He's got more of it than Black.

Noah: And what's bad about White's position?

Pat: I guess you could say he's given up squares.

Noah: Some squares. Now what's good about Black's position?

Pat: It's pretty solid. And he can, you know, attack the base of the ♙-chain with ...c5, like they always talk about in the books.

Noah: Right again. But here's the million dollar question:

What's bad about Black's position?

Pat: Got me. Black hasn't done anything yet but develop the ♗.

After he plays ...e6 it's like he's got a French but without the stupid ♗ locked in at c8.

Noah: Then that ♗ should be a key to White's treatment of the opening.

Yet through most of the 20th Century the main line people followed was 4. Bd3? – even though it trades off White's good ♗ and eliminates the only exploitable Black piece.

1. e4	c6
2. d4	d5
3. e5	Bf5

213

"If (Black) is going for victory, he is practically forced to allow his opponent to get some kind of well-known positional advantage."
– Mikhail Tal

WHAT BLACK GIVES WHITE

In many popular openings Black routinely trades concessions for counterplay. Among the concessions are:

(1) LESS SPACE: In main lines of the **Modern, Pirc, Philidor's, Alekhine's, King's Indian** and **Old Indian Defenses,** for example. Also the **Closed** (non ...dxc4) **Catalan** and **Czech (...e5) Benoni.**

(2) LESS CENTER ♙ CONTROL: In the **Scotch Game, Center Game** and **Steinitz Defense Ruy Lopez** (all with ...exd4). Also, in the **Rubinstein** and **Burn Variations** of the **French** and main lines of the **Caro-Kann** (all with ...dxe4). And in the wildly unbalanced **Noteboom-Abrahams Slav** (1. d4 d5 2. c4 e6 3. Nc3 c6 4. Nf3 dxc4 5. a4 Bb4 6. e3 b5 7. Bd2 a5 8. axb5 Bxc3 9. Bxc3 cxb5).

(3) LOSS OF TIME/ LAGGARD DEVELOPMENT: In most open **Sicilians,** the **Caro-Kann** with 4...Nd7, the **QGD's Cambridge Springs** and **Lasker Defenses,** and the **Ruy Lopez Bird's Defense.**

(4) TRADING ♗ for ♘ : In the **Nimzo-Indian, Winawer French, English Opening** with ...Bb4xc3, the **QGA** with ...Bg4, the **QGD Chigorin's Defense** (2.. Nc6/... Bg4) and the **Caro-Kann Two Knights Variation** (with ...Bg4xf3).

(5) LACK OF SOLIDITY: In the **Lopez Open Defense** and main lines of the **QGA.**

(6) LOSS OF MATERIAL: In the **Two Knights Defense** with 4. Ng5, the **Lopez Marshall Gambit** and the **Benko Gambit.**

(7) WEAKENED ♙ -STRUCTURE: In **Sicilians** with ...e5, the **Stonewall Dutch,** the **Slav Meran Defense,** and **QGD Tarrasch Defense.**

(8) LESSENED ♔ -SAFETY: In the **Meran Defense,** the **Richter-Rauzer Sicilians** with Bxf6/...gxf6, and the **Winawer French.**

(9) BAD PIECE: Black's light-squared ♗ in the **French** and some **Slav** and **QGD** lines.

Black stands excellently after 4. Bd3? Bxd3 5. Qxd3 e6.

For example, 6. f4, intending 7. f5 to attack the ♟-chain's base, allows 6... Qa5†! 7. c3 Qa6!.

Then Black either gets control of a strong diagonal or a good endgame (e.g. 8. Qxa6 Nxa6 9. Nf3 c5 10. Be3 Nh6 followed by ...Nf5 and ...h5).

Or 6. Nc3 Qb6 7. Nge2 Qa6! (and after 8. Qh3 Ne7 Black is already better).

4. Nc3   e6
5. g4

This is one of the promising anti-3...Bf5 systems that developed in the last 20 years.

White will try to exploit the ♗ after:

5. ...   Bg6
6. Nge2

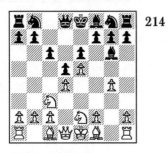

214

Followed by Nf4 and/or h2-h4-h5. For example, 6... c5 7. h4 h6 8. Be3 or 6... Ne7 7. h4 h5 8. Nf4! hxg4 8. Nxg6 with complex play.

Pat: If 4. Bd3 was so bad, why was it book?

Noah: Because the smart people said the real culprit in White's getting nothing out of the opening was 3. e5.

In fact, there's another good Caro weapon based on the "Take" principle that wasn't discovered until the 1990s.

Pat: And it's supposed to be clear to me in Diagram 215.

Noah: It should.

White's idea, popularized by Nigel Short, was to exploit the light squares and the ♗'s absence from the queenside.

For example, White plays 4. Nf3, puts his ♗ on e2 and waits for the right moment to play c4 or Nh4xf5.

Pat: Why does that work?

Noah: It works because Black usually needs the counterplay of ...c5 – the attack on the base of the ♟-chain, as you said.

But that move exposes him to risks along the a4-e8 diagonal now that his ♗ is outside the chain.

Also the b-♟ can be attacked with Qb3 – since Black doesn't want to weaken the light squares further with ...b6.

Pat: Does move order matter?

Noah: No, that's the beauty part of playing against a passive setup.

White can play Nf3, Be2, 0-0 and Nh4 or c4 in a variety of different sequences.

Pat: Looks easy to play.

Noah: Like having a substitute teacher for a month.

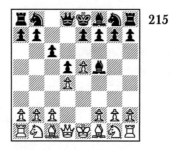

215

4. Nf3

The simplest of development.

4. ...   e6
5. Be2   c5

White has done well against 5... Ne7 6. 0-0 Nd7 7. Nh4 followed by Nxf5/c3/Bd3.

Or 6... Bg6 7. c3 Nf5 8. Qb3 b6 9. Rd1 and c4.

6. Be3

In the 1990s, before Black appreciated the strength of White's system, he got poor games after 6. c4 cxd4? 7. Nxd4.

6. ...   Ne7

Experience indicates 6... cxd4 7. Nxd4 Ne7 and then 8. c4 Nbc6 may be better.

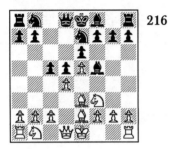

216

Now 7. dxc5 Nd7 8. 0-0 and 9. c4 or the immediate 7. c4 offers White active play in the center with mixed chances.

Pat: How does "Take what he gives you"...

Noah: Or "...what she gives you."

Pat: Have it your way. "Take what she gives you."

But how does "Take" work in a real opening? Like the Open Sicilian.

Noah: The Caro-Kann is pretty real.

But since you asked, consider Diagram 217.

Pat: This line doesn't really have a name, does it?

Noah: Not yet. Black has several choices, including 5... g6, which makes it a Dragon.

"Today... weak squares and weak pawns are self-inflicted in order to mislead the opponent, open lines are ceded so as to save the ♖s for other more promising plans..."
–David Bronstein

Or 5... a6, which turns it into a Najdorf.

Or even the flexible 5... Nc6, which delays the naming ceremony until move 6 or later.

Pat: And why should I care about 5... e5 ?

Noah: Because it makes my point about "Take."

The books used to say 5... e5 was bad because it creates a hole at d5 – but that's the same hole that Black is happy to accept in the Najdorf after 5... a6 6. Be2 e5.

Pat: So what you're saying is that what really makes 5... e5 bad is the check.

Noah: Yes, that's one thing Black's move order gave White.

As a result he has to interpose on d7 and allow the ♘ to f5.

Pat: But it's really just a tactical finesse.

Noah: True, but tactics bury a lot of promising opening ideas.

1. e4   c5

2. Nf3   d6
3. d4   cxd4
4. Nxd4   Nf6
5. Nc3

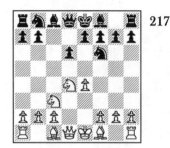

217

5. ...   e5

Trying to force White's best piece backwards.

6. Bb5†!

The only good move. Otherwise Black stands well (6. Ndb5 a6 7. Na3 b5 or 6. Nf5 Bxf5).

6. ...   Bd7

Obviously not 6... Nc6?? 7. Nxc6.

Black is positionally worse after 6... Nbd7 7. Nf5!, e.g. 7... a6 8. Bxd7† Qxd7 (8... Bxd7 9. Nxd6†)

9. Ne3.

For example, 9... Qc6 10. Qd3 Be6 11. 0-0 Be7 12 a4 and Ncd5.

7. Bxd7†   Qxd7
8. Nde2

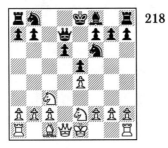

The hole at d5 will be magnified by Bg5xf6, e.g. 8... Nc6 9. Bg5 Be7 10. Bxf6 Bxf6 11. Nd5.

Pat: So I should never miss a check.
Noah: That's not the point.

Let me try a different frequency – or at least a slightly different position.

What do you see in Diagram 219?
Pat: All I see is that Black played 5... Bd7, instead of 5... e5.

Noah: But that's an improvement, since Bb5† is no longer in the cards.

Black can play ...e5 and then ...Bc6 after the N/d4 moves.
Pat: Does anybody really play this?
Noah: A few GMs – and there's a reason it's only a few GMs.
Pat: And you're gonna tell me the reason has to do with "Take."
Noah: I will. The bad thing about ...Bd7 is that it's a bit passive and denies Black the option of ...Nbd7.

White can take advantage of that with 6. Bg5, threatening to double his ♟s with Bxf6.
Pat: I see. When Black stops that with 6... e6, White can take advantage of that move by attacking a new target, the d-♟.
Noah: You've got it. This is the most forceful way of seeking an edge against 5... Bd7.

But often you have a choice of methods – and using "Take" correctly becomes harder.

1. e4   c5

2. Nf3   d6
3. d4   cxd4
4. Nxd4   Nf6
5. Nc3   Bd7

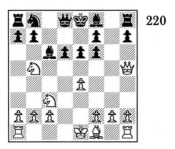

Pass-moves such as 6. h3?, allow Black to realize his plan with 6... e5 7. Ndb5 Bc6 and 8... a6.

6. Bg5

Here 6... Nbd7 is impossible and 6... e5? 7. Bxf6 Qxf6 8. Nd5 is unpleasant.

6. ...   e6
7. Ndb5!

Now 7... Bxb5 8. Bxb5† Nc6 9. Qf3!, targeting c6, favors White (9... h6 10. Bh4 Be7 11. e5!).

7. ...   Bc6

8. Bxf6   gxf6

Not 8... Qxf6?? 9. Nc7†.

9. Qh5

White, with 0-0-0 coming up, has a slight edge.

Pat: How much harder?
Noah: As hard as Diagram 221.
Pat: Another position that's news to me.
Noah: And you probably won't see it much.

Black's fifth is a waiting move, just like Najdorf's 5... a6.
Pat: At least it develops a piece – a piece can attack the e-♟ with ...Nc5.
Noah: However, as we saw with the

Caro-Kann, even a well-developed enemy piece can create opportunities for you — if you takes what's been given.

Pat: Who gives what here?

Noah: Black gives up a few things.

First, he gives up the possibility of ...Nc6xd4, which is a common idea in the Dragon and Richter-Rauzer that can greatly ease White's pressure and create counterplay for Black.

He also gives up on ...Na5-c4, a valuable maneuver to Black's best outpost square.

And it's not just this ♘ that's affected by 5... Nbd7.

Pat: Lemme guess. On d7 it gets in the way of the other ♘.

I mean, if it's attacked by a ♙.

Noah: True enough. With 5... Nbd7 Black may be vulnerable to g4-g5 because his best retreat square is occupied.

But in this case he has a well-timed answer in ...d5.

Pat: Another of those Pavlov-moves.

1. e4	c5
2. Nf3	d6
3. d4	cxd4
4. Nxd4	Nf6
5. Nc3	

One of the ideas of 5... Nc6 is to gain time with ...g6/...Bg7 and ...Nxd4, followed by a discovered attack on the ♛.

This is why 6. g3 is considered relatively innocuous (6... g6 7. Bg2 Nxd4! 8. Qxd4 Bg7).

5. ...	Nbd7

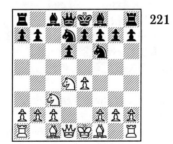

221

Among the promising options for White is:

(a) 6. Bc4 because Black lacks the ...Na5 device – and 6... Nb6 is

a poor substitute, e.g. 6... Nb6 7. Bb3 e5 8. Nde2 Be6 9. Bg5 followed by Bxf6/Nd5 with advantage to White.

(b) 6. g3 because Black doesn't have ...Nxd4, e.g. 6... g6 7. Bg2 Bg7 8. 0-0 0-0 9. Re1 a6 10. a4 and Nd5 with less play for Black than he usually gets in the Dragon.

Ditto for 6... e6 7. Bg2 a6 8. 0-0 Qc7 9. a4 Be7 10. g4.

Another idea is g4-g5, with or without the support of f3.

But Black seems to be okay after 6. g4 h6 7. h4 d5! or 6. f3 a6 7. g4 d5!.

Noah: Yes, our old friend Pavlov.

The "Take" principle is valuable when you've landed in a position that looks familiar – but is not quite part of your book knowledge.

Pat: There's an awful lot that's not part of mine.

Noah: Okay, what do think about about Diagram 222?

Pat: Hmm, maybe I've seen it be-

fore.

But maybe not – the position I know has dark-squared ♗s.

Noah: Quite true. Black was trying to improve on a book line in which 8... Nxd4 followed by 9... e5 is played to support the ♘.

Pat: Doesn't that create humungous holes at d5 and d6 ?

Noah: Yes, but the N/d4 plugs up the d-file so the holes aren't that bad.

A more serious problem with the 8... Nxd4/...e5 line, is the bad B/g7.

Pat: So, Black solves the problem with 8... Bxd4.

Noah: But that should create a new problem – if White stops to think it out.

And if he does he'll see that Black is now weak on the dark squares – a fact that can be exploited by 11. f4.

Pat: I'm not a defensive genius but it seems to me that Black can cover e5 by putting ♙s at f6 and d6.

Noah: But that gives White something else.

Pat: You mean a new target at g6.

Noah: Precisely. White ends up with a strong, effortless attack and all he had to do was apply "Take."

1. e4	c5
2. Nf3	Nc6
3. d4	cxd4
4. Nxd4	g6
5. c4	Bg7
6. Be3	Nf6
7. Nc3	Ng4
8. Qxg4	Bxd4

On 8... Nxd4 9. Qd1! White gets a nice space edge (after 9... Ne6 or 9... Nc6) or positional superiority (after 9... e5). Black has to give White something.

9. Bxd4	Nxd4

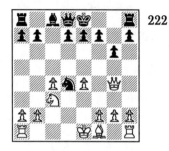

222

10. 0-0-0!

On 10. Qd1 the 10... e5 defense is stronger than in the 8... Nxd4 line and may equalize after 11. Qd2 d6 followed by ...Be6/...Rc8.

10. ...   **e5**

Now *Ninov-Ja. Meister, Correspondence 1994/5* went:

11. f4!	d6
12. Qg3	

Strong because if Black defends e5 with 12... Qe7, he invites 13. Nd5.

And 12... Qc7? is worse (13. fxe5 dxe5 14. Rxd4).

12. ...	f6
13. h4!	

Also good is 13. f5 Kf7 14. Ne2.

13. ...   **Be6**

223

14. h5!	g5
15. fxg5	fxg5
16. c5!	

With a strong attack (16...Qa5? 17. Rxd4! exd4 18. Bb5† Bd7 19. Bxd7† Kxd7 20. Qxd6†).

Pat: It can't always be that easy.

Noah: It isn't.

Sometimes the exploitation of an opponent's development requires a bit of finesse.

Pat: Sorry, I don't do finesse.

Noah: But maybe can you figure out what's wrong with White's po-

sition in Diagram 224?

Pat: It must be something about 9. Nc3 – because it says here that that's the new move.

Noah: You're on the right track. But what precisely is bad about it?

Pat: Got me. "♘s before ♗s"?

Noah: That's a slogan, not a reason.

Pat: The d-♙'s weak?

Noah: You're getting warmer.

Actually, the real difference between 9. Bb2 and 9. Nc3 is that in the game White can't reinforce his N/f3 with its brother after ...Nh4.

That means Black can trade off the best defender of d4 and get his ♛ to a great square at h4.

Pat: And White's pieces look stupid.

I mean, hello? 12. Na2 ?

Noah: He didn't have much better – because Black was alert and took what was offered.

1. e4	e6
2. d4	d5
3. e5	c5

4. c3	Nc6
5. Nf3	Bd7
6. a3	Nge7
7. b4	cxd4
8. cxd4	Nf5
9. Nc3	

Book was 9. Bb2.

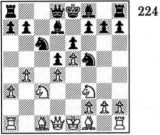

224

On c3 the ♘ enables White to anticipate an attack on d4 because 9... Qb6 can be met by 10. Na4!.

9. ...	**Rc8!**

With the idea of taking on b4 or d4 followed by ... Rxc3.

10. Bb2	**Nh4!**

In similar positions White can meet this indirect attack on d4 with Nbd2.

11. Nxh4	Qxh4

225

Now 12. Ne2? Nxb4 or 12. b5 Nxd4! 13. g3 Rxc3! (14. gxh4 Nf3†) are clearly bad for White.

In *Illescas-Speelman, Linares 1992* White played 12. Na2 and Black obtained the better game with 12... Qe4!† 13. Qe2 Qg6 14. Rc1 Be7.

Pat: We're covering a lot of ground. Caro-Kann, Sicilian, French.

Noah: "Take" applies to every opening.

Pat: And you haven't even shown me a 1. d4 game yet.

Noah: Now's a good time to start.

What do you make of Diagram 226?

Pat: Just a King's Indian with White acting weird.

Noah: But there's a method to his weirdness.

White gains space and stops the Gruenfeld Defense from happening – no 3. Nc3 d5.

Pat: I guess 3. d5 makes sense if your opponent only knows the Gruenfeld.

But I've never seen it before – so there must be something wrong with it.

That's common sense, right?

Noah: Well, I'm afraid there are a lot of openings you've never seen – and not all of them are bad.

But in this case, you're right: We should be able to use logic to exploit 3. d5.

Pat: Me first. The bad things about 3. d5 are that it loses time and makes White's center ♟s more vulnerable.

Noah: Keep going.

Pat: Black can attack the ♟s, maybe like a Benko Gambit.

Noah: Or just with 3... c6.

Even though d5 is easily protected by White, Black gets a fine game then without sacrificing a ♟.

1. d4	Nf6
2. c4	g6
3. d5	

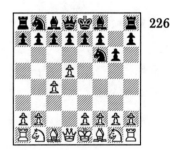

226

3. ...	c6

Black also has good play with 3... b5!? 4. cxb5 a6 5. bxa6 c6 (6. Nc3? cxd5 7. Nxd5 Qa5† 8. Nc3 Bg7 9. Bd2 Bxa6).

But a pawn is a ♟.

4. Nc3	**cxd5**
5. cxd5	**d6**

6. g3   Bg7
7. Bg2   0-0
8. Nf3

Or 8. e4 b5!? 9. Nxb5 Qa5† 10. Nc3 Ba6 with excellent comp.

8. ...   b5!

227

With great counterplay for Black – 9. Nxb5 Qa5† 10. Nc3 Ne4.

Pat: But I thought development didn't matter.

Noah: No, what I said is a big difference in development does matter.

But it only matters if you make it matter – as Black does in Diagram 228.

Pat: Whoa! Before we go there, can you please make some sense out of these moves? Like 6. Ng1 and 8... Bd6.

Noah: What happened in the first five moves is that White tempted Black's e-♟ forward so he could win it with Ne2-g3.

If he couldn't win it, he wanted to exploit 5... e4 by occupying the f4-outpost, with Ne2-f4. Therefore 6. Ng1.

Meanwhile, Black put his ♝ on d6 because it can go from there to a very active e5. Then when he plays ...d6 the ♝ has a lot more scope than it would on f8.

Pat: I guess I like Black – but I'm not not exactly sure why.

Noah: You should like Black. And figuring out why is crucial.

What White gave him in the first eight to nine moves was a lead in development. After a bit of thinking Black should realize the only way to exploit that is to open the position.

Therefore – 9... b5. You can connect the rest of the dots.

Goldin-Yakovich
Moscow 1991

1. c4   e5
2. Nc3   Nf6
3. Nf3   Nc6
4. e3   Bb4
5. Nd5   e4
6. Ng1!?

White plays to win the e-♟.

On 6. Nxb4 Nxb4 7. Nd4 0-0 and ...Na6 offers Black good play but 7... c5 may be better (8. Nb5 d5).

6. ...   0-0
7. Qc2   Re8
8. a3   Bd6!
9. Ne2

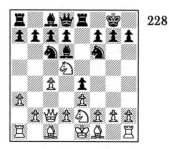

228

The e-♟ can be doomed by 10. Ng3 or 10. Nec3.

9. ...   b5!

Now 10. cxb5 Nxd5 11. bxc6 dxc6 (12. Qxc6 Nb6 and ...Ba6 or ...Bd7) or 10. Ng3 bxc4 11. Bxc4 Bb7 give Black the kind of play he wants.

10. Nxf6†   Qxf6
11. cxb5   Ne5

Taking the second ♟ is too dangerous (12. Qxe4 Bb7! 13. Qxb7 Nd3† 14. Kd1 Nxf2† 15. Kc2 Qf5† or 13. Qc2 Ng4 14. f4 Qh4† 15. g3 Qh5 with advantage).

12. Ng3   Bb7

And here 13. Nxe4 is met by

13... Qg6 (14. f3 Nxf3† 15. gxf3 Rxe4! or 14. d3 Nxd3†! 15. Bxd3 Qxg2).

13. Be2   Qh4!

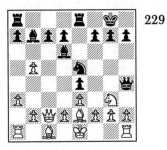

229

And Black soon had a winning attack, e.g. 14. 0-0? Nf3† or 14. Qa4 a6 15 f4 axb5 etc.

Pat: Wow. After 13... Qh4 White completely cratered.

Noah: That's a dramatic example, a big difference in development made a big payoff for Black.

More often you have to use "Take" to exploit differences that may seem minor at the time.

Pat: Like what?

Noah: Like the next example.

Pat: Why is White's sixth move wrong?

Noah: It's a waste since Black will have to trade off his B/b4 anyway if he wants to compete in the center with ...d6/...e5.

Pat: But White only wasted one move, and the position is probably gonna be closed anyway.

Noah: True, but that tempo gives Black a couple of opportunities in Diagram 230 – depending on which of two reasonable developing moves White chooses.

Pat: I see one problem.

If White plays 9. Nc3 he's walking into ...Na5.

Noah: The second problem is that by not playing Nc3 he gave Black something else, the e4-outpost.

That kind of outpost gives you at least equality – and sometimes wins games.

1. d4   Nf6
2. c4   e6

3. Nf3   Bb4†
4. Bd2   Qe7
5. g3   Nc6
6. a3?!

Book is 6. Bg2 Bxd2† 7. Nbxd2 d6 or 6. Nc3 Bxc3 7. Bxc3 Ne4.

6. ...   Bxd2†
7. Qxd2   d6
8. Bg2   0-0

230

Now 9. Nc3 e5 10. d5?! allows Black to attack c4 and b3 with 10... Na5!.

9. 0-0

This enables White to meet 9... e5, pressuring the center (10... Bg4), with an advantageous 10. d5!.

9. ...   Ne4!

This exploits the ♘'s absence from c3.

In *Shtern-Benjamin, U.S. Open 1988* Black had a fine game after 10. Qc2 f5 11. Nc3 Nxc3 12. Qxc3 e5 (and no better was 11. d5 Nd8 12. Nd4 Qf6).

Pat: I know this is supposed to be important. But somehow I've managed to win games without knowing about "Take."

Noah: Yes, but you never knew about other games you might have won.

For example, what would you do in Diagram 231?

Pat: It looks familiar – except for that ♟ on e6.

Noah: That ♟ makes a big difference.

Because Black can play ...d5, the Dragon-slaying plan with 9. f3 doesn't make as much sense.

Pat: So what's bad about 8... e6 is the hole at d6.

Then why isn't 9. Ndb5 right?

Noah: Once again, tactics prevail – they make 9... d5 a more-than-sufficient answer.

But there is a second, exploitable problem with 8... e6 – it commits Black to playing ...d5 eventually.

Pat: You mean because it just looks dumb if he only plays ...d6.

Black would be playing a Dragon and a Scheveningen then.

Noah: And that's usually a bad mix.

The reason 8... e6 is exploitable is that White hasn't commited himself yet to queenside castling or to the f3 attacking plan.

As a result of 9. 0-0!, White gets a target at d5 he can pound with heavy pieces.

Pat: Black does have a few tricks. You know, like with ...Ne4.

Noah: But structurally he's got a major problem on d5 that won't run away – and will hurt him once White completes development.

1. e4   c5

---

2. Nf3   Nc6
3. d4   cxd4
4. Nxd4   g6
5. Nc3   Bg7
6. Be3   Nf6
7. Bc4   0-0
8. Bb3

Normal here is 8... d6 (threatening 9... Ng4!).

Then 9. f3 leads to a familiar attacking system, e.g. 9... Bd7 10. Qd2 Rc8 11. 0-0-0 or 11. h4.

8. ...   e6

Some books give only 9. Nxc6 dxc6 10. e5 Qxd1 11. Rxd1 as favoring White strongly but 10... Nd5 is unclear.

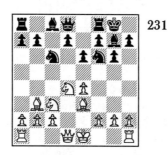

231

---

9. 0-0!

Not 9. f3, which allows 9... d5!. Then 10. Nxc6 bxc6 11. e5 Nd7 is fine for Black (and 10. exd5 exd5 11. 0-0 is only a slight edge for White).

Worse is 9. Ndb5 because Black gets strong play after 9... d5! 10. exd5 exd5 and 11... a6 (or 11. Nxd5 Nxd5 12. Qxd5 Qxd5 13. Bxd5 Bxb2 14. Rb1 Be5).

9. ...   d5

The only consistent move. Otherwise White would continue 10. h3 followed by f4 and Qf3.

10. exd5   exd5

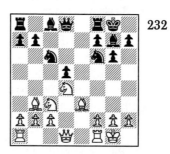

232

11. h3

White, with Qf3 and Rad1 coming up, is better.

For example, 11... Na5 12. Qf3 Ne4 13. Rfd1!. (But not 13. Nxe4 dxe4 14. Qxe4 Nxb3 15. axb3 and 15... f5.)

Noah: You'd be surprised how often the simplest move, like 0-0, is the best move.

But there are also times when you have to defer development to exploit what he gives you.

Pat: I'm sure this is leading to the next diagram.

Noah: Yes, and this exam question is a two-parter.

First, what did White give Black?

Pat: Hmm... I guess he developed his B/c1 really early.

At least it's early for a d-♟ opening.

Noah: Which is both good and bad for White.

Pat: And the bad part must be that Black can trade off the ♗ for a ♘ with ...Nh5.

Noah: But the story doesn't stop there.

Pat: You mean because Black developed a ♗, too.

Noah: Sure. White gets to play his ♕ out to b3 with tempo, attacking the b-♙.

And then White realized he shouldn't castle kingside because he has holes to grab and an enemy ♔ to attack there.

Pat: Black collapsed in record time.

Kovacevic-Bisguier
New York Open 1989

1. d4	d5
2. Nf3	Nf6
3. Bf4	c6
4. e3	Bg4

This would have been a good time to "Take" – 4... Qb6! – since 5. b3 or 5. Qc1 are clumsy defenses of b2.

5. c4	Nbd7
6. Nbd2	e6
7. Bd3	Nh5
8. Bg3	Nxg3

9. hxg3	Bd6?
10. Qb3	

Taking advantage of the ♗'s absence from the defense of b7.

10. ...	Rb8

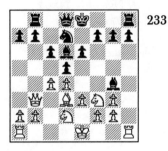

233

11. Nh2!
White has only a tiny edge after 11. 0-0 0-0.

11. ...	Bh5

Black loses a ♙ after 11... Bf5 12. Bxf5.

12. Nhf1!	Nf6

Or 12... Bg6 13. Bxg6 when 13... hxg6?? loses to 14. Rxh8†.

13. f3	Bg6

White would have forced this with 14. g4.

14. Bxg6	fxg6
15. g4	0-0
16. 0-0-0	

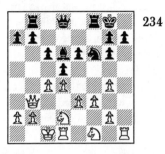

234

White had a very strong game and Black's desperation failed after 16... b5 17. c5 Bc7 18. g5 Nd7 19. f4 e5 20. fxe5!.

The rest was 20...Qxg5 21. e4 a5 22. 23. Ne3 Bxe5 24. Nxd5! Black resigns.

Noah: Not quite a record.

But very often "Take" allows you to exploit a tactical opportunity very early in a game.

The trouble is that a lot of positions don't look tactical – so what's given isn't taken, as in Diagram 235.

Pat: White's position looks fine.

Noah: It's fine from all sorts of positional points of view.

But if you also apply Blumenfeld's Law you'll see 4. d3?? is a blunder.

Pat: Whoops. I guess Black just missed 4... e4!.

Noah: What he missed was a huge window of opportunity.

It wasn't open long – just one move – before White closed it with 5. Bb2.

Chiburdanidze-Polugayevsky
Aruba 1992

1. c4	c5
2. Nf3	Nc6
3. b3	e5
4. d3??	

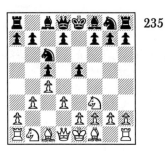

4. ...   g6??
5. Bb2   Bg7

The game was drawn in 55 moves.

But Black would be winning after 4... e4!, threatening the N/f3 as well as ...Qf6! and ...Qxa1.

White's best reply is to move the ♘ to g1 or g5 and hope for a miracle after 5... Qf6 6. d4 Nxd4.

Pat: Do these windows exist in book positions?

Noah: Some book positions, the ones that haven't been corrected yet.

An instructive example is Dia-gram 236.

Pat: Doesn't look like any book I know.

Noah: Not now, but it was fairly well known back in 1960s.

The opening starts when White tries an alternative to the usual 3. d4 and 3. c4.

In those days the book antidote to 3. Nc3 was 3... Nxc3 and ...d6xe5, which was supposed to lead to quick equality.

Pat: There must be other good moves for Black.

Noah: There are. But few people looked at them until they under-stood what Black was giving White in the diagram.

Pat: This isn't like the Caro-Kann with ...Bf5, is it?

Noah: It's similar.

The ♗ is one of the two things Black left unprotected in the dia-gram.

Pat: The other must be the b-♟.

Noah: And once someone realized how strong it was to attack both

targets with moves 7 and 8, Black's line was doomed.

1. e4   Nf6
2. e5   Nd5
3. Nc3   Nxc3
4. bxc3   d6
5. f4   dxe5

Black does better to delay this but...

6. fxe5   Bf5

... this was the book recommen-dation. Black was supposed to be equal.

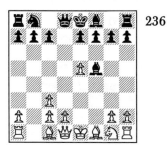

7. Qf3!   Qc8

The only other way to avoid sacrificing material is 7... Bc8.

8. Rb1!

Again attacking b7.

8. ...   c6

Or 8... Nc6 9. Bb5 threatening Bxc6† (9... Bd7 10. d4 gives White a clear edge).

"A chess optimist is one who thinks he will never do anything as stupid again."
– D.J. Morgan

8. Bd3! Bxd3
9. cxd3 e6
10. Qg3

Black has serious problems (10... Be7? 11. Qxg7) while White develops smoothly with Nf3/0-0.

Pat: Yeah, but if only Black had ...e6 in the diagram...

Noah: Windows of opportunity are all about exploiting the difference between "if only" –and the position on the board.

Quite often it's a matter of "if only I was castled" that spells defeat.

That's under the microscope in Diagram 237.

Pat: Black's position sure looks okay.

Noah: It is fundamentally sound.

But because Black hasn't had a chance to castle he's one or two moves away from true safety.

Once White realized that he knew how strong 7. Qa4 and 12. h4 were going to be.

Pat: Yet another Pavlov-move.

Noah: Right again. When Black

puts a ♘ on g6 he's giving White a great opportunity for h4-h5.

In this case 12... h5 was too weakening and going to f4 with the ♘ would have stretched Black's defenses too far.

Benjamin-Shaked
U.S. Championship 1998

1.	e4	c5
2.	Nf3	Nc6
3.	Bb5	e6
4.	0-0	Nge7
5.	Re1	Ng6
6.	c3	d5

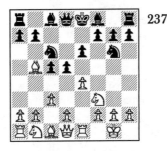

237

7. Qa4!
Now 7... dxe4 8. Bxc6† or 7...

Bd7? 8 exd5 cost a ♟.

7. ... Qd6?
But sacking with 7... Be7 (and 8. Bxc6† bxc6 9. Qxc6† Bd7) is much better here.

8. exd5 Qxd5
9. d4
White threatens 10. c4! ♛-moves 11. d5.

9. ... cxd4
10. cxd4 Be7
11. Nc3 Qd6
Or 11... Qd7 12. d5 exd5 13. Nd4!.

12. h4!
Now 12... Nxh4?? loses a piece to 13. Nxh4 Bxh4 14. d5!.

Also 12... h5 13. Ne5 followed by 14. Nxg6 favors White (or 13... Ngxe5 14. dxe5 Qc7 15. Bg5).

12. ... Bd7
13. h5 Nf8
On 13... Nf4 Black is in trouble (14. Bxf4 Qxf4 15. d5! Qxa4 16. Bxa4 or 14. Ne4 Qc7 15. Bxf4 Qxf4 16. Ne5).

14. d5!

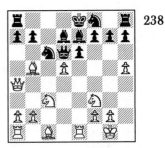

238

Since 14... exd5 15. Bf4 Qb4 16. Bxc6 or 15... Qc5 16. Rac1 Be6 17. Nxd5 Qxd5 18. Rxc6 are ugly, Black had to move the N/c6.

The game ended soon after 14... Nb4 15. Ne5 a6 16. Bxd7† Nxd7 17. Nxf7! Kxf7 18. dxe6†.

Pat: Everybody goes "Of course!" when some GM pushes his h-♟ and wins.

Noah: It's just taking what your opponent gives. Like what Black's seventh move gave White in the next example

Pat: You mean the chance to play h5xg6.

Noah: Of course. By developing the ♘ at e7 Black ruled out ...Nf6, the most economical way of ruling h5 out.

Pat: I can't buy that Black lost this game just because he put his ♘ on the wrong square.

Noah: No, but 7... Nge7 created obstacles to Black's having a happy and safe ♚-postion.

Black decided he needed ...f5 for counterplay – which he did – and could only afford that with ...0-0-0 – which he couldn't.

And ...0-0-0 gave White something else, which he took advantage of with his 14th and 15th moves.

Pat: But isn't White's ♚ in greater danger than Black's because of the ♙ at h4?

Noah: No, because White had much more operating space and time to exploit Black's weaknesses first.

Black's ♚ would have been safer after routine moves in Diagram 239. As it turned out White seized his opportunity.

Pat: Of course.

Kasparov-Speelman
Barcelona 1989

1. d4	d6
2. e4	g6
3. c4	e5
4. Nf3	exd4
5. Nxd4	Bg7
6. Nc3	Nc6
7. Be3	Nge7
8. h4!	h6

Black feels he can't afford both 8... h5 and a later ...f5.

9. Be2	f5

Much safer is 9... 0-0 10. Qd2 Kh7.

10. exf5	Nxf5
11. Nxf5	Bxf5
12. Qd2	Qd7

Black needs piece activity (12... Qf6!).

13. 0-0	0-0-0

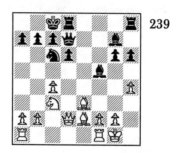

239

Understandably Black didn't want to spend another tempo (13... h5) in order to castle kingside.

Now if 14. Rad1 Kb8, Black is relatively safe.

14. b4!

Here 14... Kb8 15. b5 Ne7 16. Rfd1 and a4-a5 gives White a strong attack against a7.

14. ...	Nxb4
15. Nb5!	

Nothing saves Black now, e.g. 15... Nc6 16. Bf3 Ne5 17. Nxa7† Kb8 18. Bxb7! Kxb7 19. Rab1†!.

Or 15... Bxa1 16. Qxb4 Be5 17. Nxa7† Kb8 18. Bf3 or 15... c5 16. Rad1, threatening 17. Bxc5 dxc5

18. Qf4.

15. ...	Nc2
16. Bf3!	

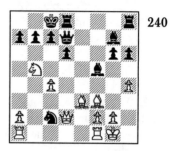

240

Black loses quickly after 16... Nxa1 17. Nxa7† Kb8 18. Qa5 or 16... Bxa1 17. Nxa7† Kb8 18. Rb1! or 16... Nxe3 17. Qxe3 Bxa1 18. Qxa7.

He kept the game alive with 16... d5 17. Bxd5 Nxa1 18. Nxa7† Kb8 – but after 19. Qb4 Qxd5 20. cxd5 he resigned in five moves.

Noah: Now before we wind up for the day...

Pat: It's about time.

Noah: ...I'd like to give you a taste

of something we'll get into another day – reevaluation.

The action begins in Diagram 241.

Pat: Looks like Black has all the action.

Noah: But looks are deceiving.

What's important to realize is that 11... Qxd5 creates tactical opportunities for both players – and that's good for White because he's the one who gets to move first in the diagram.

That means he must examine the most forceful moves – and when he does he soon realizes how strong 12. Bxf6 is.

Pat: Because it trashes Black's kingside.

Noah: Not only that. The real weakness in Black's position is something that looks like a strength – the h1-a8 diagonal.

By eliminating the N/f6 White takes advantage of the diagonal by getting in Be4.

Pat: But that's just because Black

blundered by Diagram 242.

Noah: And that's the point about reevaluation I was going to make.

Black should have realized how bad his position was getting by move 13.

If he had, he would never have tried to grab the d-♟.

Kasparov-Timman
Match 1998

1. d4	Nf6
2. c4	e6
3. Nc3	Bb4
4. Qc2	0-0
5. a3	Bxc3†
6. Qxc3	b6
7. Bg5	c5
8. e3	d6
9. Bd3	

Solid now is 9... Nbd7 10. Ne2 Ba6 and ...Rc8 with pressure on c4.

But Black chooses a logical – yet flawed – means to simplify the center and obtain counterplay.

9. ...	cxd4
10. exd4	d5?

11. cxd5	Qxd5?

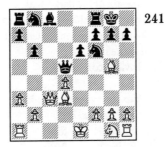

241

Black achieves his positional goal, controlling the b7-g2 diagonal, and creates a double attack on the g-♟ and B/g5.

But 12. Nf3 is not forced.

12. Bxf6!

Now 12... Qxg2 13. 0-0-0! Qxh1 loses to 14. Bxh7†! Kxh7 15. Qd3† Kg8 16. Qg3 g6 17. Qh4 and mates.

12. ... gxf6

13. Ne2!

White seizes the tactical window created by the threat of Ng3, followed by Be4 or Nh5 – or Nf4-h5.

13. ... Rd8?

Also bad was 13... Bb7 14. Nf4 Qd6 15. Nh5 Nd7 16. Qd2! and Qh6.

Best was 13... Ba6! 14. Bxa6 Nxa6 15. Rc1 with a clear White edge.

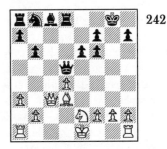

242

14. Ng3!

White is winning, e.g. 14... Bb7 15. Be4 Qd7 16. Nh5, or 14... f5 15. Be2! and 16. Bf3.

Black resigned soon after 14... Qxd4 15. Be4 Qxc3† 16. bxc3 Rd5 17. Rd1!.

"He loses all who loses the right moment."
– **Spanish proverb**

Pat: So far you've been talking about taking advantage of weak ♟s, slow development, lack of castling...

Noah: ... a well-placed ♗, and misplaced ♘s – on e7, d7, and c3.

Pat: Is there anything else you can take?

Noah: Anything that isn't nailed down. Like a good square.

Pat: It probably has to be a really good square to matter.

Noah: Sure, like d4 or e5 in the next example.

Pat: I thought you said – or was it your pal Pavlov? – that whenever White plays f3, Black should try to open the a7-g1 diagonal.

Noah: True, Black might have tried to do that with 4... c5 or 4... d6 followed by ...c6/...Qb6.

But 4... Nc6 and ...e5 is a more forcing way of taking advantage of White's fourth move.

Pat: You mean because White can't defend d4 with Nf3.

Noah: Exactly. By the time he gets

a chance to play 8. Nf3 he's already lost control of the dark squares.

White missed his last chance to be competitive when he failed to find 7. dxe5.

Pat: Pavlov scores again.

Vanderwaeren-Glek
Leuven 1995

1.	c4	f5
2.	Nc3	Nf6
3.	d4	g6
4.	f3	

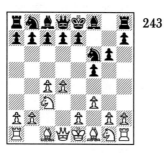

Steinitz used to build centers (5. e4) this way.

4.	...	Nc6!?
5.	e4	

Black also gets good play on dark squares after 5. d5 Ne5 6. e4 fxe4 7. fxe4 d6, e.g. 8. Nf3 Nxf3† and ...e5.

5.	...	fxe4
6.	fxe4	e5
7.	d5?	

Better is 7. dxe5! Nxe5 8. Nf3 after which Black should continue to watch the dark squares with 8... Nf7! (9. e5 Ng4 10. Qd4 d6 or 10. Qe2 Bg7).

7.	...	Nd4
8.	Nf3	Bc5!
9.	Be3	

On 9. Nxe5 Qe7 Black regains the ♟ favorably.

| 9. | ... | Ng4! |

Also good is 9... Nc2† 10. Qxc2 Bxe3.

10. Bg1

Black has too much play for the ♟ after 10. Bxd4 exd4 11. Nxd4 d6.

| 10. | ... | d6 |

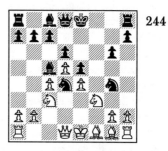

And Black stood better after 11. Nxd4 Bxd4 12. Bxd4 exd4 13. Qxd4 0-0 followed by ...Qg5 or ...Qh4†, and 11. Be2 Nxf3† 12. Bxf3 Bxg1.

Noah: He does indeed. A lot of Pavlovian reactions are perfect examples of "Take."

Black especially needs to be on the lookout for Pavlov opportunities when White grabs the lion's share of the board.

There's a good example of this in Diagram 245.

Pat: Seems like White is the one taking advantage – I mean of 8... Bd6.

Give and Take

Noah: To some degree. Thanks to 9. e4 White has two attractive alternative ways of exploiting 8... Bd6.

He can trade ♘ for ♗ with 11. Nxd6 – or try to squeeze Black with 11. c5.

Pat: I like the ♟ move.

Noah: So did I when I first looked at the position.

But you see the consequences – Black challenges the c-♟ with 11... b6.

Pat: And when White supports it with the b-♟, Black gets to attack that too.

Noah: The result is that Black can dominate the a-file and that's just enough counterplay to balance what White got in the center as a result of 11. c5.

Piket-Dreev
Nussloch 1996

1. d4	d5
2. c4	c6
3. Nf3	Nf6
4. Nc3	e6

5. Bg5	h6
6. Bxf6	Qxf6
7. e3	Nd7
8. a3	Bd6

More common here is 8... Qd8 or 8... g6.

9. e4	dxe4
10. Nxe4	Qe7
11. c5	Bc7
12. Bc4	

245

12. ...	b6!
13. b4	a5!
14. 0-0	0-0
15. Qe2	Bb7
16. Rab1	Ra7!

246

Now 17. bxa5? b5! favors Black's ♟-structure.

Play continued 17. Rfe1 axb4 18. axb4 Rfa8 19. g3 Ra3! 20. Rb3 Ra2 21. Rb2 R2a3, with equality.

Pat: Not bad. Both players got a chance to take.

Noah: That's what a lot of the sparring is like in GM games.

One final example of it is Diagram 247.

Pat: It always seems like White is delaying developing his N/b1 in the Dutch – but here he ends up fianchettoing it.

Noah: There are good reasons for that.

First, he was hoping for a chance to play Ba3xe7, trading off Black's good ♗.

Once Black anticipated that with 7... Qe7 White moved on to Plan B – the ♘ heads to d3 and then maybe to e5.

White was simply taking advantage of the Stonewall ♟-structure Black had created.

Pat: But that means there's no pressure on d5.

Noah: And Black can exploit that by blowing up the center with 10... e5.

Sosonko-Yusupov
Olympiad 1988

1. d4	e6
2. g3	f5
3. Bg2	Nf6
4. Nf3	d5
5. 0-0	Bd6
6. c4	c6
7. b3	

Preparing 8. Ba3.

7. ...   Qe7
8. Nc3   0-0
9. Na4

White can try to exploit the B/d6's inability to retreat to e7 by playing 9. Bf4.

But then 9... Bxf4 10. gxf4 loosens his ♟-structure – and 10... Ne4 followed by ...h6/...g5 or ...Bd7-e8-h5 offers Black excellent attacking chances.

Instead, White prepares Na4-b2-d3 followed by Bf4 so that he can recapture on f4 with a ♘.

9. ...   Nbd7

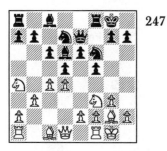

247

10. Nb2
Black can thwart the Bf4 plan

with 10... Ne4 11. Nd3 g5 but then 12. Nfe5 leaves him with many holes.

10. ...   e5!
Now Black can meet 11. cxd5 with 11... e4!, with a positionally fine game (12. Ne1 Nxd5).

11. dxe5 Nxe5
On 12. cxd5 Nxd5 13. Nxe5 and Black can choose between 13... Nc3! and the promising sacrifice of 13... Bxe5 14. Bxd5† cxd5 15. Qxd5† Kh8.

12. Qc2   Nxf3†
13. Bxf3   Be6

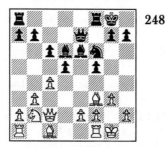

248

Black has no problems (14. cxd5 Bxd5 or 14. Bg5 d4 15. Nd3 Rad8).

Pat: You know, I could get to like playing the opening if it was all as simple as "Take."

I could even like the Queen's Indian.

Noah: Let's not go overboard, my young grandmaster.

"Take" is only one of several things you have to keep in mind in the opening.

There's something else we haven't touched on yet that you have to worry about throughout the game.

Pat: And that is...?

Noah: That is enough for one day.

In which Pat learns that anyone can offer a gambit — but greed and grabbing may be better policy.

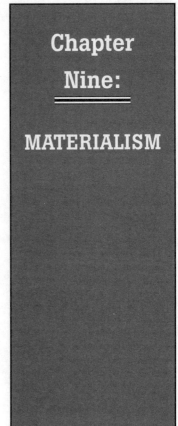

Chapter Nine:

MATERIALISM

Pat: I'm all ears. What haven't we talked about yet?

Noah: Material, as in what it's really worth in the opening.

Knowing how to strike the proper balance between time, pieces, and position is the hardest skill to acquire.

Pat: Okay, but you can skip the lecture about the evils of ♟ grabbing.

I took that course before.

Noah: Then you need a refresher – ♟-grabbing is not necessarily evil.

It's just another name for taking the other guy's pieces.

Pat: But it's got a bad reputation.

Noah: Only because of times when the grabber loses all sense of proportion and goes after a ♟ or two at the expense of everything else.

Black does this in our first example – with distinction.

Pat: When did Black start going downhill?

Noah: Around move 7. In fact, his seventh and eighth moves should share one huge question mark.

By move 10 Black has given away valuable time, made a bad ♗-for-♘ trade and left his N/e4 open to tactics.

That ain't worth a ♟.

Kasparov-Korchnoi
Horgen 1995

1. Nf3	Nf6
2. c4	e6
3. Nc3	d5
4. d4	c6
5. Bg5	h6
6. Bh4	dxc4
7. e4	Bb4

Book is 7... g5 8. Bg3 b5 or 8... Bb4 9. Bxc4 Nxe4 10. 0-0 Nxg3 (when 11. fxg3! gives White attacking chances on the f-file).

8. Bxc4	Bxc3†
9. bxc3	Qa5

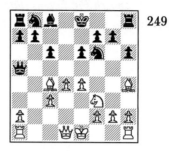

249

10. 0-0!	Nxe4
11. Ne5!	

The lost c-♟ is not nearly as relevant as the Qg4 threat.

For example, 11... 0-0 12. Qg4 f5 13. Qg6 (or 12... Nxc3 13. Bf6) and White wins.

Also bad for Black is 12... Ng5 13 f4, e.g. 13... Nh7 14. Rf3! and 13... Ne4 14. Rae1 and 13... f5 14 Qh5 Ne4 15. Be7.

11. ...	Nd7
12. Qg4	

White dominates the board after 12... g5 13. Qxe4 Nxe5 14. dxe5 gxh4 15. Rab1.

Slightly better – but still bad for Black – is 12... Nxe5 13. dxe5 Ng5 14. Bxg5 hxg5 15. Qxg5 0-0.

Noah: This is one aspect of materialism that hasn't changed much in 150 years.

Pat: That sounds like there's other things that have changed.

Noah: They have. ♟ sacrifices, for example.

♟ sacks to gain the initiative are much more common in GM chess today.

Pat: But there were always gambits, back in the days of dinosaur chess.

You know, Morphy, Chigorin, those guys.

Noah: True, but those were gambits offered by White to create an attack against a ♚.

Nowadays ♟s are sacked for purely positional reasons – Black is almost as likely to sack as White.

A good case of that is Diagram 250.

Pat: We just looked at a Sicilian like this the other day.

Noah: Yes, when we were talking the differences between ...Nc6 and ...Nbd7.

After ...Nxd4 White's ♕ is misplaced at d4 on the hot c3-g7 diagonal.

Pat: And it doesn't have a wonderful place to retreat to.

Noah: Maybe not wonderful. But by going to b4 the ♕ makes Black think twice about moving his B/c8.

And Black's not about to develop his ♕ on active squares such as a5 or b6 then.

Pat: But Black has to connect his ♖s and get on with his life. If White gets to play Bg5 and Nd5 before then, I'd love his game.

Noah: You should. That's why it makes sense for Black to harass the Q/b4 even if it costs him the b-♟.

Pat: Funny – White's okay in an equal-material position after 12... Nxd5.

But he's worse when he's a ♟ up after 12... a4.

Adams-Kramnik
Wijk aan Zee 1998

1. e4   c5
2. Nf3   Nc6
3. Nc3   d6
4. d4   cxd4
5. Nxd4   Nf6
6. g3   g6
7. Bg2   Nxd4
8. Qxd4   Bg7
9. 0-0   0-0

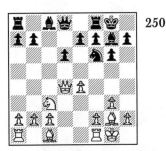

250

White fears discovered attacks – not just the traps of 10. b3? Nxe4 or 10. Be3? Ng4 but also 10... Be6 and 11... Nd5 against other moves.

10. Qb4   a5
Much better than the passive

10... Rb8.

11. Qb3   Be6!
Based on 12. Qxb7 Nd7! followed by 13... Rb8 14. Qa7 Nc5 and threat of 15... Ra8.

12. Nd5   a4!
Not 12... Nxd5 13. exd5 Bf5 14. a4 with rough equality.

13. Qxb7   Nxd5
14. exd5   Bf5

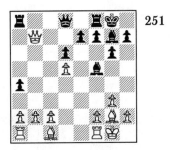

251

And the strong queenside pressure and threats (15... a3!; 15... Bxc2) gave Black a terrific edge.

Noah: A ♟ is a small price to pay for the initiative in a sharp opening. Sometimes it's worth at least two.

Diagram 252 shows an example of that in a super-sharp line.

Pat: What do you call this opening?

Noah: It's a standard slash-and-burn Najdorf position, the kind that was considered so strong that for years Black avoided it.

Pat: Why?

Noah: Because the 11. Bxe6 sack is too hot to accept.

So if Black got that far he was supposed to accept a materially even – but positionally inferior middlegame – with 11... Nxe5.

Pat: Yeah, but after 11... 0-0 Black's not only down a ♟ but he also loses control of d5.

That has to count a lot.

Noah: Not that much. Even two ♟s down Black has major threats.

White's ♔ is still in the center and his minor pieces don't protect one another.

Pat: I guess he never appreciated how much danger he was in.

Noah: And when he failed to cut his losses at move 20 the game was all over except for the scoresheet signing.

"I never make a mistake in the opening."
– Ernst Gruenfeld, when asked why he never played 1. e4.

Goloshchapov-Movsesian
Mlada-Boleslav 1995

1.	e4	c5
2.	Nf3	e6
3.	d4	cxd4
4.	Nxd4	Nf6
5.	Nc3	d6
6.	Bc4	a6
7.	Bb3	b5
8.	f4	Be7

Black usually avoids what happens now by playing 8... b4 or 8... Bb7 (and 9. e5 dxe5 10. fxe5 Ne4).

9.	e5	dxe5
10.	fxe5	Nfd7
11.	Bxe6	

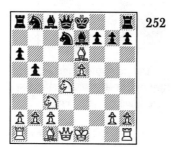
252

Now 11... fxe6 12. Nxe6 Qb6?

13. Nd5 (13... Qxe6?? 14. Nc7†) or 12... Qa5 13. Nxg7† is awful for Black.

The book line was 11... Nxe5 12. Bf4! fxe6 13. Bxe5, which favors White.

11.	...	0-0!
12.	Bd5	Ra7

White is in trouble (13. Bf4 b4) and should consider 13. 0-0 Nxe5 14. Bf4.

13.	e6	Nc5!
14.	exf7†	Kh8

Threatening to win material with 15... b4 or 15... Rd7.

15.	Bf4	Bh4†
16.	g3	b4

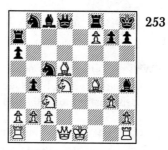
253

Black's threats, including ... Re7† and ...bxc3/...Qxd5, count more than White's.

17. Nf3

Or 17. Bxb8 Re7† 18. Kf2 bxc3 19. Nc6 Qb6.

17. ... Bf6

Black had a strong initiative after 18. Ne4 Rd7 19. Nxf6 gxf6!.

White's last chance was 20. Bxb8 Rxd5 21. Qe2 Rxf7 22. 0-0 Bh3 23. Bf4!.

Instead he tried 20. Bc4? and resigned soon after 20... Rxd1† 21. Rxd1 Qe7† 22. Kf2 Be6.

Pat: Somebody always seems to be sacrificing something in the Sicilian.

Noah: Or the King's Indian. Or the Benoni.

Or even the Catalan.

There are lots of openings in which ♙-sacrifices are simply part of the landscape.

Pat: I see you've got a Benoni set up in Diagram 254. Or is it a King's

Indian?

Noah: A King's Indian.

But before we go there you'll notice two good illustrations of the "Take" principle.

Pat: One must be 9... h5 – another Pavlov move.

Noah: Exactly. It takes advantage of White's ♘, which will get kicked back from g3 to h1.

But 8... h5 also gives White something – something he didn't take.

Pat: You're not making this easy.

Noah: It's simple. White could have restricted Black a bit with 11. Bg5!, which takes advantage of his inability to play ...h6.

But the main reason I'm showing you this position is 14... Bd4.

Pat: I really don't get that.

Black is behind in development – yet he spends a tempo to trade off his best piece and lose a ♟.

Noah: To understand why, you have to learn the basic rule of the King's Indian – Black either gets counterplay or he gets crushed.

In other words, a ♟ is chump change.

Here you see that 14... Bd4 was the best way of exploiting the king-side dark squares – which Black virtually owns after 16... Qg5.

Spassky–J. Polgar
Match 1993

1. d4	Nf6
2. c4	g6
3. Nc3	Bg7
4. e4	d6
5. f3	0-0
6. Nge2	c5
7. d5	e6
8. Ng3	exd5
9. cxd5	h5!

Now 10. h4 is a too-weakening way of stopping ... h4.

10. Be2	Nbd7
11. 0-0	a6
12. a4	h4
13. Nh1	Nh5
14. Be3	

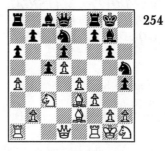

254

14. ...	Bd4!
15. Bxd4	

Refusing the offer is worse (15. Qd2? Nf4! and now 16. Bxd4 Qg5! wins for Black (17... Nh3# as well as 17... Qxg2# are threatened).

Or 16. Rf2 Bxe3 17. Qxe3 Qg5 18. Kf1 f5).

15. ...	cxd4
16. Qxd4	Qg5
17. Rad1	f5

"When the moment is right White can drop an H-bomb on Black's position."
– **Alex Yermolinsky on sacrifices on b5, e6, d5 or f5 in various Sicilian Defense positions.**

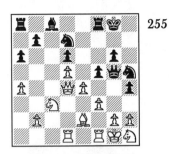

255

Black has ample compensation, e.g. 18. Nf2 Nf4 or 18. Qd2 f4 followed by ...Ne5/...h3.

The game went 18. exf5 Nf4! 19. g3 Rxf5 20. Bd3 and Black was content to draw by perpetual check (20... Nh3† 21. Kg2 Nf4† 22. Kg1 Nh3†).

Pat: You can't be saying every ♟-sacrifice is sound.

Noah: No, not every one.

And even a sound sacrifice may be a bad move because there are safer alternatives that achieve the same effect.

A good rule of thumb is:

DON'T OFFER MATERIAL WHEN YOU CAN GET GOOD PLAY THROUGH SIMPLE MOVES

You see Black violating this in Diagram 256.

Pat: I've never even seen 4. dxe6 before.

Noah: It's just a cop-out to avoid the main Benoni lines.

But it's virtually forgotten and not as bad as the books claim. White wants to pressure d5, not occupy it.

Pat: He shouldn't get much of an edge.

Noah: No, but you can appreciate Black's thinking.

When he looked at the diagram and saw that 7... d5 was risky, he became concerned.

So he tried to work it out by analogy and saw 7... b5, which looks good.

Pat: Analogy to...?

Noah: To the Blumenfeld Counter Gambit – which goes 1. d4 Nf6 2.

c4 e6 3. Nf3 c5 4. d5 b5!?.

You don't hear much about it these days because White doesn't accept the gambit.

Pat: Black's reasoning was bad?

Noah: It was a reasonable idea but it turns out that Black doesn't have enough compensation.

The real mistake here is that Black could have gotten a fine game at no expense with 7... Nc6.

1.	d4	Nf6
2.	c4	c5
3.	d5	e6
4.	dxe6	fxe6
5.	Bg5	

Another strategy is 5. Nf3 Be7 6. g3 d5 7. Bg2, to take aim at d5.

Then 7... Nc6 8. 0-0 0-0 9. Nbd2 and 10. e4! (...dxe4/ Ng5 regains the ♟).

"If you play the King's Indian don't be afraid to be a ♟ down."
— **Garry Kasparov**

5. ...	Be7

Or 5... d5 6. e4!, e.g. 6... h6! 7. Bxf6 Qxf6 8. exd5 exd5 9. cxd5 Bd6 with compensation for the ♟.

6.	Nc3	0-0
7.	e3	

"Nowadays activity and the initiative are more important than material (i.e. a ♟)."
— **Alexander Belyavsky**

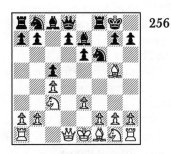

256

White can meet 7... d5 8. cxd5 exd5 with 9. Bxf6 Bxf6 10. Qxd5† Qxd5 11. Nxd5 Bxb2 12. Rb1.

7. ...　　b5?

Better was the simple and direct 7... Nc6 8. Nf3 b6 followed by ...Bb7 and eventually ...d5.

8. cxb5

Black has more for the lost ♙ after 8. Nxb5 Qb6 or 8... Qa5† 9. Nc3 Nc6 and ...Rb8.

8. ...　　d5
9. Nf3　　a6
10. bxa6　　Nc6
11. Bb5

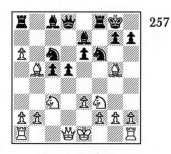

257

And Black has scant compensation for the ♙.

Pat: I'll bet there's a lot more rules about material.

Noah: Sure, but they have a bad habit of working only part of the time.

For example, Nimzovich said:

"Never play to win a ♙ while your development is yet unfinished!" – then he added that there was an exception if the ♙ was in the center and it could be grabbed safely.

Pat: But how do you know if it's safe?

Noah: Ask Nimzovich.

Or there's Capablanca, who said White – but not Black – could grab a ♙ provided it didn't delay completing development for more than two moves and wasn't otherwise dangerous.

Pat: That must leave out a lot.

Noah: You could write a book about exceptions – beginning with the Poisoned Pawn Variation of the Najdorf.

Of the old rules, a more useful one is:

THE SAFEST WAY TO DEAL WITH A GAMBIT IS TO FIND A GOOD TIME TO GIVE MATERIAL BACK

The reason this often works is that when the sacrificer tries to regain his ♙ or whatever he's given up, he has to expend some time and piece-energy.

Pat: Piece-energy?

Noah: Yes, the potential energy of his coordinated pieces.

Well-organized pieces create a pool of tactical strength – they threaten things, make double-attacks and so on.

But this strength is often wasted when one or two pieces are diverted to win back material.

Pat: You got a position that translates this for me?

Noah: Sure, Diagram 258 will explain better than words.

Pat: I've had positions like Black's after 4... dxc4.

And I never knew if I should be trying to protect the extra ♙.

Noah: Black didn't take on c4 just to win material.

He took because the vacant d5 also gives him a great ♘-outpost.

And the capture at least temporarily interrupts White's development.

Pat: You mean, no Bd3.

That must be why 5... b5 makes sense.

Noah: Yes, by stopping 6. Bxc4 it

forces White to make a choice.

He can either seek compensation for the ♟, say with Nf3-e5 and Be2-f3.

Or he can fight to get the ♟ back with 6. a4.

Pat: But 6. a4 must be a good move.

Noah: It is – but like a lot of good moves, it's not forcing enough.

Black can give the ♟ back with 6... Nf6 and throw in tempo-gainers like ...Bb4† and ...Nd5 – and end up with a great middlegame.

1. d4	d5
2. c4	e6
3. Nc3	c6
4. Bf4	

A rare alternative to 4. Nf3, 4. e4 and 4. e3.

4. ...	dxc4
5. e3	b5!

Now 6. b3 is met by the annoying 6... Bb4!.

6. a4!

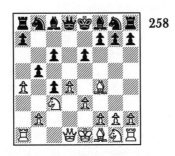

258

Now 6... Bd7? creates a development logjam.

Better is 6... b4 7. Ne4 Qd5 or even 6... Qb6 (7. Qf3 bxa4! and ...Bb4).

But most accurate is the active:

6. ...	Nf6!
7. axb5	cxb5
8. Nxb5	

White has nothing better (8. b3? Bb4 9. Ne2 Nd5 or 8. Qf3 Nd5).

8. ...	Bb4†
9. Nc3	Nd5

Now 10. Qc2! Bb7 offers Black sufficient play.

10. Ne2?!	0-0

11. Bg3	Bb7

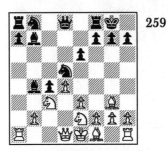

259

And White has a difficult time completing development, e.g. 12. e4 Nb6 13. f3 Nc6 14. Bf2 f5!.

Or 12. Qc2 Nc6 13. Nf4 Nxf4 14. Bxf4 Qf6 and 15... e5.

Pat: Piece-energy – I see what you mean.

White's evaporated quickly.

Noah: A ♟ grab often has that effect on your opponent's piece.

Sometimes grabbing is the only consistent move.

In diagram 260, for example, the "Take" principle applies – and that means White should grab on b5.

Pat: This must be one of those positions they analyzed to death 50 years ago.

Noah: It only looks that way.

You can probably figure out that this is actually a new position.

Pat: Why?

Noah: Because in all the other Meran Variation lines like this Black needs to preserve his b-♟ with ...a6 or ...b4 before he can get his queenside house in order with ...Bb7 and ...c5.

Here he doesn't take those precautions. So, if White let's him get away with 9... c5, Black will be a move ahead of normal.

Pat: But White doesn't get to keep his extra ♟.

Noah: No, he cashes it in for something else.

After 10. Bxb5 it's Black who has to spend some of his piece-energy to regain material equality.

By move 12 he's still in the opening – but White's pieces are ready to begin the middlegame.

1. d4	d5
2. c4	c6
3. Nf3	Nf6
4. e3	e6
5. Nc3	Nbd7
6. Bd3	dxc4

"In a gambit you give up a ♙ for the sake of getting a lost game"
– S.S. Boden, co-author of the unsound, Boden-Kieseritsky Gambit

7. Bxc4	b5
8. Bd3	

The "book" lines are (a) 8... a6 followed by 9... c5, (b) 8... b4, and (c) 8... Bb7 9. e4 b4.

8. ...	Bb7
9. e4	

On the quiet 9... Be7 White's initiative becomes too great, e.g. 10. 0-0 b4 11. Na4 Rc8 12. Re1.

9. ... c5?

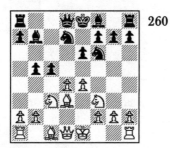

260

10. Bxb5!

Not complications like 10. e5 b4 when a simple capture is available.

10. ... Nxe4

Otherwise White keeps his ex-tra ♙ with Qe2 or increases pressure with 11. Qa4 or 11. Ne5.

And 10... Bxe4? is just a blunder (11. Nxe4 Nxe4 12. Bc6).

11. Nxe4	Bxe4
12. 0-0	

White has a strong attack at no cost.

For example, 12... Be7? 13 Ne5 or 12... Bd6? 13. dxc5 are very strong.

White stands well after 12... Bxf3 13. Qxf3 Rb8 14. a4 cxd4 15. Bf4 Rc8 16. Rac1.

Pat: Seems like there's an awful lot of chances to grab material in the openings they play nowadays.

Noah: Or to sacrifice. Or to allow the other guy to sacrifice.

Which brings up a corollary.

Pat: Again with that word.

Noah: It's a corollary to the rule about not sacrificing if you can get an equally good position for free. This one is fairly obvious and it goes:

GRAB MATERIAL IF NON-GRABBING IS JUST AS RISKY

Pat: How can non-grabbing be just as risky?

Noah: Remember what I said about the Evans Gambit?

Declining the gambit is just as hard on Black as accepting – and at least if he grabs on b4 he's a ♙ up.

Pat: Makes sense, I guess.

Noah: The key is correctly evaluating material on one hand – against time and positional values on the other.

Black failed that litmus test twice in the next example.

Pat: I see he didn't take the first ♙ White offered, at move 6.

Anything wrong with that?

Noah: No, that was fine.

But he should have jumped at the second opportunity, in Diagram 261.

White got the initiative for nothing when Black failed to play 9... dxc4.

Pat: I guess if you're going to be squeezed you deserve something for your pain.

Noah: And the pain got worse when Black missed another opportunity with 13... Qxd4.

That was worst of all because White later used the d-♟ to plug up the file and prevent Black from trading heavy pieces.

Once White stopped the only other counterplay, ...b5, Black was waiting for the axe to fall.

Anand-Granda Zuniga
Madrid 1998

1. d4   Nf6
2. c4   e6
3. Nf3   b6
4. g3   Ba6
5. b3   d5
6. Bg2

Based on 6... dxc4 7. Ne5.

6. ...   Bb4†

7. Bd2   Bd6
8. Nc3   c6
9. 0-0

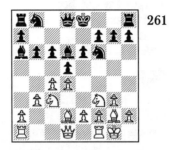

261

On 9... dxc4 White's compensation is unclear after 10. Ne5 or 10. bxc4 Bxc4 11. Ne5.

But...

9. ...   0-0?
10. e4!

Now White – with a threat of 11. e5 – can get the benefits of a gambit for free.

10. ...   Nxe4
11. Nxe4   dxe4
12. Ng5   Be7
13. Nxe4   Nd7?

Better was 13... Qxd4!, e.g. 14.

Qc2 Qd8 15. Rad1 Nd7.

14. Bf4!   Nf6
15. Qc2   Rc8

It's too late for 15.. Qxd4?? – because 16. Rad1! traps the ♛.

16. Rfd1   h6
17. a4!

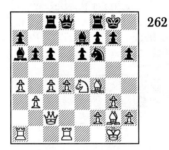

262

This stops ...b5 and prepares to open the queenside on White's terms with a5.

White soon had a paralyzing advantage (17... Nxe4 18. Bxe4 Bf6 19. Be5 Qe7? 20. a5! b5 21. c5! Rfd8 22. b4 Rd7 23. Ra3! and the ♖ transferred powerfully to the kingside.).

Pat: What bugs me is that the annotators always make it look like it was so easy for the loser to defend.

Noah: The annotators are guilty of something just as bad – when they evaluate sacrifices in pure *Informant*-speak.

Pat: I prefer English.

Noah: So do I. But *Informant* anno-

"The sacrifice of a ♟, a ♞, a ♝, or any piece confers on the (sacrificer) a small sense of transient joy, and an unpleasant sensation is experienced by the leader of the army that has to suffer it."

– David Bronstein

tators are addicted to using the infinity sign (∞) when they evaluate sacrifices.

Pat: I've seen it – infinity means the sacrificer has compensation. Nothing wrong with that.

Noah: Nothing, except when it's a way of not really evaluating the sack.

Often the sign means there is some compensation – but not necessarily enough.

Take a gander at Diagram 263.

Pat: What am I looking at?

Noah: A very double-edged position in which logic triumphed over an infinity sign.

In a previous game Black rejected the ♙ offer and got the worst of it.

White was supposed to have great comp after 13... cxd4.

Pat: So in this game Black decided grabbing was just as safe as non-grabbing.

1. d4	**Nf6**
2. c4	**e6**
3. Nc3	**Bb4**
4. e3	**c5**
5. Bd3	**Nc6**
6. Nf3	**Bxc3†**
7. bxc3	**d6**
8. 0-0	**e5**
9. Nd2	**0-0**
10. Rb1	**b6**
11. h3	**Bd7**
12. f4	

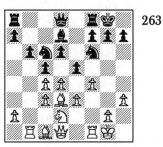

263

White stood well in a previous game that went 12... exf4 13. Rxf4 Qe7 14. Qf3 and the winner gave the alternative – 12... cxd4 13. cxd4 exd4 14. e4, followed by an infinity sign – in his notes.

12. ...	**exd4**
13. cxd4	**cxd4!**

White has little compensation after 14. exd4 Nxd4 15. Bb2 Bf5 or just 15... Ne6 and 16... Nc5.

14. e4	**Re8**

Black puts the e-♙ under pressure, leaving White to prove 12. f4 was sound.

15. Re1	**Qc7**
16. Nf3	**Bc8!**

Now if White tries to get the ♙ back with 17. Bb2 Bb7 18. Nxd4 Black has 18...Nxd4 19. Bxd4 Nxe4 (20. Qg4 f6).

17. e5	**dxe5**
18. fxe5	

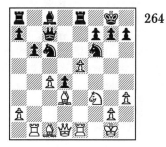

264

18. ...	**Nd7!**

And this is safety first.

Being one ♙ ahead, Black doesn't need to take further risks (18...Nxe5 19. Bf4 Nxf3† 20. Qxf3).

19. Bf4	**Nf8!**
20. Ng5	**Be6**

And in *Lugovoi-Aseev, Russian Championship 1996*, Black stood slightly better thanks to the extra ♙.

Noah: Precisely. But the real choice isn't just whether to grab – it's whether to keep.

For example, in Diagram 265 you see a world championship match game where a TN blew up in White's face.

But it happened only because Black wouldn't allow White to regain a gambit ♙.

Pat: What was the point of 15. c5 anyway?

Noah: White was trying to seal off counterplay before retaking on e4.

He assumed he could always reestablish material equality later on

–leaving himself with a bind on the queenside.

Pat: So Black ended up giving back a different ♙.

Gambit-happy H.E. Bird liked to say that as a rule he left the opening with an excellent position – but unfortunately in most cases with almost no pieces.

Noah: At interest. By move 17 Black's pieces are swarming.

Karpov-Timman
FIDE world championship 1993

1. d4	Nf6
2. c4	e6
3. Nf3	b6
4. g3	Ba6
5. b3	Bb4†
6. Bd2	Be7
7. Bg2	c6
8. Bc3	d5
9. Ne5	Nfd7
10. Nxd7	Nxd7
11. Nd2	0-0
12. 0-0	Rc8
13. e4	b5
14. Re1	dxe4

Or 14... dxc4 15. bxc4 bxc4 16. Qc2 – and even if White doesn't get to retake on c4 he has a fine game.

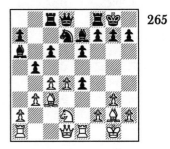

15. c5?

The usual move, 15. Bxe4, allows 15... bxc4 16. bxc4 c5!, freeing Black's game (17. d5 exd5 18. Bxd5 Bf6).

On 15. Nxe4 bxc4 White has to accept the equality of 16. Qe2. So he stopped ...bxc4 before retaking on e4.

15. ... **f5!**

Black prepares to centralize strongly with ... Nf6-d5.

16. f3 **b4!**

Now on 17. Bb2 Black has 17... Bg5 and if 18. fxe4, then 18... Nxc5! (19. dxc5 Bxd2).

17. Bxb4 **Ne5!**

And Black was winning after either 18. dxe5 Qd4† 19. Kh1 Qxb4 or 18. Bc3 Nd3 (19. fxe4 Nxe1).

Noah: You should also be aware that a lot of ♙ sacks are neither temporary – nor intentional.

Pat: How can you not know when you're sacking?

Noah: You may not know because many opening systems are based on forgotten tactical points that made certain ♙s ungrabbable.

So even GMs forget that when a similar position arises the material may suddenly be very grabbable – as in Diagram 266.

Pat: That's a pretty flaky way for White to play, 2. Ne2.

Noah: There are two ways to meet flaky moves.

You could try to punish them – that involves some risk.

The other, practical way is to transpose into something familiar. Remember analogy?

Pat: I'm trying to forget.

Noah: Hmmm, in any event you should pay attention to this –

Tigran Petrosian once reached the position after 5. c3 and didn't know what to do – so he reacted by using analogy and played 5... e6.

Pat: Even though it locked in his B/c8?

Noah: Yes, because that turns the position into a French Defense, an opening Petrosian knew how to handle.

Pat: But then White's got an extra move, Ne2.

Noah: True, but that may or or may not help White. The ♘ might be better at f3.

And either way, it won't matter much in a closed position.

The problem for Black is that from move 4 on he mistakenly as-sumed he could always regain ma-terial safely if White took on c5.

Pat: He could have gotten his ♙ back with ...Nxe5.

Noah: But that turns out badly at move six or seven.

Pat: So he was nearly busted after 6... e6. Nifty.

Short-Gulko
Horgen 1995

1. e4	c6
2. Ne2!?	d5
3. e5	c5
4. d4	Nc6

Now on 5. dxc5 Black regains the P safely (5... Qa5† 6. Nbc3 e6 and 7... Bxc5 or just 5... e6 6. Be3 Nxe5).

5. c3	Bf5

Tigran Petrosian's solution was 5... e6 6. Nd2 Nge7, e.g. 7. Nf3 cxd4 8. Nexd4 Ng6 or 8. cxd4 Qb6 and ...Nf5.

6. dxc5

Previously 6. Ng3 Bg6 7. dxc5 had been found wanting because of 7... e6 8. Be3 Nxe5 with equality.

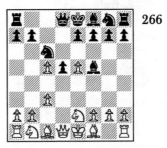

6. ... **e6?**

Black probably didn't like the disruption of his forces that follows 6... Nxe5 7. Nd4! (7... Bd7 8. Be2 e6 9. b4).

7. b4!

Now 7... Nxe5 8. Nd4 threatens 9. Nxf5 and 9. Bb5†.

7. ... **a5**

8. Nd4

The ability to occupy d4 is an-other benefit of 6. dxc5.

8. ... **axb4**

9. cxb4 **Qc7**

And here 9... Nxb4 allows 10 Bb5†.

White has the better of 9... Bxb1 10. Rxb1 Rxa2 11. Bb5.

10. Bb5

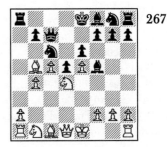

White has a clear edge after 10... Bxb1 11. Rxb1 Qxe5† 12. Be3 Qc7 13. 0-0.

Noah: He may have been surprised by dxc5, because it's a relatively rare idea.

"The 'temporarily sacrificed'
♙ *doesn't know it was only temporary."*
– Anonymous

But there are other temporary ♟ sacrifices that happen all the time and are taken for granted – like Diagram 268.

Pat: Why did White allow ...cxd4 ?

Noah: Because it's a common theme in this opening.

White expects to win back his ♟ with a great gain of time – that is, by Rad1 and Rxd4.

Pat: Okay, castling makes sense. And 11. Qe2 must've been consistent.

Noah: Consistent with the spirit of the opening.

But it's the tactics of this particular position that failed White – in particular, allowing 14... e4!.

From moves 13 to 15 White's piece-energy evaporates.

1. e4	e6
2. d4	d5
3. Nd2	dxe4
4. Nxe4	Nd7
5. Nf3	Ngf6
6. Nxf6†	Nxf6

7. Bg5	c5
8. Bxf6	

A common alternative is 8. Bb5† Bd7 9. Bxd7† followed by Qe2/0-0-0.

8. ...	gxf6

Not 8... Qxf6, which is met by the annoying 9. Bb5†!.

9. Bc4	cxd4
10. 0-0!	

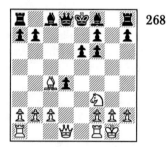

268

White's initiative is over after 10. Qxd4 Qxd4 or 10. Nxd4 Bc5 11. c3 Bxd4 12. cxd4 Qa5†.

10. ...	Bg7
11. Qe2?	

Again White has Rad1xd4 in mind. But 11. Nxd4 a6 12. c3 had to

be better.

11. ...	0-0
12. Rad1	e5!
13. c3	Qc7
14. cxd4	e4!

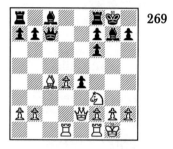

269

Now 15. Qxe4?? Qxc4 costs a ♗.

Black was better after 15. Nd2 f5 (or 15. Nh4 f5 16. Bb3 Bf6) in *Bo. Vuckovic-D. Kosic, Yugoslavia 1999.*

Pat: This must happen a lot more often in 1. e4 openings than anywhere else.

Noah: Actually, there is a temporary sacrifice that lies at the heart of 1. d4 openings that everyone takes

for granted.

Pat: What are we talking about?

Noah: We're talking about ...dxc4.

It's a temporary grab in the Queen's Gambit and in a lot of Queen's Gambit Declined lines after move 5.

You also see it in some Gruenfelds – and in Catalans, where it often turns out to be a permanent grab.

Pat: I thought White always regains that ♟. I mean the Queen's Gambit isn't the King's Gambit.

Noah: No, but consider Diagram 270.

Pat: I must've seen it before.

Noah: I bet you haven't. This may look like stereotyped book. But the white ♘ usually isn't at c3.

Pat: Having Nc3 hurts White?

Noah: An extra developing move can hurt– because he can't play Na3xc4.

In this case, White has two ways of quickly regaining the ♟ and one of them grants Black superior piece play.

Materialism

1. d4	Nf6
2. c4	g6
3. Nc3	Bg7
4. g3	d5
5. Bg2	

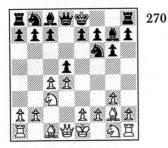

270

5. ...   **dxc4!**

Now 6. Nf3 0-0 7. Ne5 (otherwise 7... Nc6) Nfd7 is fine for Black.

6. Qa4†   **Nfd7**

So that 7. Qxc4 can be met by 7... Nb6, winning the d-♟.

7. e3

After 7. d5 0-0 8. Qxc4 Black equalizes with 8... c6 9. dxc6 Ne5.

7. ...   **0-0**

8. Qxc4   **c5**

Now 9. dxc5 Ne5! and ...Nd3†

favors Black.

Better is 9. Nf3 with rough equality (9... cxd4 10. Nxd4 Ne5 and 11... Nbc6).

9. Nge2   **Nc6**

And here White's best is to probably sack a ♟ to complete development (10. 0-0 cxd4 11. exd4 Nb6) or play the 10. dxe5 Nde5 11. Qd5 endgame.

Pat: What if you're like me – Most of my sacks are unintentional and there's no way of getting material back?

Noah: Then your assignment is to seek compensation.

It may not be there, but if you don't look, you don't find.

Even GMs often discover as soon as they land in a new position that they have to search for the comp that an infinity sign promised them in some book.

Pat: What does real comp look like?

Noah: It looks like what happens after Diagram 271.

To get there Black made a typical "Take" reaction at move 4, attacking a pawn that White left vulnerable with Bf4.

If White then tries to protect b2, he runs into development problems,

Pat: I like the 6. Rc1 trap.

Noah: Good developing moves often set traps by themselves.

The main point here is that after Black's TN at move 6, White gets into trouble if he tries to hold the b-♟.

That leaves him a ♟ down at the diagram – and seeing that his chief tactical ideas – like Rb1xb7 and Nb5 – are history.

Pat: Been there. Even the traps don't work then.

Noah: But there is compensation nonetheless.

White knows he must open the center. And when he sees that 11. e4 is flawed he found the superior 11. Be5!.

Pat: With a great game.

Gulko-Shcherbakov
Helsinki 1992

1. d4	d5
2. c4	c6
3. cxd5	cxd5
4. Bf4	Qb6

Now 5. Qd2 Nf6 6. Nc3 (else 6... Ne4) Bf5 7. e3 e6 and ...Bb4/...Ne4.

5. Nc3	Nf6
6. Rc1	

Here 6... Qxb2?? loses to 7. Na4 Qb4† 8. Bd2.

6. ...   **Bd7!**

But here 7... Qxb2 is threatened and there is no easy defense (7. Qd2 Ne4 8. Nxe4 dxe4 and ...e5!/...Bb4 or 7... e6 followed by ...Ne4 or ...Bb4).

7. e3	Qxb2
8. Bd3	e6

Now 9. Nf3 Bb4! favors Black.

9. Nge2	Qa3
10. 0-0	a6!

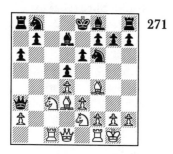

271

On 11. Rb1 b5 12. Bc7 Black loses his ♛ after routine moves such as 12... Be7?? (13. Rb3!).

But he has good alternatives, including 12... Bc6 and 13... Qe7.

11. Be5!

Exploiting Black's inability to pay ...Nbd7 and threatening to open the game favorably with 12. Bxf6 gxf6 13. e4.

On the immediate 11. e4 dxe4 Black is relatively safe (12. Nxe4 Nd5).

11. ...	Be7
12. e4	Bc6

Or 12... Nc6 13. Bxf6! Bxf6 14. exd5 exd5 15. Nxd5 and 14... Nxd4

15. Ne4.

White also has more than enough for a ♙ after 12... dxe4 13. Nxe4 Nxe4 14. Bxe4 or 13... Nc6 14. Rc3! Qa5 15. Nd6†.

13. exd5	exd5
14. Ng3	

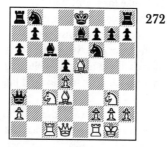

272

With Nf5 coming up White has a promising game (as he also would have after 14. Bxf6 Bxf6 15. Nf4).

Noah: A good enough game.

Even if you're sure you have adequate compensation you shouldn't assume you'll end up with more than equal chances down the road.

And you still have to find concrete moves to make the compensation real. The next example shows how sensitive this is.

Pat: Is Black's game really so bad after 6... Ne7 ?

Noah: No, but a lot of players would feel a lot more comfortable by sacking a ♙ than by retreating the ♘.

In Diagram 273 you can see Black's comp.

Pat: Sure. He rules the dark squares.

Noah: A lot of dark squares. But until this is translated into counterplay, Black's compensation is one big infinity sign.

What would make it real is rapid development – say with ...Bb4† and ...0-0 – and an attack on d5 – with ...c6.

Pat: So he starts with the check.

Noah: Because it's faster than 8... c6 – and in gambit positions faster is usually better.

You see a good illustration of how not to use compensation in the Karpov game.

Pat: I see what you mean – after 10.

Qe5†! it's all downhill for Black.

1. d4	d5
2. c4	dxc4
3. e4	Nc6

"It is a very well-known matter of experience that losing a ♙ in the opening by mistake is often the involuntary equivalent of playing a quite promising gambit' – **Jacques Mieses**

4. Be3   Nf6
5. f3   e5
6. d5   Nd4

More in the spirit of counterattack than 6... Ne7 7. Bxc4 a6 8. a4.

7. Bxd4

It's better to grab a ♙ if the alternative is just as risky, e.g. 7. Bxc4 Bc5 and White has tactical problems on the g1-a7 diagonal.

The game *Yermolinsky-D. Gurevich, U.S. Championship 2000* went 8. Bf2 c6! 9. dxc6 Qb6 10. cxb7 Bxb7 with a stronger attack than in the text below.

7. ...   exd4
8. Qxd4

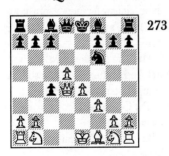

273

8. ...   Bb4†

On 8... c6 9. Bxc4 Bb4† 10. Nc3 0-0 Black stands well.

Better is 9. Nc3!, to meet 9... Be7 with 10. 0-0-0 (threat: 11. d6).

Also 9... Bb4 can be met by 10. Qe5†! *(Karpov-Piket, Gröningen 1995,* which White won after 10... Qe7 11. Qxe7† Kxe7 12. dxc6 bxc6 13. Bxc4 Nd7 14. 0-0-0).

9. Nc3   0-0

Black doesn't have time for moves that allow 10. Qe5 with check.

10. 0-0-0

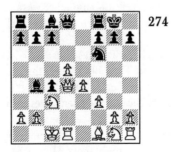

274

Now 10... c6 allows a strong 11. d6.

10. ...   Bxc3!

This makes ...c6 stronger. Black has enough for the ♙ after 11. bxc3 c6 12. dxc6 Qa5! or 11. Qxc3 c6 12. dxc6 Qb6!.

Noah: Remember, comp may amount to nothing more than having the initiative, a kind of short-term momentum.

And often the only way to keep that momentum is to pitch more ♙s and pieces into the pot.

Pat: Otherwise what?

Noah: Otherwise your window of opportunity closes and the only thing on the board that matters is material.

The next game is a dramatic illustration of how to raise the ante.

Pat: I'd never think of 13. Nd5.

Noah: You would if you applied "Take."

Black correctly stopped 13. e5, which would have left White with a substantial space edge and strong attacking chances.

But there was a downside to 12...

Nd7 – allowing Nd5. White realized that this window was only going to be open for a move or two.

Pat: As the game goes Black kept trying to give back material.

Noah: Yes, and 14... Nc5 would have been a saving defense – if White had played 15. Re3 or later 16. Rd1.

As it was, he disregarded material until move 19 when he could cash in his chips.

Akopian-Volzhin
Ubeda 1996

1. d4   d5
2. c4   dxc4
3. e3   Nf6
4. Bxc4   e6
5. Nf3   c5
6. 0-0   a6
7. Bb3   Nc6
8. Qe2   cxd4
9. Rd1   d3

Preventing White from retaking on d4 with a ♙.

10. Rxd3   Qc7

11. Nc3   Be7
12. e4   Nd7!

Stops 13. e5 Nd7 14. Bf4, which would be dangerous after say 14 ...0-0 15 Re3!.

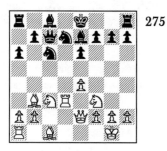

275

13. Nd5!

Exploiting the ♘'s retreat.

13. ...   exd5
14. exd5   Nc5!

White's attack is too strong after 14... Nce5 15. Nxe5 Nxe5 16. Bf4 (16...Bd6 17. Bxe5 Bxe5 18. d6).

Or 15... Qxe5 16. Re3 Qd6 17. Bd2 and Re1.

15. d6!   Qd8
16. Ng5!

Better than 16. Rd1 Nxb3 17.

axb3 0-0 since White has nothing better than material – and positional – equality (18. dxe7 Qxe7).

16. ...   Nxd3
17. Nxf7!   Qd7!

The complications of 17... Nxc1 18. Rxc1 Qd7 19. Nxh8 favor White.

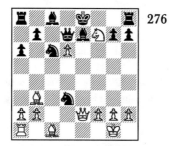

276

18. Bg5!

Better than 18. Nxh8? Qxd6 as played in the game.

White keeps a strong attack even after the superior 18...Nc5! 19. Nxh8.

He won after Black played 18... Rf8 19. dxe7 Rxf7 20. Bxf7† Kxf7 21. Qh5†.

Noah: But when the ante goes up, so do the risks.

It becomes easier then for the defender to give back material to beat off the attack – because he has more material to return.

Pat: That sorta makes sense.

Noah: Material is such a broad subject we can only touch on it today.

But maybe this final example will sum it up.

After 8... Nxe4 the position is highly charged and extremely hard to evaluate.

Nevertheless, White decided to offer a ♟ because other ways of defending c3 seemed to give Black an easy game.

Pat: I'm with you so far.

Noah: Then Black made the correct decision to grab.

Pat: Because the alternatives were just as scary.

Noah: Right. The key decision for White came at move 11.

He could have limited his risk to a ♟, with 11. Rb1.

Pat: I don't see enough comp then if Black castles.

Noah: Neither did White. So he looked at sharper moves that left the R/a1 hanging.

The most dangerous try, 11. Qg4, doesn't work – not because it costs the Exchange but because it allows castling.

Pat: That only leaves 11. Ba3. The kind of move Morphy liked to play.

Noah: Unfortunately for White there's no Morphy-finish because Black didn't have to grab the Exchange immediately.

That's something a sacrificer often forgets when he leaves something hanging for more than a move.

Pat: There's an awful lot of analysis here.

Noah: The position deserves it.

Pat: And in the end White still has comp if he plays 13. Qd5!.

Noah: Comp for a few ♟s, maybe even for a piece.

But not for a ♖ – and that's what loses games.

Sutovsky-A. Mikhalevsky
Israel 1998

1. e4	e5
2. Nf3	Nc6
3. Bb5	a6
4. Ba4	Nf6
5. Nc3	Bc5
6. Nxe5	

A typical fork-trick to dissolve Black's center. It's much more ambitious than 6. d3 d6 7. Be3.

6. ...	Nxe5
7. d4	Bb4

Black plays for more than what the book move, 7... Bd6, offered.

8. dxe5	Nxe4

Now 9. Qd4 Nxc3 10. bxc3 Be7 promises White little.

9. 0-0!?

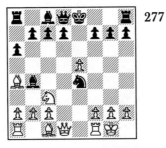

277

9. ...   Nxc3!

Other answers to the threat of 10. Nxe4 lose time or incur as much or more risk than 9...Nxc3 (9... Bxc3 10. bxc3 Nxc3? 11. Qg4 Nxa4 12. Qxg7!).

10. bxc3

On 10... Be7 Black has an inferior version of 9. Qd4 and can get into trouble after 11. Qg4 or 11. f4.

10. ...   Bxc3!

Now after 11. Rb1 0-0 the onus is on White to show his compensation.

11. Ba3

Also in the gambit style is 11. Qg4, hoping for pretty finishes such as 11... Bxa1 12. Qxg7 Rf8 13. Ba3! or 11... Bxe5 12. Bf4! Bxa1 13. Re1† Kf8 14. Bxc7! Qxc7 15. Qb4† and mates.

But Black has 11... 0-0! and then 12. Bh6 Bxe5 or 12. Bg5 d6! (e.g 13. Qh4 f6 or 13. Qg3 Bxe5).

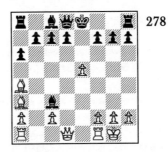

278

Now on 11... Bxa1 12. Qd5 or 12. Qxa1 and White can exploit Black's inability to castle (12. Qxa1 Qh4 13. e6! Qxa4 14. Qxg7).

11. ...   Qh4!

This stops 12. Qg4 while attacking the B/a4.

12. f4   Bxa1!

Now 13. Qxa1 b5! and White is well short of compensation (14. e6 f6! and Black wins).

Better is 13. Qd5!, preparing to pressure d7 with 14. Rd1, or to take on f7 after 14. Bb3.

But after 13... Bc3! Black is winning, e.g. 14. Rd1 Qg4 or 14. Bb3 Kd8! or 14. Qc5 b5 15. Qxc3 bxa4.

Pat: I thought I understood more about material before we started this afternoon.

I must be making negative progress.

Noah: As I said it's a very difficult subject – a tricky balancing act with material in one scale and time and positional values in the other.

And you might as well start appreciating this balancing act because it only becomes harder in the middle game.

Pat: Tell me about it.

Noah: I will – but not today.

The McFarland Connection

Grandmaster Soltis has written several fine titles for the North Carolina publisher, McFarland Company.

The two which have received the greatest fanfare from the chess press are: The 100 Best Chess Games (of the 20th Century) and Soviet Chess 1917-1991.

Andy wants me to reassure you that he made six trips to the former Soviet Union to gather material for his "Soviet Chess" book and that he didn't rely on expatriates from the NYC area. The four page bibliography is outstanding. Also included is the unheralded, but important, pronunciation guide to the names of former Soviet chess greats, living and deceased.

In which Noah shows how ♖s move mysteriously, ♔s can castle manually, and ♗s are questioned carefully.

Chapter Ten:

═══

GETTING LATE

Pat: We must have covered everything by now.

Noah: Almost, but not quite.

There are still a few decisions you have to make late in the opening that I'd like to tackle today.

Pat: Beginning with ...

Noah: Beginning with castling.

Pat: What's there to say – If you don't castle, you lose.

End of story.

Noah: Actually, there are three more subtle errors you can make with castling.

The first is doing it too early.

This doesn't occur as often as castling too late – but it can be just as fatal, as in Diagram 279.

Pat: Why is it too early?

Noah: Because Black had more important business to take care of first.

He should have developed more of his minor pieces – and traded off at least one of White's.

Pat: But I see White wasted no time castling.

Noah: He has that luxury.

As a wise man once said, "Black is not White."

Pat: I'll try to ignore that.

Besides, I'd never be able to calculate all those sacks on e6 and f7.

Noah: Maybe not now, you're still young.

But the point here is that sacks like those are going to succeed when White has three developed minor pieces plus ♕ and ♖ to attack with – and Black has nothing with which to defend.

Slobodian-Kaminsky
Halle 1995

1.	e4	e6
2.	d4	d5
3.	Nd2	c5
4.	Ngf3	cxd4
5.	exd5	Qxd5
6.	Bc4	Qd8
7.	0-0	a6
8.	Nb3	Qc7
9.	Qe2	Bd6
10.	Nbxd4	Ne7

11. Re1

279

11. ...	0-0?

Correct was 11... Nbc6, preparing to castle safely, e.g. 12. h3 Nxd4! 13. Nxd4 0-0.

12. Ng5!

White threatens strong sacks on e6 or f7 – and inserting ...Bxh2†/Kh1 doesn't change that.

Black loses after 12... Nbc6 13. Ndxe6! (e.g. 13... Bxe6 14. Bxe6 fxe6 15. Qxe6† Kh8 16. Qh3 h6 17. Ne6 Qa5 18. Bxh6!).

12. ...	h6

13. Nxf7!

Now 13... Rxf7 14. Nxe6 is strong.

White won after 13... Kxf7 14. Nxe6 Bxe6 15. Qxe6† Ke8 16. Bxh6!.

For example 16... gxh6 17. Rad1! Qd7 18. Qxh6 with terrific threats, or 16... Rf6 17. Qg8† Kd7 18. Rxe7†! followed by a ♖-check on d1 or e1.

Pat: Yeah, really.

Noah: And even when all your minor pieces are in play it may be wrong to castle.

Pat: Black must have castled at the right moment in the next example.

I mean he couldn't wait around for Nb5-d6†.

Noah: Yes, it's White that I'm interested in.

He felt – correctly – that he should get an edge out of the opening after 7... Na6.

But when he examined the position further he saw that 13. 0-0? allows Black to solve his one problem, the misplaced N/a6.

Pat: Seems like White had one of

your big windows of opportunity – five forcing moves in a row.

Noah: And when they were over, White could take time to castle.

After that Black quickly fell apart.

Kharlov-Yarats
Biel 1997

1. d4	Nf6
2. c4	e6
3. Nc3	Bb4
4. e3	c5
5. Ne2	b6
6. a3	Ba5
7. Bd2	Na6?
8. Ng3	0-0

Not 8... Bb7 9. Nb5! Bxd2† 10. Qxd2 and the threat of Nd6† gives White the upper hand (10... d6 11. dxc5 or 10...Bc6 11. Nd6† Ke7 12. d5!).

Best is 10... d5 but then 11. cxd5 exd5 12. Nf5 or 11... Nxd5 12. e4 or 11... Bxd5 12. Nc3! favors White.

9. Bd3	d5
10. cxd5	cxd4
11. exd4	Bxc3

12. bxc3	Qxd5?

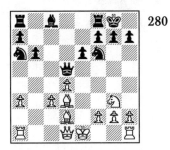

280

13. Qe2!

Not 13. 0-0? Nc5! 14. dxc5 Qxd3 or 14. Bc2 Nce4.

13. ...	Nc7
14. Ne4!	Nce8

Not 14... Bb7 15. Nxf6† gxf6 16. Bh6 or 16. Qg4† Kh8 17. Qh4 f5 18. Bh6.

15. c4!	Qxd4

Black has no compensation for the lost Exchange after 15... Qd8 16. Bb4.

16. Bc3	Qd7
17. Rd1	Qc7

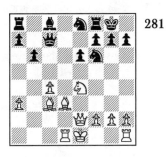

281

18. 0-0!

Now was the right time. On 18. Bb4 Bb7 19. Bxf8 Kxf8 Black is alive.

After 18. 0-0 White won: 18... Bb7 19. Nxf6† Nxf6 20. Bxf6 gxf6 21. Bxh7†! (21...Kxh7 22. Qh5†, 23. Qg4† and 24. Rd3).

If White had played this combination at move 18 Black could have defended better at the end with ...Qe5†-g5.

Pat: You mentioned three castling errors. What's the second?

Noah: Number two is believing your ♔ is automatically going to be safer on g1 than on e1.

Or, if you're Black, safer on g8 than on e8.

This is particularly common in the Sicilian, when you're often better off not castled, such as in Diagram 282.

Pat: Before that – what's 6... Bb4 all about?

Noah: It's about disrupting White's development.

White ends up with an extra tempo but it's the less-than-useful Bd2.

Pat: And you're saying Black can safely sack the Exchange after 11... b5.

Modern castling was introduced more than 500 years ago as a two-step procedure – that is, K/e1-to-g1 was one move, and R/h1-to-f1 was another.

Noah: It's not much of a sacrifice.

GMs recognize that as the kind of sack that always works over the board.

Pat: I'll take your word for it. But in the diagram does it make sense that Black's ♔ is safer in the center than on g8?

Or that it's safe on the kingside later on after ... g6?

Noah: Yes, it would have been quite secure after 11... h5, followed by queenside castling – or no castling at all.

A WAITING MOVE

Castling is often used as a waiting move, e.g. 1. d4 Nf6 2. c4 e6 3. Nc3 Bb4 4. Qc2 c5 5. dxc5 and now 5...Na6 6. a3 Bxc3+ 7. Qxc3 Nxc5 8. f3! is considered inferior for Black.

Better is 5... 0-0 and then 6. Nf3 Na6!.

As for 15 ... g6, that was just a good way of defending the ♔-position.

Pat: I guess the way things went White's attack played itself.

Fedorov-Khurditse
Russia Cup 1998

1.	e4	c5
2.	Nf3	e6
3.	Nc3	a6
4.	d4	cxd4
5.	Nxd4	Qc7
6.	g3	Bb4
7.	Bd2	

Other defenses to 7... Bxc3† are no better.

7.	...	Nf6
8.	Bg2	Nc6
9.	Nb3	Be7

On 9... d6 White gets the two ♗s with 10. a3!.

10.	f4	d6
11.	0-0	

282

Black needn't fear 11... b5 12. e5 because of 12... dxe5 13. fxe5 Nxe5! 14. Bxa8 Qa7†.

11.	...	0-0?
12.	g4!	b5
13.	g5	Nd7
14.	a3	

After 14... Re8 15. Rf3 Black missed his last (!) good defense chance – 15... g6! followed by ...Bf8-g7 and ...Nf8.

He played 15... Bb7? 16. Rh3 g6 17. Qe1 b4 and was lost after 18. Qh4 h5 19. Bf3! and Bxh5, e.g. 19... bxc3 20. Bxh5 cxb2 21. Bxg6!.

Noah: Just about.

And sometimes proper ♔-play requires subtle treatment such as castling by hand.

Pat: Hand?

Noah: Sure, and Diagram 283 illustrates it.

Pat: I see GMs making moves like 11. h4 all the time. What gives?

Noah: A couple of things are happening here.

White recognizes the dangers to his ♔ after 11. 0-0 – as well as the benefits of securing f4 for his ♘ by ruling out ...g5.

Pat: I guess his ♖ can always come out by way of h3.

Noah: In fact, it will be quite well-placed at g3.

And the ♔ can find complete safety at g1 – just as if it went there in one move with 0-0.

That's what we call castling by hand.

Adams-Lputian
Pula 1997

1.	e4	e6

2. d4	d5
3. e5	c5
4. c3	Nc6
5. Nf3	Nh6

Even though 6. Bxh6 gxh6 rids White of his bad ♗, Black would be in fine shape.

6. Bd3	cxd4
7. cxd4	Nf5
8. Bxf5	exf5
9. Nc3	Be6
10. Ne2	h6

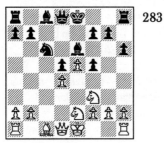

283

Now on 11. 0-0 Black has 11... g5! with excellent prospects.

11. h4!	Qa5†
12. Kf1!	

Better than 12. Bd2 Qa6.

12. ...	Be7
13. Kg1	Rc8
14. Nf4	g6

And now 15. Rh3 followed by Rg3 favors White slightly.

Pat: And what's the third castling mistake?

Noah: Number three is choosing wrong in the short-versus-long debate.

Castling short – that is, kingside – is the right way to go in the vast majority of cases.

But there are distinct exceptions, such as Diagram 284.

Pat: Why is 0-0 wrong here?

Noah: It's wrong for two – or maybe three – reasons.

First, the black ♚ becomes a target on g8 and would be safer on the queenside.

Pat: I guess the second reason is that after ...0-0 Black has no kingside counterplay.

Noah: Correct. And the third reason is that after 11... 0-0 White

saves a tempo.

He doesn't have to play f3 because ...Bxg2 is too dangerous.

As the game goes White had his choice of strong plans.

Toshkov-Kosten
Yurmala 1987

1. d4	Nf6
2. c4	e6
3. Nc3	Bb4
4. Nf3	b6
5. Bg5	Bb7
6. e3	h6
7. Bh4	Bxc3†
8. bxc3	d6
9. Nd2	Nbd7
10. a4	a5
11. Rb1	

The **latest** anyone has ever castled in a tournament game was 48... 0-0, *Neshewat-Garrison, Detroit 1994.* Black won eight moves later.

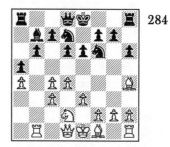

284

11. ...	0-0?!

Better was 11...Qe7 with ...0-0-0 in mind (12. f3 g5! 13. Bf2 0-0-0 14. e4 Nh5).

12. Bd3!

Too dangerous for Black now is 12... Bxg2 13. Rg1 Bb7 14. Ne4.

12. ...	Qe8

Black gets out of the pin and anticipates e3-e4-e5.

13. 0-0

Play continued 13... e5 14. e4 Nh7 15. Bg3 c5 16. Re1 Qe6 17. f4 f6 with good play for White after either:

(a) 18. dxe5 dxe5 19. f5 followed by Nf1!-e3-d5, or

(b) 18. d5 followed by f5, Bf2 and Re3-g3! with a strong attack on g7.

Pat: I always thought that when the ♔s end up on opposite wings, the guy with fewer ♟ weaknesses just wins.

Noah: Not exactly.

Whether it's White's ♔ that survives or Black's also depends on whose attack proceeds unhindered.

All it takes is strong counterplay to do the hindering – as in Diagram 285.

Pat: That looks like pretty risky play for Karpov.

Noah: There was no one better at deciding what to do with his ♔.

In previous games in this line Black automatically castled long – even though he kept losing.

It took this game to show that short was better.

Pat: Because?

Noah: Because for the one billionth time a wing attack is met strongly

by counterplay in the center.

Black's play against d4 was so swift that White never had enough time to train his pieces on the K/g8.

Kamsky-Karpov
FIDE World Championship 1996
12th game

1. e4	c6
2. d4	d5
3. Nd2	dxe4
4. Nxe4	Nd7
5. Ng5	Ngf6
6. Bd3	e6
7. N1f3	Bd6
8. Qe2	h6
9. Ne4	Nxe4
10. Qxe4	Nf6
11. Qe2	Qc7
12. Bd2	b6
13. 0-0-0	Bb7
14. Rhe1	

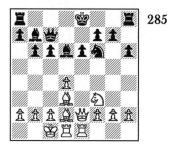
285

14. ... **0-0!**

Experience shows that 14... 0-0-0 15. Ba6! Bxa6 16. Qxa6† Kb8 17. Qe2 Nd5 18. c4 favors White.

15. g4 **c5!**

Not 15... Nxg4 16. Rg1 Nf6 17. Qe3! (not 17. Bxh6 Bf4†) Kh8 18. Rxg7!.

16. g5 **hxg5**

17. Nxg5

Black safely wins at least a ♟ after 17. Bxg5 Bf4†!.

17. ... **Bf4!**

18. h4

286

Here Black thought a long time about 18... cxd4 – then decided on a more active move.

18. ... **Rad8!**

And Black has the better of 19. dxc5 bxc5 20. Be3 Rd4!.

Pat: Neat. The center's way more important than the kingside.

Noah: Of course, the case of wing-attack-vs.-wing-attack is more common.

The next example shows the dangers of queenside castling.

Pat: What's with Bb5 and the ...Na7 moves?

Noah: Just a little skirmishing based

on "Take what he gives you."

White's seventh move gave Black a chance to wreck the queenside with ...a4-a3.

Pat: But Black's ninth move also gave White something – control of b5.

Noah: Very good.

Yet when he occupied b5, that gave Black a chance to harrass the ♗ with ...Na7.

Basically what Black is saying with his moves 10-12 is that he's willing to draw – and that it's up to White to take the risks to continue to fight.

Pat: Which White does.

Noah: He does indeed – and it costs him.

Later there's a tactical version of "Take" – at move 16 Black threatens a strong Exchange sack on c3.

Pat: It would never occur to me to put my ♕ on b8.

Anand-Kramnik
Melody Amber (blindfold) 1999

1. e4	c5
2. Nf3	Nc6
3. d4	cxd4
4. Nxd4	Nf6
5. Nc3	d6
6. f3	e5
7. Nb3	Be7
8. Be3	0-0
9. Qd2	a5

Book was 10. a4.

| 10. Bb5 | |

White grabs a fine square and stops 10... a4.

10. ...	Na7
11. Be2	Nc6
12. Bb5	Na7
13. Ba4	Be6
14. Bxa7	

On 14. 0-0 Black has 14... Bc4! and 15... b5.

| 14. ... | Rxa7 |

In **grandmaster slang,** "I castled" means he lost two games in a row (00) — and "I castled long" means three losses.

| 15. Qf2 | Ra8 |

287

16. 0-0-0?

White is slightly worse after 16. 0-0.

| 16. ... | Qb8! |

Black threatens ...Rc8xc3 followed by ...b5.

| 17. Bb5 | Rc8 |

Even on 18. a4 Black can play 18... Rxc3! 19. bxc3 Qc7 and ...d5, with excellent compensation.

| 18. Na4 | d5! |
| 19. Nb6 | a4! |

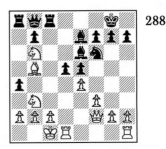

288

White is losing after 20. Nxc8 Qxc8 21. Nd2 a3 or 20. Nxa4 dxe4.

The game ended with 20. Bxa4 Qa7! 21. exd5 (or 21. Rhf1 d4! 22. Nxc8 Rxc8) Bd8! 22. dxe6 Bxb6 23. exf7† Kxf7 24. Nc5 Qxa4 White resigns.

Noah: Well, that leads us into a second major area of late-opening decisions – What to do with the heavy pieces.

Pat: I thought heavy pieces were easy:

You just put the ♖s on open files and stick the ♕ somewhere on the second or third rank.

Noah: But if you follow that credo, trouble is bound to arise when you find you just don't have open files – or a good square for the ♕, as Black does in Diagram 289.

Pat: He shouldn't have problems with the ♖s. He can put 'em on d8 and e8 or double on the d-file.

Noah: But after Black missed a chance to get the ♕ to g6, he was scrambling for a way to connect his ♖s.

The solution he chose only put his heavy pieces in harm's way.

Kamsky-Short
PCA Candidates match 1994
first game

1. d4   d5
2. c4   dxc4
3. e4   e5
4. Nf3   Bb4†
5. Nc3   exd4
6. Nxd4   Ne7
7. Bxc4   Nbc6
8. Be3   0-0
9. a3   Bxc3†

10. bxc3   Na5
11. Be2   b6

Better is activating the R/f8 with 11... f5 or gaining space with 11... c5.

12. 0-0   Bb7

Again 12... f5 is better, or 12... Ng6.

13. Qc2!

289

Now 13... c5 is too late because of 14. Nb5 followed by Rad1 and Nd6.

But Black can still activate his ♕ with 13... Qd6 14. Rad1 Qg6.

13. ...   Qe8
14. Rad1   Rd8?
15. Bf4!

Black has no easy way of defending c7 (15... Rd7 16. Bg4 or 15... c5 16. Nb5 and Nd6 or Nc7).

15. ...   Ng6
16. Bxc7   Bxe4
17. Qb2!

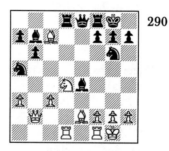

290

Black sacked the Exchange (17... Rxd4 and lost) because 17... Rd7 18. Bb5 or 17... Rc8 18. Bd6 were even worse.

Noah: This business of placing the heavy pieces has gotten a lot more subtle in the last 30 years.

Pat: How so?

Noah: It used to be that in some openings, the ♖s automatically ended up on certain squares.

For example, in the Open Sicilian, Black always used to put his ♖s on c8 and d8.

But more often nowadays a GM will put one ♖ at e8.

Pat: Just to protect e6?

Noah: And also to prepare ...d5 or ...e5.

He might also put the other ♖ at b8, to support ... b5-b4, rather than at c8.

And you should be aware that there are perfectly equal positions in which Black has no good ♖-squares at all.

Pat: Show me.

I'll believe it, but show me.

Noah: Okay, try Diagram 291 on for size.

Pat: I understand what Black was thinking – he took what White gave him with Bg5.

I just don't like what he did.

Noah: You should. He's equal after 11... Bd7 despite appearances.

The two ♗s will count for something in the middlegame even if Black has to keep his ♖s for a while at d8 – after ...0-0-0 – and h8.

1. d4	Nf6
2. c4	g6
3. Nc3	Bg7
4. Nf3	d6
5. Bg5	h6
6. Bh4	g5
7. Bg3	Nh5
8. e3	e6!

It's important to find a square for the ♕ such as e7, e.g. ...Nc6, ...Bd7 and ...Qe7.

9. Be2	Nc6
10. Nd2	Nxg3
11. hxg3	Bd7

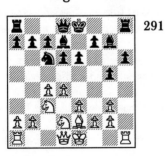

291

Black will castle queenside and play for ...f5, with good chances despite his ♖s' lack of open files for several more moves.

Pat: Must be another case of your opening imbalances.

Noah: Exactly, Black knows the player with the ♗s is usually the player with a future.

And the space-challenged player should always be looking for a creative way to get his ♖s into play.

Pat: I'm sure this is leading to Diagram 292.

Noah: It sure does. Because of the ♙-structure Black has problems developing four of his pieces.

Pat: He solves one problem at move 9.

Noah: Yes, you don't see it much in the Dutch, but ...Nc6-e7 works here.

As for Black's heavy pieces, there are three ways of getting them into play.

The traditional Dutch method is ...Qe8-h5 and ...Rae8.

But here that would leave White with too much space in the center and queenside.

Pat: I'll buy that.

Noah: The second method is ...Qc8-b7 – a good idea but it leaves the future of the ♖s uncertain.

Pat: What's left?

Noah: The ...b5 break to open the b-file. It looks odd – but it works.

M. Gurevich-Kengis
Bad Godesburg 1995

1. c4	b6
2. d4	Bb7
3. Nc3	e6
4. a3	

Another safety-first move. After 4. e4 Bb4! Black can complicate (5. Bd3 f5; 5. Qc2 Qh4).

4. ...	f5
5. Nf3	Nf6
6. g3	Ne4
7. Bd2	Be7
8. Bg2	Bf6
9. Rc1	Nc6!

An excellent way of developing

the N with tempo – Black threatens 10... Nxd4! 11. Nxd4 Nxc3 and ...Bxg2.

"Do you know my theory of how Capablanca played? He always tried to exchange one ♗, so that he should have no problems about how to arrange his ♙-chain. Then he exchanged one ♖, if possible. Then he had no problems about which ♖ to place on the only open file."
–David Bronstein

10. Be3	0-0
11. 0-0	Ne7
12. Nxe4	Bxe4
13. Qd2	

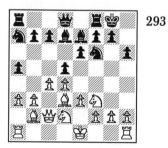

292

13. ...   Rb8!

With ...b5 Black will try to activate the R/b8 and secure d5 for his ♘.

14. Bg5

Or 14. Rfd1 b5 (15. Bf4 bxc4 16. Rxc4 Nd5).

14. ...	Bxg5
15. Nxg5	Bxg2
16. Kxg2	b5!

And Black has adequate play (17. b3 bxc4 18. bxc4 Rb3 19. Rc3 Qa8† and ...Rfb8).

Or 17. b4 bxc4 18. Rxc4 Nd5 or 17. c5 Nd5.

Noah: Turn the board around 180 degrees and you get something like the next example.

Pat: Another case of Black playing weird... what's 10... Na7 about?

Noah: It's Black's attempt to get control of light squares such as b5 and, indirectly, d5.

Pat: Didn't work.

Noah: It didn't work because it was much slower than White's g4-g5.

Black's 11th move only ensured that at least half the g-file would be opened.

Pat: And Black only lasted nine more moves.

Wilder-Kogan
U.S. Championhsip 1987

1. d4	Nf6
2. c4	e6
3. Nf3	Bb4†
4. Nbd2	d5
5. Qa4†	Nc6

6. a3	Be7
7. e3	0-0
8. Qc2	a5

At the time book regarded a waiting policy as best – 8... Re8 9. b3 Bf8 and ...g6/...Bg7.

9. b3	Bd7
10. Bb2	Na7

Black intends 11... a4 and, if 12. b4, then 12... dxc4 13. Nxc4 Bb5 or ... Nb5/...Bc6.

11. Bd3

White prepares 12. g4 and 13. g5 (since 12... Nxg4? 13. Bxh7† favors his attack).

11. ...   h6

293

12. Rg1!   c5

13. dxc5	Bxc5
14. g4!	

White was winning after 14... dxc4 15. Bxc4 Rc8 16. g5 hxg5 17. Nxg5, threatening 18. Nh7! Be7 19. Ne4!. The game ended with 17... Re8 18. Nxf7! Qe7 (18... Kxf7 19. Qg6† and Qxg7†) 19. Ne4! Kxf7 20. Nxf6 Resigns.

Noah: As you probably know, there are two basic errors you can make with ♖s – misplacing them and using the wrong ♖ on the right square.

Pat: You mean like when the annotators give some move a question mark and says "Wrong ♖."

Noah: Correct. That's the type of error the player with more freedom makes.

And the player who is cramped makes the kind of mistake that Black does in Diagram 294.

Pat: I hate positions like that. What's the ♗ doing on b7?

Noah: It was hoping for a chance to

play ...exd4 and ...c5.

White avoided that with 12. dxe5 and Black seized his opportunity to trade a pair of ♘s.

But Black went wrong with the R/a8.

Pat: Why was it wrong to support ...c5 ?

Noah: It was wrong simply because ...c5 never happened.

If Black had realized that, he would have put the ♖ where it would have done some good, lined up against the white ♙ at b4.

Krasenkov-Hickl
Jakarta 1996

1. d4	d6
2. Nf3	Nf6
3. c4	Nbd7
4. Nc3	c6
5. e4	e5
6. Be2	Be7
7. 0-0	0-0
8. Qc2	a6
9. Rd1	Qc7
10. Rb1	b5

11. b4	Bb7
12. dxe5	Nxe5!

Once again exchanges ease the defender's task. Black has a harder task after 12... dxe5 13. c5 or 13. a4.

13. Nxe5	dxe5
14. Be3	

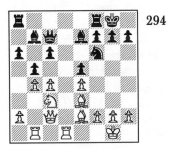

294

The positionally attractive 14. c5 allows Black counterplay with 14... a5.

White will go after his only target, b5, with 15. a4.

But 14... Rab8! is a good counter-idea, so he can continue 15. a4 bxc4 16. Bxc4 Bc8 and b4 becomes a target for Black.

14. ...   Rac8?

15. a4!	bxc4

When he made his 14th move Black may have miscalculated the result of 15... c5 16. bxc5!.

Then 16... bxc4 17. Rb4! and Rxc4 which favors White (or 16... Bxc5 17. Bxc5 and 18. axb5).

16. Bxc4

Now 16... c5 17. b5! is a positional edge for White.

16. ...   Ng4

17. Bc5

With a clear White edge due to his space and the bad B/b7.

Noah: When the imaginative deployment of a ♖ pays off, it pays off royally – as in Diagram 295.

Pat: What's going on before then?

Noah: White made another of the crucial decisions that regularly arise in the late opening – When and how to change the ♙-structure.

Pat: You mean like at move 9.

Noah: As well as at move 11.

Those are good changes for White because the B/b7 becomes buried,

" 'The white ♕ does not feel comfortable when staying on the same file as the black ♖,' one of the commentators assures us. I must confess that I omitted to ask my ♕ how she was actually 'feeling' and moved her for a concrete reason."
– Alexander Alekhine on one of his world championship games

he gets f5 for his pieces and he can open the kingside with fxe5.

Pat: Seems like a lot of ♟-action that early in the game.

Noah: But it's good ♟-action. And White's 13th is very important because it stops the only queenside counterplay, ... b5, and also gives him an alternative way of completing development.

Pat: That's cute.

Instead of getting stuff off the first rank, he brings the ♗s back and uses the second rank for his ♖.

Noah: So, by Diagram 296 White's development is as complete as he needs for this middlegame – even though two of his minor pieces are still on the first rank.

After 17. Bb1 he threatens, among other things, Nxf4-h5 followed by a sacrifice on f6.

Yusupov-Rozentalis
Elista 1998

1. d4	Nf6
2. Nf3	e6

3. e3	b6
4. Bd3	Bb7
5. 0-0	c5
6. c4	Be7
7. Nc3	cxd4
8. exd4	d6
9. d5!	

A window of opportunity: White locks in Black's B/b7 based on 9... exd5 10. cxd5 Nxd5?? 11. Bb5†.

9. ...	e5

Not 9... 0-0 because of 10. dxe6 fxe6 11. Nd4!.

10. Ng5	Nbd7
11. f4!	Rc8
12. b3	a6
13. a4!	0-0

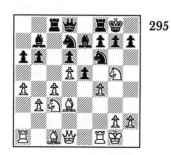

295

14. Ra2!	

White has g4 and Rg2 in mind.

14. ...	h6

Black hopes for 15. Nge4 Nxe4 16. Nxe4 f5!, greatly improving his ♟-structure and counterplay.

15. Raf2!	exf4

Not 15... hxg5 16. fxg5 Ne8 17. Qh5 with a crushing attack.

16. Nh3	Ne5

Defending the ♟ with 16... g5 provokes a strong 17. Nxf4 sacrifice (17... gxf4 18. Bxf4 Kg7 19. Bxh6†! Kxh6 20. Qd2† Kg7 21. Qg5† Kh8 22. Rxf6! with the idea of Qh6† and mates).

17. Bb1!

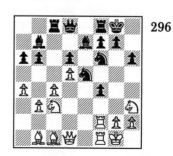

296

Again 17... g5 18. Nxf4 gxf4 19. Bxf4 is strong (19... Nfg4 20. Bxe5 Nxf2 21. Rxf2 dxe5 22. Qg4† and Qf5-h7).

Black played 17... f3 but that only gave White a better attacking file (18. gxf3 Re8 19. Rg2! Kh8 20. f4 Ned7 21. Ng5! and wins).

Pat: At least that example was sort of easy to follow.

White just found the fastest way to get his ♖ to the kingside.

Noah: Harder to understand are the so-called mysterious ♖-moves.

Pat: Mysterious?

Noah: Mysterious because the ♖s aren't developed on open files.

Nimzovich used the term to mean putting a ♖ on a file that wouldn't be opened without your opponent's help.

Pat: Why would he help anyway?

Noah: Because otherwise he has even less operating room than you do.

Maybe Diagram 297 will clarify

this a bit.

Pat: Hold on. What's with 6... d5 ?

Noah: Black felt it was worth a tempo to stop 7. e4 – while preparing ...e5 on his own.

But then the mysterious 10. Rad1 has its effect.

Pat: I see. Black didn't want to justify the ♖-move by playing ... e5.

Noah: And yet that refusal to play ...e5 gave White a free hand to dominate the center – with Ne5 followed by f4 and eventually e4.

Ovechkin-Kruppa
St. Petersburg 1999

1. d4	Nf6
2. Nf3	g6
3. g3	Bg7
4. Bg2	0-0
5. 0-0	d6
6. Nc3	d5
7. Be3	c6
8. h3	Nbd7
9. Qd2	Re8

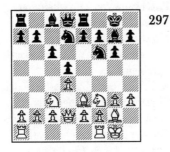

297

10. Rad1!

A mysterious but useful ♖-move.

On Black's intended 10... e5? White gets a terrific game from 11. dxe5 Nxe5 12. Nxe5 Rxe5 13. Bf4 Re8 14. e4!.

10. ...   Qb6

A bit better is the quiet 10... b6 and ...Bb7.

11. b3   Qa5

12. Ne5!

The R/d1 will come to life after 12... Nxe5 13. dxe5 Nd7 14. f4.

12. ...   Nf8

13. f4

And White stood better after

13... Qa3 14. g4! e6 15. Bf2 N6d7 16. e4.

Noah: Nowadays "mysterious ♖-move" is also used to describe not-so-mysterious situations in which a player puts his ♖ behind a ♙ he'd like to push.

For example – Diagram 298.

Pat: This is what my openings look like – no files for my ♖s.

Noah: True, but there are squares where the ♖s may have a future file.

In this case we have an illustration of a good mysterious move for Black – as well as a bad one.

Black's ♖s would have had a future after ...Re8, but not after ...Rc8.

Pat: It's funny how quickly that hurt him.

Noah: Yes, by Diagram 299 his heavy pieces are in a mess because of the pinned ♘s.

Van Wely-Timman
Match, Breda 1998

1. Nf3	Nf6
2. c4	e6
3. Nc3	Bb4
4. Qc2	0-0
5. a3	Bxc3
6. Qxc3	d6
7. d4	b6
8. Bg5	Bb7
9. Nd2	Nbd7
10. f3	d5
11. e3	

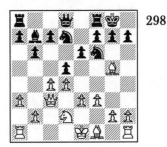

298

Here 11... Re8!, preparing ...e5, was good.

For example, 12. Bd3 h6 (deflecting the ♗ in order to weaken e3) 13. Bh4 e5!.

Then Black is equal after 14. 0-0 exd4 15. exd4 dxc4 16. Nxc4 Nf8 and ...Ne6.

Or 14. cxd5 Nxd5! 15. Bxd8 Nxc3 16. Bxc7 Nd5.

11. ...   Rc8?

Black dreams of ...c5 but...

12. cxd5   exd5
13. Bd3   h6
14. Bh4   Qe7
15. Bf5!

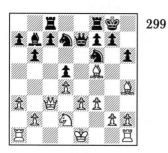

299

White threatens 0-0 and e3-e4-e5, as well as Bxd7.

Black lost after 15...Rce8 16. Bxd7 Qxd7 17. Bxf6 gxf6 18. Kf2, preparing Nf1-g3-h5.

Better was 15... g5 16. Bf2 c5 – but White is clearly better after 17. h4.

Pat: What about ♕s? Any special rules for developing them?

Noah: Usually ♕s are not a problem.

Ninety percent of the time, finding a good first-square for the ♕ is easy.

Pat: I guess I knew that.

Noah: Moreover, the difference between the best square for the ♕ and the second-best square is relatively minor.

An instructive exception is Diagram 300.

Pat: This must be one of those plus-over-equals positions that White always gets after 1. d4.

Noah: It's not all that good for him – if Black is alert.

It's true that Black has the infamous hanging ♙s to worry about and that the R/d1 is lined up against his ♕.

Pat: I know you. This where you say "But..."

Noah: But ... there's a great square for the ♕ that solves all Black's problems.

In fact, once Black secures that square, his ♙s are perfectly safe – and his advantage in space begins to turn the game in his favor.

Pat: I get it – e6. Cool maneuver.

Lautier-Short

Pamplona 1999/2000

1. d4	e6
2. Nf3	Nf6
3. c4	d5
4. Nc3	Be7
5. Bg5	h6
6. Bh4	0-0
7. e3	b6
8. Bd3	Bb7
9. 0-0	Nbd7
10. Bg3	c5
11. Qe2	Ne4
12. cxd5	exd5
13. Rad1	

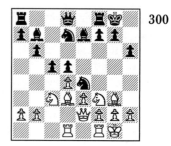

300

13. ...   Qc8!

Now 14. Rc1 can be met by 14... Ndf6 15. Rfd1 Qe6!, when Black's center has been turned from a weakness into a strength.

14. Bb1

Or 14. dxc5 Nxc3 15. bxc3 Nxc5 and Black stands a bit better.

14. ...   Ndf6
15. Qc2   Re8
16. Be5   Qe6!

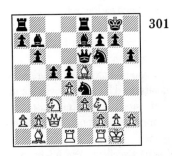

301

The attempt to exploit Black's last move, 17. Nb5 Bd8 18. dxc5 bxc5 19. Nc7, only favors Black after 19... Bxc7 20. Rxc7 Rac8.

In the game Black had the edge after 17. dxc5 bxc5 18. Qa4 Ng5! 19. Nxg5 Qxe5.

Noah: Yes, quite nice.

And as you know from experience, ♛s are often the next-to-last piece to be developed.

Pat: Just before the second ♖.

Noah: In fact, sometimes they're the last piece developed.

But there are many exceptions when the ♛ can do something

useful before the ♖s can.

Pat: Like what?

Noah: Like the three Hs of a good defender – hinder, harass and hamper.

Black does a good job of that in Diagram 302.

Pat: Isn't b6 just a dumb square for the ♛?

I mean, Black's supposed to play for ...b5, right?

Noah: Usually, but you have to remember that the opening isn't just a matter of reaching your goal.

It's also about stopping your opponent from reaching his.

Pat: Especially if you're Black.

Noah: Precisely.

Here White would have an ideal setup with excellent chances for kingside attack if he had been allowed to play 12. Nc3 and f4.

Pat: But Black can't stop Nc3 forever.

Noah: Of course not.

But the preparatory moves White needs to get that in, such as Nc2 or

Rfd1, don't fit in with the plan he wanted to follow.

A bit more harassment at move 13 provoked White into a bridge-burning middlegame that offered Black good chances.

Plaskett-Sadler
Hastings 1998-9

1. e4	c5
2. Nf3	d6
3. Bb5†	Bd7
4. Bxd7†	Nxd7
5. 0-0	e6
6. b3	Ngf6
7. Qe2	Be7
8. Bb2	0-0
9. c4!	

Having traded light-square ♗s, White wants to build a ♙-center on light squares.

9. ...	a6
10. d4	cxd4
11. Nxd4	

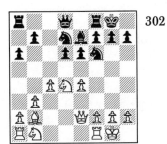

302

11. ...	Qb6!

White would have a fine game after 11... Qc7 12. Nc3 Rac8 13. Rad1 and f4.

12. Kh1

Or 12. Nc2 Rac8 13. Nc3 Rfe8 and 12. Rd1 Rfe8 13. Nc3 Rad8 14. Rab1 Bf8, with roughly equal play.

12. ...	Qc5

Preparing ...b5.

13. Nd2	Qh5!

Before White can play f4/N2f3, Black interrupts him with a threat to trade into an even endgame.

White avoids: 14. f3 and after 14... Rfe8 15. g4!? Qg5 16. Rg1 Ne5! 17. Raf1 Ng6 Black is well.

Pat: Is there anything else I should worry about in the late opening?

Noah: Three things, one minor the other two major.

Pat: What's the minor?

Noah: The old business of putting-the-question-to-the-♗.

Challenging a white ♗ after it lands on g5 – or a black ♗ on g4 if you're White – may seem routine.

Pat: When I do it it's usually just weakening. Or a waste of time.

Noah: But often the pin-challenging moves, such as h3, are remarkably useful.

Unlike when White plays the safety-first h3 before ...Bg4, it's a forcing move after ...Bg4.

And what it forces is the ♗ to choose a diagonal.

Look at the mess White gets into in Diagram 303.

Pat: Black can really get away with 11... g5 ?

Noah: He can because the B/g5-pin was the best thing about White's position.

And when it was broken, Black turned out to have a murderous attack.

Timman-Karpov
FIDE World Championship
Jakarta 1993, 15th game

1.	d4	Nf6
2.	c4	e6
3.	Nc3	Bb4
4.	Qc2	0-0
5.	a3	Bxc3†
6.	Qxc3	b6
7.	Bg5	c5
8.	dxc5	bxc5
9.	e3	Nc6
10.	Nh3	

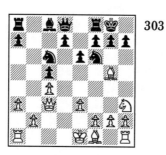

303

| 10. | ... | h6! |

Here 11. Bxf6 Qxf6 12. Qxf6 gxf6 is painless for Black.

11.	Bh4?	g5!
12.	Bg3	Ne4
13.	Qc2	Qa5†

Now 14. b4 Nxb4! 15. Qxe4 Nd5†! loses to a ♞-fork.

| 14. | Ke2 | f5! |

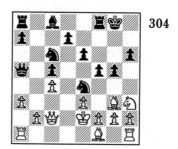

304

And White was clearly losing after 15. f3 Nxg3† 16. hxg3 Rb8 17. Nf2 Ba6.

Pat: If that's the minor thing I have to worry about, what are the majors?

Noah: One of the majors is what I mentioned earlier today, changing of the center.

Remember what I said about center *zugzwang*?

Pat: You said most centers are predetermined by book moves – and that usually there's no reason to change the center until the middlegame.

Noah: Excellent. You might turn out to be a good opening player after all.

A useful rule of thumb is to be very suspicious about any ♟ move that closes the position after move six – as in Diagram 306.

Pat: Don't GMs always talk about how good it is to have a queenside majority?

Noah: That's a good thing to have in the ending – if you live that long.

Here Black forgets about a basic corollary of ♟ play.

Pat: Which is?

Noah: Mobility matters.

After 8... c4 White's kingside ♟s become mobile – while Black's

THE IMPACT OF ...h6

In some openings the addition of ...h6/Bh4 improves Black's position significantly by gaining space or reducing White's options: In the Najdorf Sicilian (1. e4 c5 2. Nf3 d6 3. d4 cxd4 4. Nxd4 Nf6 5. Nc3 a6) the line 6. Bg5 e6 7. Qf3 used to be considered very dangerous for Black.

305

For example, 7... Nbd7 8. 0-0-0 Qc7 9. Qg3 b5 10. Bxb5! with great compensation or 7... Be7 8. 0-0-0 Qc7 9. Rg1 and 10. g5. But 7... h6! is the antidote — 8. Bxf6 Qxf6 9. Qxf6 gxf6 is at least equal and 8. Bh4 Nbd7 9. 0-0-0 Ne5! 10. Qe2 g5 11. Bg3 Bd7 is fine for Black.

Also, the original Tartakower Defense of the QGD (1. d4 d5 2. c4 e6 3. Nc3 Nf6 4. Bg5 Be7 5. e3 0-0 6. Nf3 b6) is considered favorable for White after 7. cxd5 exd5 8. Bd3 Bb7 9. Qc2 Nbd7 10. h4!.

With the addition of 6... h6 7. Bh4 b6 the comparable line, 8. cxd5 exd5 9. Bd3 Bb7, is fairly even.

queenside pawns just sit and wait.

It follows that a wing attack with ♙s becomes strong if your opponent can't break in the center.

That explains the strength of 10. g4!.

Kasparov-J. Polgar
Tilburg 1997

1. c4	e6
2. Nc3	d5
3. d4	Bb4
4. e3	c5
5. a3	Bxc3†
6. bxc3	Nf6
7. cxd5	exd5
8. f3	

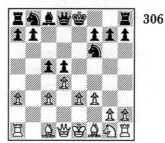

306

8. ...   c4?
Better was 8... Qc7 followed by ...b6/...Ba6. (Note that 9. Bd3? would walk into 9... cxd4 10. cxd4 Qc3†).

9. Ne2	**Nc6**
10. g4!	**h6**
11. Bg2	

White has a powerful position with prospects for both g5 and e4 – and no Black counterplay to worry about.

The trend was clear after 11... Na5 12. 0-0 Nb3 13. Ra2 0-0 14. Ng3 Bd7 15. Qe1 Re8 16. e4! dxe4 17. fxe4 Nxg4 18. Bf4 followed by 19. h3 Nf6 20. e5.

"A mobile ♙-majority on the kingside is as a rule much more advantageous than a less mobile one on the queenside."
– Ludek Pachman

Pat: So, when I think "♙ move" I have to think about whether it creates counterplay for me. Or kills it.

Noah: That's one set of criteria.

But there are also times when it's valuable to change the ♙-structure with an ugly move – because it means killing the enemy counterplay.

Like Diagram 307.

Pat: Ugly is right. That B/c4 is great – until White turns it into a giant ♙ when he plays 12. d5.

Noah: But he stops Black's main idea, ...d5!.

Once that's off the radar screen there's only one thing that matters – White's edge in space.

Pat: Then he can just roll Black off the board with his kingside ♙s.

Dolmatov-Romanishin

Olympiad 1992

1. e4	e5
2. Nf3	Nc6
3. d4	exd4
4. Nxd4	Bc5

5. Be3	Qf6
6. c3	Nge7
7. Bc4	Nxd4?
8. cxd4	Bb4†
9. Nc3	Bxc3†

"Since the whole career of a ♙ is limited to five or six irreversible moves, every ♙ advance needs to be weighed most carefully."
– Max Euwe

| 10. bxc3 | Qc6 |
| 11. Qd3 | Qg6 |

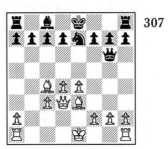

White would like to castle somewhere and begin his attack – but Black threatens to equalize at least with 12... d5.

For example, 12. 0-0 d5! 13. exd5 Bf5! 14. Qd2 Be4.

Or 12. 0-0-0 d5! 13. exd5 Qxd3 14. Rxd3 Bf5 15. Rdd1 Be4.

| 12. d5! | d6 |
| 13. 0-0-0! | Bd7 |

Now 13... Qxg2 14. Rhg1 and Rxg7 or 13... f5? 14. Bb5† c6 15. dxc6 bxc6 16. Ba4 are unappealing.

On 13... 0-0 14. f4 Black is worse

after 14.. f5 15. e5 – and lost after 14... Qxg2? 15. Rdg1.

14. f4

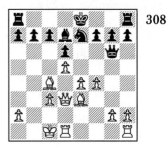

White won after 14... f6 15. f5 Qf7 16. g4.

Pat: I always end up arguing with myself when I'm ready to push a ♙.

Noah: That's a good debate to have – because there are usually trade-offs you have to evaluate accurately.

If you gain space in the center, you'll probably have to give up squares.

Pat: As you said, every move has its minuses.

Noah: In this case, it was Bobby Fischer who said it better.

But you have to beware of giving up too many squares – as White does in Diagram 309.

Pat: What's the point of 8. e5 ?

Noah: White wanted to meet the ...Nxe4 threat – with a gain of time and a gain of space.

Pat: He got both.

Noah: True, he did get e4 for his pieces.

But it turns out that d5, the square he gave up, was more valuable.

The result is that White's pieces were in a mess by move 10.

Pat: And White had such a nice center before 8. e5.

Gulko-Miladinovic
Elenite 1995

1.	d4	d5
2.	c4	Nc6
3.	Nc3	dxc4
4.	Nf3	Nf6
5.	e4	Bg4
6.	Be3	e6

7.	Bxc4	Bb4

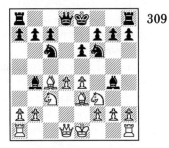

309

Book here was 8. Qc2.

8. e5?   Nd5

9. Qd3

White is preparing to castle and play Ne4, with a fine game.

9. ...   Na5!

But the positional threats of ... Nxc4 and ...Bxf3 are too hard to meet.

For example, 10. Bb5†? c6 11. Ba4 Bf5! loses for White (12. Qd2 Nc4 13. Qc1 Nxb2).

In the game Black had superior light-square play after 10. Bg5 Qd7 11. Bxd5 Qxd5! 12. 0-0 Bxc3 and ...Bxf3.

Noah: What makes this subject so hard is that there are times when ugly moves work and attractive moves fail.

And even if there is a center *zugzwang* situation you can sometimes profit from changing it: You can favorably capture or push – provided the timing is exactly right.

Pat: What makes the timing right?

Noah: A variety of things.

For example, in Diagram 310 Black gives up the center because he can create a lot of problems for White on e4.

Pat: See what you mean.

It's not easy to protect the e-♙.

Noah: And Black has all sorts of annoying tactical shots, like ...Nc5-e6 and ...Ng4, to prevent White from unraveling his pieces. Had White managed to unravel them, he would have had the better game because of his better center and greater space.

Pat: But by Diagram 311 Black stands well.

Atalik-Naiditsch
Budapest 1998

1.	d4	Nf6
2.	c4	g6
3.	Nc3	Bg7
4.	e4	d6
5.	Nf3	0-0
6.	Be2	Na6
7.	0-0	c6
8.	Re1	

This natural move seems to

"To get squares you gotta give squares."
– Bobby Fischer

solve whatever problems White might have had defending e4. But...

8. ...   **e5**
9. Be3?

310

Now 9... Ng4 is good harassment (10. Bg5 Qb6) but Black has a better idea.

9. ...   **exd4!**

Now 10. Nxd4 Re8 is uncomfortable for White (11. f3 Nc7 and 12... d5!, or 11. Bf3 Nc5 12. Qc2 Bg4!).

10. Bxd4   **Re8**

The e-♟ is attacked and on 11. Bf1 Black has 11... c5!, gaining the two ♗s – or a ♟ (12. Be3 Nxe4).

11. Nd2

Black's pieces are much too active after 11. Qc2 Nc5! 12. Bf1 Ne6 13. Be3 Ng4 14. Bd2 Nd4!.

11. ...   **Nc5**
12. Bf1

Not 12. e5? Nfd7, which favors Black.

12. ...   **Ne6**
13. Be3   **Nc7**

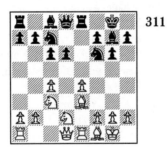

311

And 14... d5 or 14... Ng4 will equalize at least.

Pat: So I have to worry about when to close the center – as well as when to open it.

Noah: And that's only two of the basic center changes you should

consider.

Sometimes you're presented with a golden opportunity to build a strong center where nothing previously existed.

Pat: Why do I think this is leading up to Diagram 312?

Noah: Probably because it's a splendid example of center-building.

Pat: I don't get this one. Black's ♘ looked awesome on e5.

So why shouldn't the other ♘ go to c6?

Noah: Actually, Black's play is quite logical.

After 6. b3 he has the makings of a big spatial edge – provided he can stop White from playing d4 and controlling the long b2-g7 diagonal.

That means Black needs a ♟, not a ♘, on e5.

1. e4   **Nf6**
2. Nc3   **d5**
3. e5   **Nfd7**
4. Nxd5   **Nxe5**

5. Ne3   **c5**

White would stand well after 5... Nbc6 6. b3.

For example, 6... g6 7. Bb2 Bg7 9. d4 Nd7 10. Nf3.

6. b3

312

Now 6... g6 7. Bb2 Bg7 8. Nc4 favors White and 6... Nbc6 7. Bb2 e6 8. f4 Ng6 9. g3 (or perhaps 9. Bb5 Nxf4 10. Qf3) are about equal.

6. ...   **Nec6!**
7. Bb2   **e5!**

Black had a superior position in *Groszpeter-Suba, Kecskemet 1979,* which went 8. g3 Bd6 9. Bg2 0-0 10. Ne2 f5 11. Nc4 Bc7 12. d3 Be6.

Pat: I'm always stumped when some GM retreats a perfectly good piece.

You know, they've got a ♗ on d3 or c4 and they bring it back to f1.

Noah: Retreats are often cryptic because they violate the ancient rule against moving a piece twice in the opening.

Pat: That one I've heard.

Noah: It's a rule with more than a germ of truth.

That germ proved terminal to White in Diagram 313.

Pat: How much of this is book?

Noah: Most all of it up to move 18 – when White erroneously followed the "Take" principle.

Pat: You mean he occupied e6 because Black gave up control of it the move before.

Noah: Exactly. White wanted to confuse Black's pieces with the threat of 19. Rxd6.

But he overlooked Black's reply and the result, four moves later, was hugely one-sided.

Pat: Sure was. All of Black's remaining pieces were developed then – and none of White's.

Noah: And that meant even a retreat, like 23... Bc8!, could be powerful.

Anand-Nunn
Wijk aan Zee 1990

1. e4	e5
2. Nf3	Nc6
3. Bb5	a6
4. Ba4	Nf6
5. 0-0	Be7
6. Re1	b5
7. Bb3	0-0
8. c3	d5
9. exd5	Nxd5

Powerful retreats

...occur in several closed openings.

For example: 1. c4 Nf6 2. Nc3 c5 3. Nf3 b6 4. e4 Bb7 5. e5 Ne4? — and now 6. Nb1! wins material (7. d3).

---

10. Nxe5	Nxe5
11. Rxe5	c6
12. Bxd5	cxd5
13. d4	Bd6
14. Re3	Qh4
15. h3	g5
16. b3	f5
17. Qf3	Bb7

Now 18. Ba3 is consistent.

18. Re6?

Perhaps expecting 18... Bb8, after which 19. Ba3 is stronger than 18. Ba3 would have been.

If Black defends the ♗ instead with 18... Rad8, his plan of ...Rae8 is out of the question.

18. ...	Rae8!

Since 19. Rxd6 Re1† 20. Kh2 Rxc1 is horrible White had to play:

19. Rxe8	Rxe8

And Black's attack (threats: ...Re1 mate or ....g4) steadily grew:

20. Kf1 g4 21. Qxf5 gxh3 22. Qxh3 Qxh3 23. gxh3 Bc8! etc.

Pat: You don't really mean I should never move a piece twice in the opening.

Noah: Heavens no. Not at all.

Just think of those Ruy Lopez lines where White plays B/b5-a4-b3-c2 and N/b1-d2-f1-g3-f5.

Pat: When he hasn't even touched the B/c1 or R/a1.

Noah: Correct. The point is you don't want to develop pieces or ♟ s until you know where they belong.

And at the same time it pays to move other pieces a second or third time in order to prevent your opponent from putting his ♟ s and pieces where he wants them.

As Diagram 314 shows.

Pat: I understand 10. Qa4 – it attacks a ♙.

But what's with 11. Qa5 ?

Noah: White's on the verge of a middlegame battle that was strategically defined by 7. Nxc6.

The capture messed Black's ♙s up a bit. But if he can perform a bit of reconstruction, with ...c5 and ...d6, he should stand well.

Pat: He never got that far.

Noah: No, White's ♕-maneuver neatly stopped ...c5 and set c7 and d6 up as targets for his ♖s and ♗.

Psakhis-Ekstrom
Dresden 1998

1. c4	Nf6
2. Nc3	e5
3. Nf3	Nc6
4. g3	g6
5. d4	exd4
6. Nxd4	Bg7
7. Nxc6	bxc6
8. Bg2	0-0
9. 0-0	Rb8
10. Qa4	a6

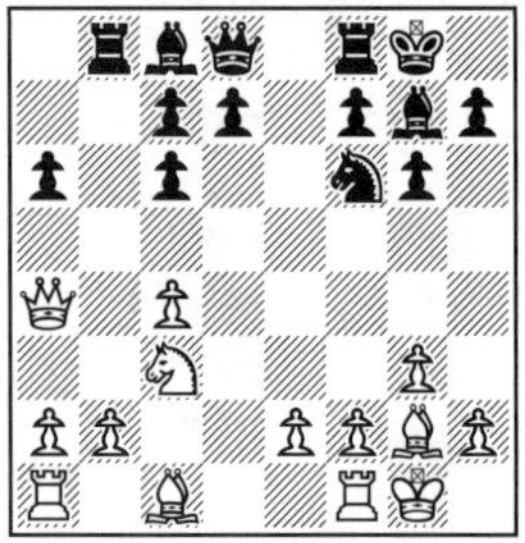

[diagram 314]

Black prepares 11... c5 followed by ...d6 and ...Rb4 or ...Bb7.

11. Qa5!

This keeps Black constricted (11... d6 12. Bxc6 or 11... c5 12. Qxc5).

11. ...   **Bb7**

No better is 11... Ne8 12. b3 c5 because 13. Ba3 d6 14. Rad1 favors White.

12. c5!   **d6**

Or 12... Nd5 13. Nxd5 cxd5 14. Bf4 Rc8 15. Rad1.

13. Rd1   **Qe7**

14. Bf4

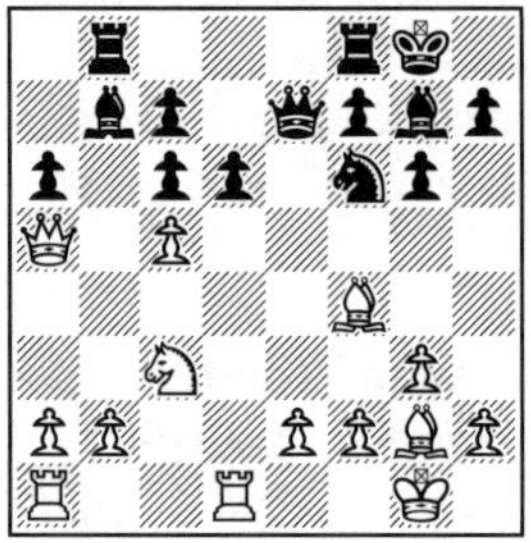

[diagram 315]

White has continuing pressure (14... Nd5 15. Nxd5 cxd5 16. cxd6 cxd6 17. Rd2).

Pat: Are there any real rules about when to move a piece a second time?

Noah: Nothing you can carve in stone.

But there's one that always helped guide me:

Don't move a developed piece until you've gotten the maximum use out of it.

Pat: How am I supposed to know when it's the maximum or not?

Noah: Maybe Diagram 316 will help.

Pat: That's one I've seen a few quintillion times.

> "Never move a piece twice until you've moved it once."
> — Anonymous

Noah: But you probably haven't seen 8... Na5 – even though it was the main line of the Lopez for years and years.

Pat: What's wrong with it?

I mean, it's kind of forcing – White's got nothing if he allows ...Nxb3.

Noah: Very true. But what's wrong is that Black shouldn't move the N/c6 until there is no prospect of using it to pressure d4.

Only after White spends a tempo on h3, a good safety-first move, does it pay for Black to play ...Na5 and put pressure on the center with

Getting Late

...c5 and ...Nc6.

1. e4	e5
2. Nf3	Nc6
3. Bb5	a6
4. Ba4	Nf6
5. 0-0	Be7
6. Re1	b5
7. Bb3	d6
8. c3	

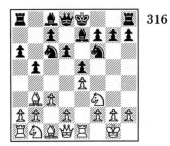

316

The accurate continuation is 8... 0-0! so that 9. d4 can be met by 9... Bg4!, with pressure against d4.

Theory regards 9. h3 as better, and then one key line goes 9... Na5 10. Bc2 c5 11. d4 Qc7 12. Nbd2 with a very slight edge for White.

8. ...	Na5?

The book-favored move in the 1930s and '40s.

9. Bc2	c5
10. d4	Qc7

White has saved a move (no h3) and can begin his middlegame with 11. a4!:

(a) 11... Bb7 12. Nbd2 0-0 13. dxc5 dxc5 14. Nf1 and Ng3-f5, or

(b) 11... b4 12. cxb4 cxb4 13. Nbd2 0-0 14. h3, with a fine game in either case.

Pat: So this rule is all about timing.
Noah: Basically true – and it applies most often to ♘ moves.

Diagram 317 shows another common mistake with a black ♘ – and a cute dance by the ♗s.

Pat: I thought that whenever Black gets a ♟-structure like that he should shoot for ...f5 and ...Nf4.
Noah: He should – but at the right moment.

The point is that Black only has one target in the diagram, at e4.

So he should get the maximum use out of his N/f6 by attacking the ♟ with ...Nc5.

That way he forces White into a defensive move that makes a later ...f5 more effective than an early one.

Pat: What's going on with the ♗s?
Noah: That's also pretty instructive.

First White took advantage of 7... Nh5 by developing his B/c1 with a gain of time, 9. Bg5.

That was good because none of the blocking moves – 9... Ndf6, 9... Bf6, 9... f6 and 9... Nhf6 – were useful to Black.

Pat: But a trade of ♗s would be good for him, right?
Noah: Right. That's why White avoided both 10. Bxf6 and 10. Bh6 Bg7!.

White waited for Black to retreat the ♗ to e7 before going to h6.
Pat: In the end, Black's minor pieces aren't too badly placed.
Noah: Yes, but by then White's got

a terrific plan in the works.
Like I said, it's a matter of timing.

1. d4	Nf6
2. c4	g6
3. Nc3	Bg7
4. e4	d6
5. Nf3	0-0
6. Be2	e5
7. d5	

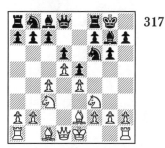

317

7. ...	Nh5?

Better is 7... a5, securing c5 for a N, e.g. 8. Be3 Na6 9. 0-0 Nc5.

Then after 10. Nd2 it's time for 10... Ne8 (11. Qc2 f5 12. exf5 Bxf5 with an equal game).

8. g3!	Nd7

On 8... f5 9. exf5! Black gets a bad game (9... Bxf5 10. Nh4 or 9... gxf5 10. Ng5).

9. Bg5!	**Bf6**
10. Be3!	**Be7**
11. Bh6!	

Now 11... Re8 misplaces the ♖.

11. ...	**Ng7**
12. h4	

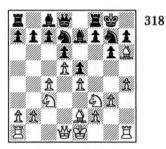

318

White has a clear edge after 12... Nf6 13. Nd2 Kh8 14. h5 *(Gligoric–Donner, Lugano 1970).*

Noah: The mark of a strong player is knowing when to rearrange the furniture.

Pat: What furniture?

Noah: I mean to shift the bulk of your army to better squares.

Maybe I should finish up today with an example of that.

Pat: You mean like in Diagram 319.

Noah: Yes. This was a very theoretical line in the late '90s.

Pat: Very theoretical?

Noah: That's another way of saying super-GMs made a living by using it – and by convincing fans that they understood it.

Even though the GMs felt White's position was essentially superior to Black's no one was able to prove it with the natural moves, such as 0-0 at move 14 or 15.

Pat: So where's the furniture?

Noah: There are several pieces of it:

For example, the b-♙ is advanced to stop ...Nc4.

Pat: And then the ♘-retreat clears d4 for the ♗ that wasn't doing anything on f2.

Noah: Right, and finally the N/c3 is repositioned on e3 to cover c2

and prevent a buildup against c3.

When it's all in place Black's threats have been neutralized one by one. Without having done anything dramatic, White quickly obtained a big edge against the World's No. 1 player.

Anand-Kasparov
Frankfurt rapid 1998

1. e4	**c5**
2. Nf3	**d6**
3. d4	**cxd4**
4. Nxd4	**Nf6**
5. Nc3	**a6**
6. Be3	**Ng4**
7. Bg5	**h6**
8. Bh4	**g5**
9. Bg3	**Bg7**
10. Be2	**h5**
11. Bxg4	**Bxg4**
12. f3	**Bd7**
13. Bf2	**Nc6**
14. Qd2	**Ne5**

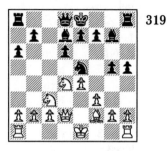

319

15. b3!

This neutralizes the N/e5 – and, despite appearances, makes it safer to play 0-0-0.

15. ...	**e6**
16. Nde2!	**Rc8**
17. Bd4	

This defangs Black's strong B/g7.

17. ...	**b5**
18. Nd1!	

And the Black pressure on the c-file evaporates once this ♘ lands on e3.

18. ...	**Rg8**
19. Ne3	**a5**
20. 0-0-0!	

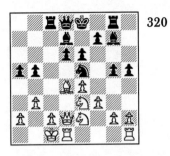

320

White had a clear edge and eventually won after 20... a4 21. Kb1 axb3 22. cxb3! Ra8 23. Bc3 Ra6 24. Nc2! Bf8 25. Nb4.

Pat: When you break it down like that, it all seems so simple.

Noah: If it was that simple, the GMs would have figured that opening out long before 1998.

But that's the way you have to train yourself to think in the opening.

Pat: I don't know if I'll ever do that.

Noah: Well, maybe not as well as a GM.

But you have to be cheered by one thing today, Pat.

Pat: What's that?

Noah: We've covered just about everything you need to worry about in the opening.

Pat: And that means...

Noah: That means after tomorrow you can start worrying about the middlegame.

The Third Book

This title is our third publication with GM Andrew Soltis, and we are pleased to offer it to the chess public.

In 2003 we will be revising GM Soltis' "Confessions of a Chess Grandmaster," with a new format, and 50 additional pages.

The first edition of *Confessions* sold pretty quickly and got great reviews. It was one of the few times a modern day grandmaster has let you inside his head, his experiences, and his laboratory. Since then a number of GMs have done the same thing.

Whether you realize it or not, Soltis is a trailblazer. Many opening variations were played by the NY GM long before they became popular and when they did, he dropped them. His variation in the Dragon inspired a large book on this subject, published by Hypermodern Press: *The Soltis Variation of the Yugoslav Attack.*

In which Pat learns when panic is good, how some games are really lost in two moves and why "15 in 30" is a rule to live by.

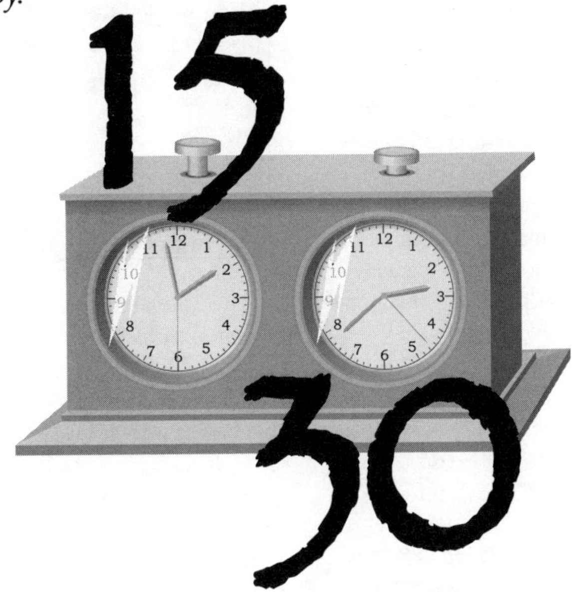

15

30

Pat: Are we there yet?

Noah: Almost. Today I just wanted to finish up a few loose ends – some practical, some psychological.

Pat: I thought everything we covered was supposed to be practical.

Noah: Hopefully it was.

But there are some vital subjects that are not treated adequately in any opening book and, well, you might as well hear about them from me.

Pat: I'm all ears.

Noah: The first item is how to deal with the clock.

When play begins you find yourself trying to get into the rhythm of making moves.

Pat: You mean like – Think. Move. Hit the clock. Write it down.

Noah: Exactly. But until you get into a comfortable rhythm, there's a tendency to think too much or too little.

Pat: For me it's usually too much – and I don't find that out until it's too late.

Noah: It's no better if you find out that you've moved too soon, as White did in this first example.

Pat: What happened?

Noah: White made his fifth move quickly – the position just seemed to him to be obviously book.

Black was so surprised he took 15 minutes to reply.

Pat: Fifteen minutes seems like a lot.

Noah: Ordinarily it would be.

But here it didn't matter – because the game is virtually over after 5... b5!.

Szabo-Keres
Candidates Tournament 1953

1. d4   d5
2. Nf3   Nf6

White "is giving ... ♗ and move, just like in the handicap tournaments for masters against weaker players in Chigorin's day."
– **David Bronstein's sarcastic comment on 5. Qa4†.**

3. c4   dxc4
4. Nc3   a6

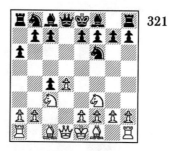

The normal moves here are 5. a4 and 5. e4 b5 6. e5.

5. Qa4†??

White confuses this with a line that begins with 4. Qa4†.

5. ...   b5!

Since 6. Nxb5? Bd7! costs a piece, White retreated the ♕ – and waited until the 41st move to resign.

Pat: Don't the GMs take a lot of long thinks?

I mean I've heard of 2600-players taking more than an hour on a move.

Noah: Not any more. Or at least, not very often.

The faster time controls of today mean that it just isn't cost effective to make a big think.

There are opening moves worth an hour – but...

Well, consider Diagram 322.

Pat: Was there something wrong with 9... Qe7?

Noah: The move is fine.

What made it disastrous was the cost – 50 minutes.

For a move to be worth 50 minutes it has to have a significant impact – say, the difference between an equal sign and plus-over-minus.

Pat: Looks like the real lemon was at move 10.

Noah: Yes, that was inconsistent considering that Black's previous move was designed to preserve and protect the ♗.

But what damaged Black the most was those lost 50 minutes.

TIME USE

Even in book positions GMs used to spend enormous amounts of time:

Paul Keres took about two hours against Laszlo Szabo at Budapest 1950 to reach 1. e4 e5 2. Nf3 Nc6 3. Bb5 Bc5 4. 0-0 Nf6 5. Nxe5 Nxe4.

Boris Ivkov spent 95 minutes over 11.c5 (after 1. d4 Nf6 2. c4 g6 3. Nc3 Bg7 4. e4 d6 5. Nf3 0-0 6. Be2 e5 7. dxe5 dxe5 8. Qxd8 Rxd8 9. Nd5 Rd7 10. Nxf6† Bxf6) at Bled 1961 against Mikhail Tal. (He lost.)

Bobby Fischer thought for more than an hour at Portoroz 1958 after Oscar Panno played (as Black) 1. e4 c5 2. Nf3 Nc6 3. d4 cxd4 4. Nxd4 g6 5. Nc3 Bg7 6. Be3 Nf6 7. Bc4 0-0 8. f3? Qb6!. (He managed to find 9. Bb3 Nxe4 10. Nd5! and drew.)

Lautier-Belyavsky
Belgrade 1997

1. d4	Nf6
2. c4	e6
3. Nc3	Bb4
4. e3	c5
5. Ne2	b6
6. a3	Ba5
7. Rb1	Na6
8. Qa4	Bb7
9. Bd2	

322

9. ...	Qe7

Black may not have liked 9... Bc6 10. Qc2 0-0 11. Ng3 but it's the sort of low-risk continuation that takes no time off the clock.

10. Ng3	Bxc3?

Inconsistent – 10... 0-0 was the common sense move.

11. Bxc3	cxd4
12. exd4	0-0
13. Bd3	

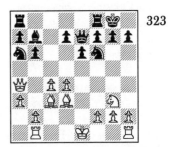

323

White has a very promising game which grew, thanks in part to the clock, after 13... Nc7 14. 0-0, e.g. 14... d5? 15. Bb4 or 14... Rfd8 15. d5! exd5 16 Nf5.

Pat: Is there a good formula to follow – I mean so I won't be thinking too much?

Noah: That's something each player has to figure out for themselves. We all think differently.

Pat: That's a big help.

Noah: But there is one time budget that was recommended by Mikhail Botvinnik and later by Garry Kasparov.

They told their young students to follow the "15 in 30 rule."

Pat: Meaning?

Noah: Meaning:

Try to make your first 15 moves in 30 minutes.

That leaves 1.5-2 hours for the later, more difficult moves of a game played at a normal tournament time control.

Pat: What if you're in a faster time limit?

Noah: Botvinnik and Kasparov didn't say. But I suggest the same proportion should apply:

Take no more than one fourth of your alloted time for the opening.

Pat: There's gotta be a lot of exceptions to that.

Noah: Not that many.

You can afford a big think only when it creates – or is a reaction to – a significant change in the course of the game.

Which brings up Diagram 324.

Pat: White just miscalculated, right?

Noah: Not just miscalculated.

White erred because he didn't appreciate this was one of those crisis moments of the game – there's usually only a few of them – that are worth a big think.

He chose a practical move when the position demanded an exact one.

Black understood that, White didn't.

Pat: How come? Black was still lost after 14... Rxf3 – a second-best move.

Noah: But he appreciated that it was the point in a game when spending 50 minutes on a move is worthwhile – because the game was about to be decided.

White's reply showed he was fumbling – the ♙ capture that would

have won at move 14 move turned the game around at move 15.

Lautier-Leko
Tilburg 1997

1. d4	Nf6
2. Nf3	g6
3. c4	Bg7
4. Nc3	d5
5. Qb3	dxc4
6. Qxc4	0-0
7. e4	a6
8. Qb3	b5
9. e5	Nfd7
10. h4	c5
11. e6	fxe6?

Necessary was 11... c4.

| 12. h5 | cxd4 |
| 13. hxg6! | Nc5? |

And here 13... Nf6 was essential.

"Perceiving when a game reaches a crisis is one of the greatest skills in chess."
– Ludek Pachman

324

14. Qc2?

Here 14 gxh7†! wins, e.g. 14... Kh8 15. Nh4! (threatening Ng6#) Rf6 16. Qd1! followed by Qh5.

For example, 16... Qd6 17. Qh5! Nbd7 18. Qe8† Nf8 19. Ng6†! Rxg6 20. Qf7! and wins.

14. ...   Rxf3

A bit better was 14... h5 15. Rxh5 Rf5.

15. gxh7†?

Too late. After 15. gxf3 dxc3 White can play 16. gxh7† Kh8 17. Rg1! and he is also winning after 15... d3 16. Qd2! hxg6 17. Qg5.

| 15. ... | Kh8 |
| 16. gxf3 | d3! |

17. Qd1   Nc6!

325

After White failed to develop with 18. Be3!, Black's pieces took over – 18. Bh6 Bxh6 19. Rxh6 Bb7 20. Bg2 Ne5! 21. Rh3 Qd4 22. Rg3 Nc4.

Pat: So there are opening moves worth a half hour.

Noah: Yes, but you have to beware of the Big Think Trap.

Pat: Trap?

Noah: Yes, it occurs when you go into a trance considering some dramatic move – and then decide you have to play it because otherwise you've just wasted those 30 min-utes.

Pat: Sounds like you're saying it's better to play a lot of solid, quick moves.

"I thought for 50 minutes over a tempting piece sacrifice, each minute becoming more and more convinced that it would not work.
And when everything was quite clear, I suddenly became angry with myself for wasting such a lot of time – and sacrificed!"
– Mikhail Tal, explaining one of his losses.

Noah: Nine times out of ten it is.

And there's a related clock problem, what I call "Believing him."

Pat: Translation?

Noah: It's the dilemma you face when your opponent comes up with a surprise move.

You ask yourself whether it's worth spending 20 or 30 minutes to find a refutation – or just trust that his move is sound.

Pat: I believe everything.

Noah: That's a pretty good policy against masters – and against a lot of non-masters, provided the cost of believing them in this or that particular position is minor.

You can see this policy in action in Diagram 326.

Pat: Black must have been surprised by 7. Nc4.

Noah: He was – for a moment.

But as soon as he saw the Nd6 mate trick he realized he had to decide whether it was worth calculating the complications of 7... Nxe4 8. Qe2 Bg7.

He correctly came to the conclusion that it just wasn't worth the time and replied quickly with a safe move.

Pat: And White didn't gain much from his finesse.

"As sometimes happens, a long think in the opening is followed by unsound strategical decisions, as the player feels somewhat compelled to justify his investment of time by unusual play."
– Joel Lautier

Noah: No, after 8. Bd3 he had just transposed into a position that could have occured after 7. Bd3 d6 8. Nc4.

Kramnik-Leko
Dortmund 1998

1. **d4**	**Nf6**
2. **c4**	**c5**
3. **d5**	**b5**
4. **Nd2**	**bxc4**
5. **e4**	**c3**

Black's improvement over 5... g6 6. Bxc4 d6 7. b3 Bg7 8. Bb2, which slightly favors White.

6. **bxc3**	**g6**

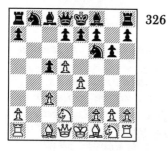

326

Now 7. Bd3 and Nc4 is normal.

7. Nc4
Played quickly.

7. ...   d6!
Ditto: He saw that 7... Nxe4 8. Qe2 the ♘ can't retreat (8... Nf6?? 9. Nd6#).

If Black had examined further he would have seen 8... Bg7 9. Qxe4! (9... Bxc3† 10. Bd2 Bxa1 11. Ba5!).

The upshot is that it was White who erred first, after 8. Bd3 Bg7 9. Nf3 0-0 10. 0-0 Nbd7 11. Bd2 Nb6 12. Na5? c4! (13. Nxc4 Nxc4 14. Bxc4 Nxe4 or 13. Bc2 Qc7! intending ...Nbxd5).

Pat: You got any other practical tips like that?

Noah: Well, we're moving now from the practical into the psychological.

There are a few times when it's worth spending time – 10, 20, even 30 minutes – if it upsets your opponent's preparation.

Pat: Because that makes a significant

change in the situation.

Noah: Right. This is what they call playing the man and not the board.

A fine example of that was Diagram 327.

Pat: Is 3... e5 sound?

"The most successful thing is to destroy the preparation of your opponent.
Here it's important not so much to play the objectively strongest move as much as an unexpected and unpleasant one."
– Judit Polgar

Noah: It looked sound at the time – but Black couldn't be sure.

The reason he chose it – after thinking half an hour – was that it was the one move "most suited to annoy a player like" his opponent, who thrives on attack and initiative.

Pat: It sure worked.

Noah: It worked spectacularly because White failed to do something else that becomes important in the latter stages of the opening – taking stock.

After 5... Nc6 White felt he should be standing well. Yet his only compensation for his development problems was the extra ♟.

Pat: So he held onto it – with two hands.

Noah: But what White should have done – once he knew he was out of book and after the position had clarified a bit – was evaluate his chances.

If he had looked at the position objectively he would have seen that he had no edge and that a neutral move like 6. Nf3 was best.

de Firmian-Granda Zuniga
Amsterdam 1996

1. e4	d5
2. exd5	Qxd5
3. d4	

327

An usual move in place of 3. Nc3, which gains time but slightly misplaces the ♘.

3. ...	e5!?
4. dxe5	

Black felt 4. Nf3 was best.

4. ...	Qxd1†!
5. Kxd1	Nc6
6. f4?	

Better was 6. Nf3 Bg4 or 6. Bf4.

6. ...	Bf5
7. c3	0-0-0†
8. Ke1?	

His last try for equality may have been 8. Nd2.

328

8. ...	f6!

White is worse after 9. exf6 Nxf6 followed by ...Bc5/...Rhe8†.

9. Bb5	fxe5

Black had the edge after 10. Bxc6 bxc6 11. fxe5 Bc5 12. Nf3 Nf6! and now 13. exf6? Rhe8† or 13. Bg5 h6 14. Bh4 g5.

Pat: I'm not sure I'm getting this taking stock business.

Noah: It's actually quite simple.

At some point in the later stages of the opening you should ask yourself what's happened so far –

Did I succeed in getting an edge? (if I'm White)
Or:
Did I equalize? (if I'm Black)

Pat: Why is that important? After all, if you're equal, you're equal.

Noah: But what if you think you're more than equal, and you're really not – like White in the last example?

Then you're bound to make bad decisions.

Pat: Why?

Noah: Because you'll reject good moves that lead to an even game – since you've convinced yourself you deserve more.

That's what ruined White's day in Diagram 329.

Pat: I don't like his third move.

Noah: It's just a way of avoiding the Benoni. The only downside to it is that it gives Black a free hand in the center.

The key moment comes later, after 10... cxd4.

Both players saw that 11. exd4 leads only to equal chances.

Pat: You could have fooled me.

Noah: The problem is that White felt he should have had more.

So he played the only alternative at move 11– and paid the price of misevaluation.

Pat: He missed some later chances, too.

Noah: He may even have thought he was winning after 14. b3, because of the 15. Ba3 threat – but by Diagram 330 he was losing.

Yusupov-Hertneck
Munich 1994

1. d4	Nf6
2. c4	c5
3. e3	g6
4. Nc3	Bg7
5. Nf3	0-0

6. Be2　　　d5

Transposing into a quiet Gruenfeld line (1. d4 Nf6 2. c4 g6 3. Nc3 d5 4. Nf3 Bg7 5. e3 0-0 6. Be2 c5).

7. 0-0

White has nothing much after 7. dxc5 dxc4 8. Bxc4 Qa5 or 8. Qxd8 Rxd8 9. Bxc4 Nbd7.

7. ...　　　dxc4

Also good is 7... cxd4 8. exd4 Nc6 – the reversed Tarrasch Defense again.

8. Bxc4　　Nbd7
9. Qe2　　　a6
10. a4　　　cxd4

329

On 11. exd4 Nb6 12. Ba2 Black equalizes after 12... Nbd5 and ...Be6

(since 13. Nxd5 Nxd5 14. Bxd5 Qxd5 15. Qxe7 Bg4! is excellent for Black) or 12... Bg4.

11. Nxd4?

A positional gamble – since the best aspect of White's position was his ♟-center.

11. ...　　　e5!
12. Nf3　　　e4!
13. Ng5

Consistent with his plan to get an edge – but again 13. Nd4 (and 13... Ne5 14. Ba2) was best.

13. ...　　　Qe7
14. b3?

Even here 14. Qc2 Nc5 15. b4 holds – 15... Nd3 16. Ba3!.

14. ...　　　Qe5!

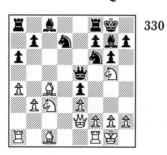

330

Black had the edge after 15. Nxf7 Rxf7 16. Bb2 Qe8 17. Rad1 Nf8 (18. Bxf7† Qxf7 19. b4 Be6).

Pat: I thought you're always supposed to be evaluating your position.

Noah: It helps. But usually you don't start judging things until you're out of book and thinking without a safety net.

Unfortunately, that's also when you make some of the most commiting moves of the game.

Pat: Both players do.

Noah: Both players can.

Unfortunately a player who thinks he has an edge is more likely to make a bad commitment – like a faulty change in the ♟-structure or a poor trade of minor pieces.

A good case of this is Diagram 331.

Pat: Pretty even so far.

Noah: White didn't seem to think so.

His problems began when he

delayed planting a ♘ on c5.

Pat: You mean 11. Na4 was best.

Noah: Right, and when your opponent blocks your first plan of the game – as Black did with 11... b5 – it's a good time to take stock.

Pat: What should he have done?

Noah: Something like 13. h3, even though it promises little.

White probably decided that only 13. f3 and Nf4 would give him what he felt he deserved.

Pat: But he did win a ♟ by Diagram 332.

Noah: Yet he was already worse then because of the e3 problem he'd created five moves before.

Mozetic-Shirov
Tilburg 1993

1. d4	d5
2. c4	c6
3. cxd5	cxd5
4. Bf4	Nc6
5. e3	Nf6
6. Nc3	a6
7. Bd3	Bg4

8. Nge2   e6
9. 0-0   Be7
10. a3   0-0
11. b4   b5!

Clearly better than 11... Rc8 12. Na4 a5? 13. b5.

12. Rc1   Rc8

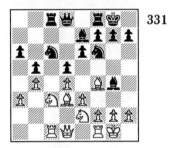

331

13. f3?

White tries to demonstrate he has a significant edge with Nf4 – at the cost of weakening e3.

He may have considered 13. h3 Bh5 14. Bg5 followed by Qd2 and Nf4 – and rejected it because Black stands well after 14... Nd7 15. Bxe7 Qxe7.

13. ...   Bh5

14. Bg3?   Bg6
15. Nf4   Bxd3
16. Nxd3   Nd7
17. Nc5   Nb6!
18. Nxa6   Nc4

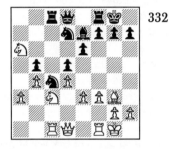

332

White has no easy way of defending e3 (19. Bf4 g5 or 19. Qd3 Ra8 20. Nc7 Rxa3 21. N7xb5 Nxb4 with advantage to Black).

Black won soon after 19. Qe2 Ra8 20. Nc5 Rxa3 21. Nxb5 Rxe3 22. Qf2 Qb6! (23. Nc7 Nxd4! 24. Nd7 Qxb4).

Pat: What about that second magic question of yours – "Did I equalize?"

Noah: That's just as important.

The flip side of failing to understand that you're only equal is failing to realize when you're getting the worst of it.

Pat: How do I learn how to avoid that?

Noah: That takes experience – which is another way of saying a lot of middlegame losses.

Pat: It usually takes me until the endgame to realize I'm losing.

Noah: True, but often you're dead by move 20 – even though you aren't buried until move 40.

Like the next game.

Pat: Doesn't look like much is happening in Diagram 333.

Noah: But it's all about to happen to Black.

White has the makings of a paralyzing queenside bind.

Pat: So which move was Black's mistake?

Noah: It wasn't a particular move.

Black's mistake was failing to panic.

Pat: I see, Black never got a chance for ...f5 until it was too late.

Noah: And by Diagram 334 White ruled the queenside and could take time repositioning ♖s and preparing the decisive b4-b5.

Qin Kanying-Wang Pin
Shanghai 1992

1. e4   c5
2. Nf3   d6
3. d4   cxd4
4. Nxd4   Nf6
5. Nc3   a6
6. g3   e6
7. Bg2   Bd7
8. 0-0   Nc6
9. Nxc6   Bxc6
10. a4   Be7
11. Be3   0-0
12. a5   Nd7
13. Qe2   Qc7
14. Rfb1

333

334

Since there is no chance for getting ...d5 or ...b5 in safely (14... b5 15. axb6 Nxb6 16. Rxa6) Black must find counterplay somewhere else.

14. ...   Bf6?

No sense of danger. Black should prepare ...f5, for example, with ....Rae8 and ...Ne5.

15. Na4!	**Rac8**
16. c3	**Bb5**
17. Qd1!	**Nc5**
18. Nb6	**Rcd8**
19. c4	**Bc6**
20. Qc2	**Nd7**
21. Rd1	**Qb8**

22. Rab1!

After long preparation – and little distraction from Black – White's advantage was obvious.

It grew quickly after 22... Nxb6 23. Bxb6 Rc8 24. Qd3 Be7 25. b4 f5 26. Re1 fxe4 27. Bxe4 Bxe4 28. Rxe4 e5 29. Rbe1 Kh8 30. Qd5! and White won.

Pat: So I should learn how to panic?

Noah: Or "become alarmed," if you prefer.

In either case, you have to know how to recognize a change of fortune – and react to it.

Otherwise you end up losing a game that lasts only two moves.

Pat: The only two-move game I know is the Fool's Mate.

Noah: There are many, many others that really last only two moves beyond where the book ends.

Diagram 335 shows you one.

Pat: White sure went down the tubes fast after 13... Rg6.

Noah: And there are a variety of reasons why.

In terms of strategy it was a mistake to open the g2-b7 diagonal.

In terms of calculating, it was wrong to assume Black would retake on e6 with the ♖.

But...

Pat: But what?

Noah: But White would have sur-

vived into the middlegame – and perhaps prospered – if he had reassessed the situation at move 15.

Pat: Maybe he didn't believe he could be in that much trouble one move out of book.

Noah: Or maybe he rejected 15. Ne1 because Black can virtually force a draw.

In any event, it was a delusion that did him in, not just a miscalculation.

Gelfand-Illescas
Madrid 1996

1. d4	**Nf6**
2. Nf3	**e6**
3. c4	**Bb4†**
4. Nbd2	**b6**
5. a3	**Bxd2†**
6. Qxd2	**Bb7**
7. e3	**0-0**
8. Be2	**d6**
9. 0-0	**Nbd7**
10. b4	**Ne4**
11. Qd3	**f5**
12. Bb2	**Rf6**

13. d5

335

13. ...   Rg6!

The book move had been 13... e5, after which 14. Nh4! (threatening 15. Nxf5 or 15. f3 Ng5 16. f4) favors White.

14. dxe6?

Much better was 14. Nd4!.

14. ...   Nf8!

White may have counted on 14... Rxe6 15. g3, safeguarding g2 and preparing Nd4.

Now he faces a dangerous plan of ...Nxe6-g5 or ...f4.

15. c5?

On 15. Ne1 and 16. f3 he can still fight – although Black has at least a draw with 15... Qh4 16. f3 Rh6!.

15. ...   Nxe6

336

The game ended abruptly with 16. cxd6 cxd6 17. Rad1 Kh8 18. Ne1? N6g5! 19. Kh1 Nh3! White resigns – the threat is 20... Nexf2† and 19. gxh3 allows 19... Nxf2#.

Pat: I know that feeling when you realize something's gone way wrong.

Noah: But if you feel it in time you can usually do something about it before it's time to stop the clock and shake hands.

A case in point is Diagram 337.

Pat: What got White into trouble?

Noah: His eighth move was a slightly dubious case of "Take."

Pat: You mean he thought that because there's no pressure on his center, g4-g5 had to be good.

Noah: And because he saw that Black had no good retreat square for the N/f6.

But it turned out that White's ninth was the main culprit.

Pat: So what saved him?

Noah: As soon as White saw how strong 11. Be3 Bb4! would be, he knew it was time to panic.

What's instructive about this game is that after White responded to the crisis correctly, it was Black's turn to take stock.

Pat: Looks like he failed the test.

Noah: Yes, he may have appreciated that White had good compensation for his lost ♟ after 13... Nc5 14. Bxc5 – so he rejected that line.

And he didn't try 13... Bb4† 14. c3 Be7 – perhaps because 15. Bf3 d5 is complicated.

But either line was better than what Black ended up doing.

Pat: It doesn't seem right he should lose.

Noah: Black deserved to lose – because even as late as Diagram 338 he continued to play as if he had nothing to worry about.

Shirov-Zviagintsev
Biel 1995

1. e4	c5
2. Nf3	e6
3. d4	cxd4
4. Nxd4	Nc6
5. Nc3	Qc7
6. Be2	Nf6
7. Be3	b6
8. g4	

More solid was 8. f4 or 8. Ndb5.

| 8. ... | h6 |
| 9. Qd2? | |

Better was 9. f3.

| 9. ... | Nxd4! |

Now 10. Qxd4 Bc5 and a trade of ♝s leaves White with dark-square problems.

10. Bxd4   e5

337

White will be in trouble after
11. Be3 Bb4! – 12. f3 or 12. Bf3 are
met by 12... Bb7 and 13... Rc8.

11. Nb5!   Qb8
12. Be3

White has taken some of the
sting out of the pin (12... a6 13. Nc3
Bb4 14. f3) because there isn't as
much pressure on c3.

12. ...   Nxe4
13. Qd3   a6?

Better was 13... Nc5 – although
White is back in the game after 14.
Bxc5 Bxc5 15. Bf3 Bb7 16. 0-0-0.

And 13... Bb4† 14. c3 Be7 is
unclear – 15. Bf3 d5! (not 15. Qxe4?

Bb7).

14. Bf3!   axb5
15. Bxe4   Ra4
16. Bd5!

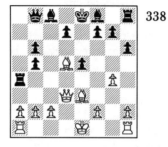

338

After this move, which both
defends a2 and attacks f7, White is
better.

Black continued 16...Bc5 17.
0-0-0 0-0? 18. g5! hxg5 19. Rhg1
g4? and was soon lost (20. b3!
Rxa2 21. Rxg4 with a winning attack).

*"If you don't know where
you're going, you'll end up
somewhere else."*
– Yogi Berra

Noah: The bottom line is – When
you realize you're slipping into
danger, you have to look for an
escape.

Pat: What kind of escape?

Noah: An escape can come about
from a good defensive scheme or
even a single tactical trick.

Often there's a clever tactic that
can solve your crisis – if you know
it's time to look for it.

I suspect that's what proved fatal
to Black in Diagram 339.

Pat: How so?

Noah: Black, a veteran GM, might
have felt at ease there because he
was holding the two-♗s edge
against a teenager.

But when he examined the natural move, 12... 0-0, he began to see
a White bind in his future.

Pat: Why is it a bind?

Noah: Because Black doesn't have a
good square for his ♛.

As I said the other day, that can
lead to a traffic jam for your heavy
pieces.

So, Black should have looked for
a tactical escape.

Pat: The move he chose looks okay:
he attacks the N/c4 and gains time
to castle and retreat the ♛ to g6.

Noah: But the same tactical sense
that failed him once – by missing
12... 0-0/13... b5! – failed him a
second time.

Pat: You mean when he misjudged
the strength of 13. Nd6†.

Svidler-Taimanov
St. Petersburg 1995

1. e4	c5
2. Nf3	e6
3. c3	Nf6
4. e5	Nd5
5. Bc4	d6
6. d4	cxd4
7. cxd4	dxe5
8. dxe5	Bb4†
9. Nbd2	Nb6
10. 0-0	Nxc4
11. Qa4†	Nc6
12. Nxc4	

339

On 12... 0-0 White has 13. Rd1! (which is strong after 13... Qe7 14. a3!).

White has a bind after 13... Qc7 or 13... Bd7 because of 14. Bf4 followed by Rac1.

12. ...   Qd3?

The tactical escape was 12... 0-0 13. Rd1! b5!, since 14. Qxb5?? Qxd1† loses and 14. Rxd8 bxa4 is nothing special for White.

White can try 14. Qc2 Qe7 15. Nd6 but then 15... Nxe5! 16. Nxe5 Bxd6 is fine for Black.

13. Nd6†!   Bxd6
14. Rd1

Now 14... Qg6 15. Rxd6 leads

to a bind, e.g. 15... 0-0 16. Be3 followed by Rad1. Black has problems solving the B/c8 development problem.

In the game Black fled into the endgame with 14... Qa6 15. Qxa6 bxa6 16. exd6 e5 but he was still worse.

Pat: I always have a problem evaluating positions – even in openings I should know.

Noah: But there are certain moments when you need to sense that the stakes have risen.

One of the things that makes a GM a GM is that he's developed a sense of recognizing when the game is entering a critical stage.

You can see Black do that in Diagram 340.

Pat: There's an awful lot going on before that.

Noah: True, White doubles his c-♟s in order to make 11. c5 strong and there's a battle over control of d6.

But the key position arises after

14. Nd2. Black evaluated it correctly – and realized he had to take action.

Pat: You mean he couldn't allow Nc4 or Rab1/Qb2.

Noah: Yes, and by move15 he had seized the initiative.

Black won because he sensed a crisis and then survived it – and because White didn't realize when his own crisis arose in Diagram 341.

Vyzhmanavin-Tseshkovsky
Moscow 1991

1. d4   e6
2. c4   f5
3. Nf3   Nf6
4. Nc3   Bb4
5. Qb3   Qe7
6. g3   a5
7. Bg2   a4
8. Qc2   d6
9. 0-0   Bxc3
10. bxc3

The point of this is...

10. ...   0-0

11. c5!

Now 11... dxc5 12. Ba3 Nbd7 13. Ne5 gives White positional play for a ♟.

11. ...   e5
12. Ba3   e4
13. cxd6   cxd6
14. Nd2

Or 14. Ne5 Qe6! and the ♘ has no retreat.

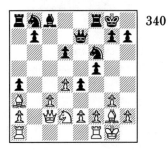

340

14. ...   b5!

Black should not allow Nc4 and wants to prevent White from mounting b-file pressure.

15. c4   Nc6!

Now 16. Qc3 Ba6 is fine for Black.

16. cxb5	Nxd4
17. Qc4†	Ne6
18. Rfd1	Bb7

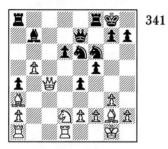

341

The chances are roughly equal if White enters the complications of 19. Bxd6 Qxd6 20. Nxe4.

But he tried for more with 19. Nf1 and lost after 19... Rfc8 20. Bxd6 Qf7 21. Qb4 Nd5 22. Qb2? (22. Rxd5!) Nc3.

Noah: Another point to remember is that taking stock is particularly useful when you reach a position new to you in an opening you think you know.

Pat: Why? I'd bet that it's more important in an unfamiliar opening.

Noah: Yes, but in an unfamiliar opening you may be more likely to realize when things are going wrong.

Familiar openings, on the other hand, have a way of lulling players to sleep – when they should be panicking.

Just like Black did in the next example.

Pat: When should he have started to worry?

Noah: At move 12.

That's when he should have realized, from his experience and book knowledge, that the normal move in similar positions, 12... g6, doesn't work well in this one.

By the time Black reached the diagram he should have accepted the likelihood of a small disadvantage, which he'd have after defensive moves such as 14... Nf8 or 15... Ne4.

Pat: But he played routine developing moves instead.

Noah: And paid the usual price.

Kramnik-Serper
Dortmund 1993

1. d4	d5
2. c4	e6
3. Nf3	Nf6
4. Nc3	Bb4
5. Bg5	Nbd7
6. cxd5	exd5
7. Qc2	

Book was 7. e3 c5.

| 7. ... | h6 |

The game now transposes into a 7. e3 c5 position but with the extra moves ...h6 and Bh4.

8. Bh4	c5
9. e3	Qa5
10. Bd3	0-0
11. 0-0	c4
12. Bf5	

The usual move in similar positions of this opening – that is, without ...h6/Bh4 – is ...g6.

But here White could meet 12...

g6 with a promising sack on g6.

Or with 13. Bxd7 Nxd7 14. e4, after which Black has problems completing development.

12. ...	Re8
13. Nd2	Be7
14. Rae1	

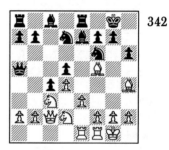

342

| 14. ... | Nb6? |

Better was 14... Nf8 and then 15... g6! (or 15. Bxc8 Raxc8 16. Qf5 g6!)

| 15. a3! | Be6? |

Simplifying was best – 15... Ne4! 16. Bxe4 Bxh4.

16. Bxe6	fxe6
17. Bxf6!	Bxf6
18. f4!	

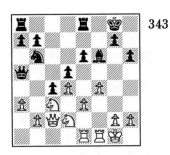

343

With Black's ♛ and ♞ offsides, White has a fierce attack: 18... Nc8 19. g4! Nd6 20. Qg6 or 18... Nd7 19. Nf3 Qc7 20. e4.

Pat: This all gets back to one of the first things you told me, right?

I mean, that you should play for the edge you feel you deserve based strictly on the position.

Noah: So, these little chats we've been having haven't been a waste of time?

You're right, of course. You have to follow what your objective assessment tells you – even if it means taking major risks.

That's what Alexander Alekhine did in the next example.

Pat: You mean because he had another of those, what do you call them, windows of opportunity?

Noah: Exactly. White took stock in the diagram and recognized he had a big lead in development.

But as he examined specific variations – such as those that spring from 10. Bd2 and 10. d5 – nothing good turned up.

Pat: And he knew his window was about to close.

Noah: Therefore logic told him that there was something both unusual and strong there for White.

As Alekhine put it, he decided he had to "search for a combative solution."

Pat: He took what Black gave him.

Noah: Pat, you've made my day.

1. e4	c5
2. c3	d5
3. exd5	Qxd5
4. d4	Nc6
5. Nf3	Bg4
6. Be2	cxd4
7. cxd4	e6
8. Nc3	Bb4?

Since Black doesn't want to take on c3 unprovoked, the immediate 8... Qa5 is better.

| 9. 0-0 | Qa5 |

344

Now 10. Bd2 Nf6 11. a3 offers White nothing after 11... Be7! 12. Nb5 Qd8.

Also unavailing is 10. d5 exd5 11. Nxd5? 0-0-0! or 11. Qxd5 Bxc3 12. Qe4† Be6 13. bxc3 Nf6.

10. a3!

White wants to use the b-file after 10... Bxc3 11. bxc3 Qxc3 12.

Rb1, e.g. 12... 0-0-0 13. Qa4, threatening 14. Bd2 or 14. d5, or 12... Nge7 13. Rxb7.

| 10. ... | Nf6 |
| 11. d5! | |

Now on 11... 0-0-0 White has 12. Qb3!, threatening both 13. dxc6 and 13. axb4! Qxa1 14. Be3, trapping the ♛.

| 11. ... | exd5 |

After 11... Nxd5 12. Nxd5 exd5 White still plays 13. axb4!, e.g. 13... Qxa1 14. Qb3 Bxf3 15. Bg5! with strong threats.

| 12. axb4! | Qxa1 |
| 13. Nd2 | |

345

The threats of 14. Nb3 and 14.

Bxg4 give White a crushing initiative.

The game didn't last long after 13... Bxe2 14. Qxe2† Ne7 (or 14... Kf8 15. Nb3 Qa6 16. b5) 15. Re1.

Noah: One more thing.

You often have to take stock more than once in the opening.

Pat: Let me guess – that's what Diagram 346 is going to show.

Noah: It does indeed.

First, White misunderstood how balanced matters were.

Pat: Yeah, he's got more space as well as the two ♗s.

Noah: But objectively that doesn't count for much here.

The trouble is that he saw that 15. f3 Nf6 would be great for him.

He also saw that 15... Nd6 would allows him to play 16. c5, an attractive move from a positional point of view, and that he could do it with tempo.

Pat: But 16. c5 backfired tactically.

Noah: And that led to White's sec-

ond error.

He should have realized his position was unraveling – and that he should cut his losses with 17. Bb2.

Pat: I can see why he didn't.

Black has a great game then after 17... axb4 and 18... Nc7.

Noah: But it's not nearly as great as it was after 17. Qc4?.

White made it even worse two moves later, in Diagram 347.

Pat: And the massacre was on.

Shirov-Adams
Germany 1997

1. d4	Nf6
2. c4	e6
3. Nc3	Bb4
4. Qc2	0-0
5. a3	Bxc3†
6. Qxc3	Ne4
7. Qc2	f5
8. g3	b6
9. Bg2	Bb7
10. e3	c5
11. Ne2	cxd4

Better was 11... Nc6, keeping

the c1-h6 diagonal closed for White's ♗.

12. exd4	Nc6
13. 0-0	Rc8
14. b4!	a5

So that on 15. b5 Ne7 Black targets c4 (...d5, ...Bd5, ...Nd6).

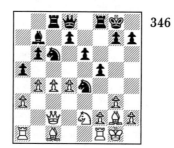

346

15. f3?

With 15. Qb3 White preserves a slight edge, e.g. 15... axb4 16. axb4 b5 17. c5!.

But not 17. cxb5 Ne7 with excellent compensation for the ♟, such as the use of d5.

15. ...   Nd6!

Not 15... Nf6 16. b5 Ne7 17. a4 with a clear advantage.

16. c5

Not 16. b5 Ne7 when Black wins a ♟.

16. ...	Nb5
17. Qc4?	Ba6
18. a4	d5!

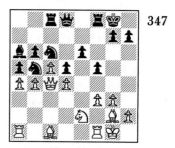

347

19. cxd6?

As bad as 19. Qd3 Nxb4 20. Qe3 Na7 21. Qxe6† Kh8 was, it's better than:

19. ...	Ncxd4
20. Qd3	Nc3!

Black won quickly: 21. Qxa6 Ndxe2† 22. Kh1 axb4 23. Be3 Qxd6, e.g. 24. Bxb6 Rc6 or 24. Qxb6 Qxb6 25. Bxb6 b3.

The game ended with 24. f4 b3

25. Rae1 Nd4! 26. Bc1 Nc2 27. Re5 Nb4 White resigns.

Noah: And that's what the opening is really all about.

Pat: There's so much I still don't understand.

Noah: Perhaps. But, you know, there is a tournament at the club this weekend and...

Pat: You think I ought to play.

Noah: I think now is the time to start applying what you've learned.

You'd be surprised how much that is.

Pat: Yeah, I guess my openings are better now. At least they don't suck as much as they used to.

Noah: Then my work here is done.

"This is not the end.
It is not even the beginning of the end.
But it is, perhaps, the end of the beginning."
– Winston Churchill after the WWII Battle of El Alemein.

Making a Comeback

The first edition (1997) of GM Soltis' **Grandmaster Secrets: Endings** went out of print in 2001. However, a slightly revised edition will be printed later in 2002. The revisions refer to two corrections noted by GM Kavalek. GM Karsten Mueller has read the book and thinks Soltis' endgame book is excellent also.

In fact, many were pleasantly surprised to see that it contained a number of novel ideas (such as elbowing and the mismatch). This book on openings is no different, and was a joy to play through and study.

It is not common for books to take a Socratic approach to learning and yet that is what every mentor or teacher does with a student—real questions looking for real answers.

Perhaps in 2004 we will see the conclusion to the trilogy, Grandmaster Secrets: Middlegame.

The chess club, five days later. Pat is talking about the tournament, in which he tied for first with a score of 3.5-0.5

At Last! Now I Can Leave The Building!

Chapter Twelve:

THE CHESS CLUB

Noah: ...And you think the only things you were doing different were in the opening?

Pat: I don't know – I guess I just felt more comfortable at the board.

Noah: I was watching your first game and your first few moves really surprised me.

Pat: Well, I just didn't want to play into his book. Like, I know how much he loves the Budapest and the Benko.

And I know I'm never gonna have the time to keep up with all the 3. d5 theory.

Noah: Not bad, you found your own weapon – and you stayed in character.

Pat: I realized he could have transposed into a Caro-Kann with 3... cxd4 – but I also know he never plays that opening.

Noah: You mean you played the man, not the board.

1. d4	Nf6
2. Nf3	c5

3. e3

Now 3... cxd4 4. exd4 d5 leads to an offbeat Caro-Kann (5. c4 or 5. Bd3).

3. ...   g6

Playing as if it's a normal King's Indian or (with ...d5) a Gruenfeld.

4. dxc5

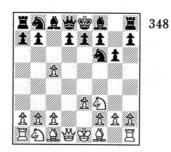

348

Pat: It got kinda interesting when I took on c5.

He suddenly realized that I could keep that ♙ if I got to play b4 and a3.

Noah: That's one of those temporary sacrifices that may not turn out to be temporary.

Pat: He used his ♛ to retake on c5

but then I got to kick it around with 7. b4.

Noah: I noticed that you didn't move the B/f1 until all the other minor pieces were out.

Pat: Well, you know it's funny but there were other things more important than developing it and castling.

I mean I wanted to control d5 and the diagonal from b2 to f6.

Noah: I'm impressed.

4. ...	Qa5†
5. Nbd2	Bg7
6. a3	

Threat of 7. b4.

6. ...	Qxc5
7. b4!	Qc7

Or 7... Qc3 8. Rb1 and Bb2.

8. Bb2	0-0

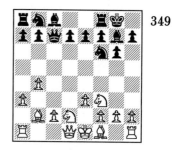

349

9. c4

Later, in the tournament's third round Pat reached the same position and his opponent played 9... d5 10. cxd5 Nxd5 11. Bxg7 Kxg7.

But after 12. Bc4 Nb6 13. Ba2 Nc6 14. Rc1 White stood well, with ♖ lined up against ♛.

After 14... Qd8 15. 0-0 Black quickly got a bad game and ultimately lost: 15... Bg4 16. Qc2 Rc8 17. b5! Na5 (17... Nd4? 18. Qb2) 18. Qb2† Kg8 19. Ne5! Bd7 20. Qb4.

Noah: I liked the way Black found himself with no good squares for his B/c8 or R/f8.

Pat: All my pieces seemed to have good squares – except one. I didn't really have to think much until move 13.

Noah: Interesting choice you made.

Pat: I figured I'd gotten all I was gonna get out of the ♘ on d2 – and it was time to get it going to d5.

Noah: You made another major decision on the next move – by changing the ♙-structure and stopping ...d5.

Pat: It sorta made sense that I deserved an edge out of the opening.

And I remembered how good the Maroczy Bind is.

Noah: You thought by analogy.

Pat: After all, the center does matter, you know.

Noah: I've heard.

9. ...	**d6**
10. Bd3	**Nc6**
11. 0-0	

Here 11... Bg4 12. h3 Bxf3 13. Nxf3 is basic plus-over-equals.

11. ...	**b6**

12. Rc1	**Bb7**

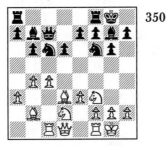

350

13. Nb1!	**Rfd8**
14. e4	

Pat: It seemed like he was ahead in development for a while – but it didn't seem to matter.

Noah: Squares mattered more.

Pat: Only one of his ♖s had a file and his ♛ eventually had to watch out for Nd5.

Noah: But despite all that you were suddenly behind on time by move 17.

Pat: Yeah, but I realized it was because he wasn't really thinking until he saw he was in trouble.

He just blitzed off his moves because he thought my moves were junky.

Noah: And he never stopped to evaluate the outcome of the opening.

Pat: Until it was too late.

14. ...	**Rac8**
15. Nc3	

Threat of 16. Nd5 Nxd5? 17. cxd5.

15. ...	**Qb8**
16. Qe2	**a6**
17. Nd5	

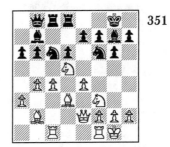

351

White has a great game. On 17... Nd7 18. Bxg7 Kxg7 19. Qb2† Kg8

he played 20. Ng5 followed by f4/Rf3-h3 and won.

Noah: That was as far as I saw. What happened after that?

Pat: In the second round I had Black and tried something else new.

Noah: I've never seen you play the French before.

Pat: Just something I found in a book. It's not even covered in some things, like *MCO*.

Noah: You ignored fashion, I like it.

Pat: I know there's an old rule about not blocking your c-♙.

But 3... Nc6 gives Black some funny pressure in the center.

Noah: True enough – every rule has to respect its exceptions.

1. e4	**e6**
2. d4	**d5**
3. Nc3	**Nc6**

Black threatens to grab (4... dxe4 and 5... Nxd4).

4. Nf3	

Or 4. e5 Black continues 4...

Nge7 5. Nf3 b6 followed by ...Nf5/...Bb7.

4. ...   Nf6
5. e5

No better is 5. Bg5 Be7 6. e5 Ne4!, e.g. 7. Bxe7 Qxe7 8. Bd3 Qb4, with counterchances.

5. ...   Ne4!
6. Bd3!

Black has a fine game after 6. Ne2 f6! or 6. Nd2 Nxf2! (7. Kxf2 Qh4†).

6. ...   Bb4

Pat: Even when I decided to trade off the N/e4 and retreat the B/b4 I thought I had a good game.

Noah: In a closed center like that you can get away with a lot.
Pat: But I couldn't have opened up things with ...f6 if I wanted to – at least not after his 12th move.
Noah: Which was actually a mistake.

He missed a chance for a creative ♖-lift.
Pat: Yeah, I guess I knew he was playing too defensively, like with his 13th.
Noah: A safety-first move.

But you're right. He should have been playing for more.
Pat: Of course, because White isn't Black.

7. Bd2   Nxd2
8. Qxd2   b6
9. a3

A good time to put the question to the ♗ (9... Ba5?? 10. b4).

9. ...   Be7
10. 0-0-0   Bb7
11. Qf4!   Na5

There was no rush to castle.

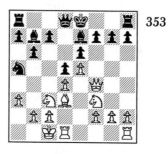

12. Rhe1

Better is 12. h4 with the ideas of Ng5 and Rh3-g3.

12. ...   c5
13. Kb1

So White can move N/f3 and avoid ...Bg5, winning the ♕.

Noah: I'm a little surprised you castled short. You could have tried ...Qd7 and ...0-0-0.
Pat: But I felt I needed counterplay.

And that meant either ...c5 or a queenside attack. Or both.

And I couldn't afford either of those ideas if I castle long.
Noah: So once he stopped ...f6 you

went after the one target he gave you.
Pat: Then I took a long time – 15 minutes – on 14... c4.

I mean, I knew that's a major step because neither of us wanted to change the center.
Noah: Quite right. White didn't want to play dxc5/...bxc5.

And you didn't want to give him an outpost on d4 by playing ...cxd4 or shutting down his counterplay with ...c4.
Pat: Another of your center zugzwangs.

I also had my doubts about it because there were no files at all for my heavy pieces.
Noah: So you created one. I liked that mysterious ...Rb8 – it set the stage for ...b5-b4.
Pat: It had a big effect on my opponent – he grabbed on b5.
Noah: And went splat.

13. ...   0-0

Now's the time.

14. h4

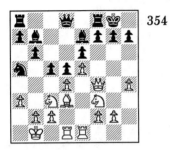

354

14. ...   c4

The immediate 14... Rb8 15. Qg4 c4 invites a dangerous 16. Bxh7†! Kxh7 17. Qh5† Kg8 18. Ng5 with a winning attack.

15. Bf1   Rb8!

16. Qg4

Intending Qh5. Unavailing was 16. Ng5 h6.

16. ...   b5

With the idea of ...b4, opening up the queenside.

17. Nxb5?   Bc6

18. Nd6

Or 18. Nxa7 (18. Nc3) Bxa3. And 18. a4 a6.

18. ...   Qb6

355

And Black's attack won.

Pat: In the last round I didn't get anything out of the opening and only drew.

Noah: You still have to be pretty satisfied: 3.5-0.5.

Pat: Yeah. But I was thinking –

If I improved so much just by not messing up in the opening, imagine what my rating would be if I only learned how not to screw up the middlegame.

Noah: Well, Pat, there's a few pointers I could offer. But...

Pat: But what?

Noah: But that would take another whole book.

Index

Symbols

♟ chain / base 119, 146, 148
♟ center 218
♟ grabbing 65, 86, 166
♟ sacrifices 166, 168, 170
  temporary 178
♟ structure (s) 26, 29-32, 67, 76, 83, 112,
  116-117, 122, 147, 163-164, 195-196,
  202, 207, 218, 231
♟s (weak, weakened) 147, 162

♘ fork 183, 200
♘ on the rim 96
♘s before ♗s 152

♗ for ♘ (trading) 147

1. a3 33-34
1. b3 38
1. c4 38
1. g3 38
1. g4 74
1. Nf3 38, 78
15 in 30 rule 211, 214
1953 Candidates 16
2800 rating 19

A

a3 112
abnormal move 135
active plan of development 26
Adams, M 20
aggressive moves 40
*Albin Counter Gambit – with colors
  reversed 128*
Alekhine, A 59, 75, 105, 195, 225

Alekhine-Chatard Attack 39
Alekhine's Defense 38, 66, 147
alternating simultaneous exhibition 59
ambition 35
analogy 16, 24-30, 33-34, 40, 177
analyzed book 60
Anand, V 47, 51, 60, 91
annotators 174
anti-book opening 24
anti-positional 131
antideluvian prejudices 87
arsenal of lines 73
assess the outcome 9
asterisk(s) 88, 90, 95-96, 98-99
attack on the base of the ♟ chain 148
attack with an attack 21
avoiding sharp lines 79
avoids surprises 73
awful positions 10

B

bad analysis 56
bad piece 147
Balashov, Y 55
Bareev, E 76
base of the ♟-chain 146
basic principles 132
basic tactics 44
battle of the tempo 121

BCO 52
behind in development 169
Belgrade Gambit 71
believing him 215
Belyavsky, A 170
*Benko Gambit 18, 20, 30, 64, 66, 72, 142-
  143, 147, 153, 230*
*Benoni Defense 30, 64-65, 76-77, 97, 113,
  168, 170, 217*
  Czech 79, 147
  Modern 30, 38, 66, 138, 147
Berra, Yogi 222
best defense 61
  move 61
biased 50
Big Think Trap 215
bind 176, 222
Bird, H 176
Bishop's Opening 50, 64
Bishops-of-opposite-color v
biting on granite 139
bizarre move 23
Blackmar-Diemer Gambit 72-73
Blumenfeld, B 112, 133
Blumenfeld Counter Gambit 170
Blumenfeld's Law/Rule 127, 133, 157
blunder(ed) 11, 14, 16
Boden-Kieseritzky Gambit 173
Boden, S 173

Bogo-Indian Defense 64
Bogolyubov, E 132
Boleslavsky, I 49
book 38, 44-45, 128, 134, 153, 168, 173,
  179, 183, 207, 212, 218
  analysis 74
  antidote 158
  knowledge 23
  memory 32
  moves 19
  position(s) 128, 158
  reason 23
Botvinnik, M 32, 38, 62, 68, 80, 214
**Bronstein, D 36, 40, 68, 91, 149, 174,
  192, 212**
Budapest Defense 63, 230
budgeting your study time 68-69
bungling move 50

C

calculate (-ing, -tion) 133, 186, 215, 220
Candidates match 131
Candidates semifinals match 44
**Capablanca, J 65, 75, 77, 112, 131, 136,
  192, 220**
Capablanca's Rule 127, 131-132, 135
*Caro-Kann 38, 58, 64, 66-67, 75-77, 79,
  82, 95, 146-149, 151, 153, 158, 230*
  4... Nd7 147
  Advance 146
  Two Knights Variation 147
castle manually (by hand) 185, 188
castling errors 187
Catalan 75, 80, 168, 178
  Closed 147
category openings 75

cautionary tale 51
celebrated repertoires 79-80
Center Game 147
center closed 12
 squares 92
 zugzwang 200, 203
center-building 204
chess character 58
 optimist 158
Chigorin, M 61, 212
choices 34, 72, 104
chump change 169
Churchill, Winston 226
clock 212, 213
closed center 232
clumsy defenses 157
colors reversed 25, 29, 30, 117
 positions 40
commiting moves 108
common sense 19, 21-22, 24, 33, 46, 48,
 94, 131-135, 137, 153
compare the analysis 49
compensation (comp) 34, 66, 131, 136, 154,
 170-171, 175, 179-183, 187, 191, 216, 226
competitive chess 22
Complete Black Defensive System with 1...
 d6 54
Complete Defence to 1. P-K4 53
complications 173
computer 49
concentrating like crazy 10
confidence 73
contradict 98
control of diagonal/squares 11, 67
control (s, -ling) the center 101, 105
correspondence openings 74

Corzo, J 136
counter-moves 116
counterattack 181
counterbalance 19
counterchances 232
counterplay 28, 32, 35, 39, 48, 89, 94, 119,
 141, 147, 151, 154, 160, 169, 174-175,
 180, 189-190, 196, 202, 220, 232
cowardly strategy 50
crushing initiative/sacrifice 41, 226

D
danger signs 50
dark squares 11
dated 50
dead even (equality) 41, 45
defer development 156
developing moves 22
dicey line 66
dinosaurs 43
dogmatic 50, 52
dominate the center 40
double attack 161
Double Fianchetto 30
double-edged position 175
download (ing, s) 14, 51, 60
Dragon player 71
draw agreed 51
drawable with best play 47
drawing ability 75
dumb 10
dumbed-down generalizations v
Dutch Defense 64, 77, 80, 106, 163, 193
 Antoshin 62
dynamic imbalance 146

E
ECO Volume C 53
ECO Volume D 53
edge 67
 clear 142
 getting 61
 small 40, 51, 97
 space 118, 138, 181
 terrific 167
 tiny 42, 157
ego trip 50
semi-zugzwang 118
English Opening 30, 45, 50, 76, 78-79,
 93, 111, 135, 147
repertoire 73
equal (-ize, [-ing]) 45-46, 219
escape 222
Euwe, M 202
evaluate (-ing) 182, 216, 218, 231
Evans Gambit 61, 173
excellent drawing chances 47
exceptions 97
expansion on the queenside 41
explosive position 45

F
fanatic openings 72
fancy moves 22
fashion 59, 77
faulty analysis 49
favorable complications 21
feeling 33, 195
fight (-ing) for equality 20-21
fine position/strategy 40, 75
finesse 107, 112, 152, 215
Fischer, B 76, 99, 108, 203, 212

flaky moves 176
Fool's Mate 220
foremost opening theoretician 49
fork-trick 183
Four Knights Game 53, 80
fragile 71
freeing maneuvers 44
French Defense v, 23-24, 39, 58, 62, 64, 73,
 95, 118, 146, 153, 177, 231
 Advance 23
 Burn 147
 Classical 39
 Exchange 77
 MacCutcheon 62
 Milner-Barry 75
 neo-Rubinstein 62
 Rubinstein 147
 Tarrasch 62, 77
 Tartakower 62
 Winawer 79, 80, 108, 147
Fried Liver Attack 21
Fritz 87
frontal attack 137

G
Gallagher, J 111
gambit lines 44
gamesmanship 129
Giuoco Piano 21, 117
Gligoric, S 124, 138
GM a GM 223
going blind 61
going for a kill 38
good doesn't mean great 41
good opening decisions 125
grab 182

grandmaster draws   51
  openings   75
  slang   190
greed and grabbing   165
Gruenfeld Defense   10, 31, 62, 65-67, 78, 82,
  90, 135, 153, 178, 218, 230
  Exchange, Modern   65
  non-Exchange   62
Gruenfeld, E   168

H

handshake   51
heavy pieces   191, 192, 222
heavy thinking   67
hinder, harass and hamper   199
hole(s)   49, 98-99, 106, 124, 149-151, 157
hypermodern openings   50, 123
hypnotic effect   55

I

ignorance   44
illogical moves   22
IM disease   11
imbalance (s)   146, 193
immense complications   67
improvement   46
Indian   117
infinity sign   175, 179, 180
Informant   46-48, 51, 55, 60, 69
Informant-speak   174
initiative   35, 167
islands   94
Italian game   21, 117
Ivanchuk, V   73
Ivkov, B   212

J

Janowsky, D   104
Janowsky Variation   104

K

**Karpov, A   11, 24, 60, 73, 77, 90, 180,
  190**
**Kasparov, G   16-20, 51-52, 58, 61, 76,
  170, 214**
Keres, P   75, 132, 212
Khalifman, A   55
King's Indian Defense   55, 64-68, 72, 78-79,
  113, 134, 147, 153, 168, 170, 230
  Fianchetto   64, 80
  Saemisch   76
King's Gambit   30, 52, 68, 96, 178
King's Indian Reversed   66, 79-80
kingside attack   22
know the traps   42
knowing fewer openings   56
Korchnoi, V   24, 52, 68, 91, 125
Kramnik, V   76, 78

L

lack of castling   162
lack of solidity   147
laggard development   147
lame-o   34
Landau, S   59
Larsen, B   22, 66, 106-107
Lasker Defenses   147
Latvian Gambit   74
Lautier, J   18, 215
less center/space   147
lessened King safety   147
life of its own   49

liquidate the center   41
little mistakes   8
logic (al)   19-24, 43, 124, 134-135, 175
  common sense   16
  defense   21
  move   133
long diagonal   12
long memory   73
long think   215
long weekend (variations)   68-69, 77
looking at the board   9, 14
loopholes   135
loss of material   147
low maintenance   64
  profile   66
  risk (continuation)   64, 66-67, 213

M

Maroczy Bind   41, 47-48, 50, 71, 231
Marshall Attack   44
Mason, J   105
masters   212
material   166, 173
  equality   172, 175
MCO   64, 231
memor(y, -ize)   9, 16, 18-19, 24, 44, 45, 73
Meran Defense   26, 54, 64, 80, 147, 172
microscope   159
Mieses, J   180
Miles, T   66
million dollar question   146
minor advantage   41
  sin   44
minority attack   v
misevaluat (-ion, -ed)   55, 217
modern opening   146

moral   56
Morgan, D   158
Morphy, P   16, 61, 94, 182
Morra Gambit   75
mysterious   196, 197

N

Najdorf, M   106
Napier, W   86
natural defenses   21
nerves   128
Neverhurdovich   51
New In Chess   66
new move   23
nice diagonal   41
Nimzo-Indian   34, 58, 66, 72, 76, 78, 80,
  90, 136, 147
  Saemisch   72, 85
Nimzovich, A   171, 196
non-commital move   9
  -developing moves   20
notebook   16
novelty   100
Nunn, J   71

O

obvious defense   45
Old Indian Defense   79, 147
one good defense   38
one opening system as White   38
only moves   69
OOR   73, 74, 76, 77
Opening-Think   142
openings   34
  cult   74, 77
  experts   74

familiar 224
fashionable/trendy 65, 60
name 11
sharp 44-45, 67
unfamiliar 224
out of repertoire (OOR) 73
oversight 59
oversimplifying 142

P

Pachman, L 201, 214
pain 174
panic 219-220, 224
Panno, O 212
passive middlegame 26
Pavlov (ion) 103, 113-114, 116, 125, 134, 162
move (s) 151, 159, 169
reactions 162
personality traits 58
Petroff Defense 69, 75, 78
Petrosian, T 44-45, 60, 74, 77, 79, 90, 177
PGN 87
Philidor's Defense 147
piece developments and plans 26
energy 172, 178
Pillsbury, H 86
Pirc Defense 20, 147
Plaskett, J 10
playing the man 216
plus-over-equals position 48
plusses and minuses 130
poisoned pawn 86
Poisoned Pawn Variation 171
poker variation 73

Polerio 21
Polgar, J 216
Ponziani Opening 50, 117
popular stuff 60
Portisch, L 40
positional lines 13
good 12
point of view 26
themes 68
values 183
post-mortem 110
postal chess 74
powerful retreats 204
practical tips 216
premature commitment 105
preparation 138, 140, 216, 220
prepared openings 16
pressuring the center 155
procrastination 104
promising gambit 139
protected squares 131
Pseudo Lopez 68
psychological 212, 216
impact 133
trap 60
weapon 112

Q

QGA, main 29-30, 64, 72, 112, 119, 147
...Bg4 147
QGD 26, 29, 34, 38, 44, 67, 71, 76, 79, 80, 82, 104, 113, 121, 141, 178
Cambridge Springs 147
Chigorin 62, 147
Exchange 72, 80, 104
Janowsky 142

Makagonov 77
Tarrasch 25, 77, 147, 218
Tartakower Defense 201
Tartakower-Makogonov 77-79
Queen Pawn's Game 128
Queen's Gambit 21, 178
Queen's Indian Defense 66-67, 72, 76, 78-80, 111, 164
Deferred 30
Petrosian 112
question to the ♗ 232

R

radar screen 202
ready-made plan 72
real lemon 212
variation 22
recommended line 46
record for victims 43
rediscovered 62
reevaluation 161
refusing the offer 169
refutation 82, 134-135
refute most bad openings 22
repertoire 76, 77
reputations 50
Réti Opening 30, 76, 80
retreats are often bad 22
Reuben's Rules 82
rhythm 212
right to move first 41
risk (y) 63, 65, 124, 134
in the long run 13
incredibly 130
tolerance 66
Riumin, N 108

Romanishin, O 66
rough equality 167, 179
routine moves 14
Rudensky 9
rule (s) 97, 171, 176, 231
of thumb 108
Ruy Lopez 21, 27-28, 44, 50, 62, 67-69, 72, 79-80, 96, 99, 109, 116, 135, 205-206
Bird's Defense 147
Dilworth 69
Exchange / Delayed 64-65
Marshall Gambit 68, 147
Open 68, 80 147
Riga 69-70
Schliemann 68
Siesta 74
Steinitiz Defense/Deferred 27, 75, 147

S

sacrificial lines 73
Sadler, M 61
safety first 109, 111-112, 125
net 218
Salov, V 76
Sanakoev, G 26
SAT word 73
Sayre, Pat 7, 15, 37, 57, 81, 127, 165, 211, 229
scariest line 65
scoresheet signing 168
Scotch Game 147
Seirawan, Y 76, 100
seize the advantage 42
Semi-Slav 68, 76
Botvinnik 68, 74
Semi-Tarrasch 76

sharp tactical eye   13
sharper position   109
Sherwin, J   87
Shirov, A   62, 97
Short, N   125, 134, 148
short-versus-long debate   189
Sicilian   16, 28, 38-39, 53, 58-60, 63-64,
67, 73, 77-78, 92, 99-100, 110, 147, 153,
166, 168, 187, 220
Alapin   77
Boleslavsky   29
Closed   67
Dragon   10, 50, 66, 68, 72, 77, 80, 92,
130, 149, 151, 155-156
Gambit   73
Keres   132
Najdorf   60, 68, 71, 74, 77, 79, 111,
149-150, 167, 171, 200
Open   147, 149, 192
Poisoned Pawn Variations   71
Polugayevsky   71
Richter-Rauzer   64, 104, 109, 147, 151
Scheveningen   30, 38, 156
Siesta   53
Sozin Velimirovic   71
sign of maturing   58
similar opening   28
simple development   33
simplify the center   161
simplifying trick   29
slash-and-burn   167
Slav   38, 44, 62, 77, 79, 95
Abrahams   74
Exchange Variation   32, 44, 77, 80
Marshall Gambit   74
Meran   77, 147

Noteboom-Abrahams   147
slight inferiority   21
slow development   162
small popularity   68
smothered mate   v
Smyslov, V   18-19, 77
snap judgment (s)   52, 55, 129
Sokolov, I   18
sound sacrifice   170
Spanish TV   19
Spassky, B   100
specialized repertoires   77
squeezed   51
standard plan   24
state secret   90
steadily improving his position   42
Steinitz, W   58, 94, 98, 120, 162
stereotyped book   178
Stonewall   108
♙-structure   163
Attack   75
Dutch   147
formation   107
strange stuff   60
Strauss, D   48
strong center   134
strongest move   61
openings   21-22
study 20 hours a week   72
stupid rules   82
sub-sub-variations   44
substitute for thinking   18
Sultan Khan   112
super-GMs   208
super-sharp line   60, 167
superficial evaluations   52, 55

superior piece play   178
suspicious   48
symmetrical position   42
Szabo, L   140, 212

T

tactical (-ly)   44, 77
bad   12
escape   222
failure   22
finesse   149
hole   43
ideas   44
opportunity (-ies)   157, 161
problems   21
quotient   13
sound
terrible
trumps logic   133
trick   222
window   161
Take   149-150, 152, 162, 164, 169, 179, 191,
205, 221
Tal, M   27, 42, 58, 61, 63, 91, 146, 212,
215
Tall, Noah   vi, 7, 45, 103, 145, 185
Talmudic scholar   67
Tarrarsch, S   27, 50, 52, 56, 110, 142
Tarrasch Trap   27
Tartakower, S   73
tension   140
tempo
battle   121
extra tempi (o)   46
loss of time (tempi)   41, 110, 147
wasted time/tempo   22-23, 109-110

thematic maneuver   18
theory   230
debate   67
novelties   138
think (-ing)   18, 23-24, 34, 39, 67, 154, 213,
218, 233
for myself   76
Think. Move. Hit the clock   212
three Hs   199
time controls   212
efficiency/use   124, 212
unlimited   140
waster   110
Timman, J   18, 76
tired   11
TN   31, 68, 71, 100, 130, 146, 175, 179
proof   71
Torre Attack   90, 91
tournament life   18
transparent   131
transposition   28, 38, 50, 112
tricks   76
trap (-py)   12, 27, 42, 44, 52, 132, 134, 167,
174, 179, 215
unknown   43
tricks   74
Trompowsky   128
trust book   45
published analysis   45
reputation   49
Two Knights Defense   11, 21, 50, 62, 147
typical opponent   68

U

ungrabbable   176

V

Vaganian, R   73, 74
Vienna Game   64, 73
Viking chess   176

W

waiting move   188
   policy   194
watching and waiting   137
Watson, J   13, 16, 108
weapon (s)   30, 61, 77, 134, 230
   no-risk weapon   65
weird stuff   12
Wilder, M   22
willing to draw   191
window (s) of opportunity   157, 187, 196
world championship finals   91

Y

Yudasin, L   65
Yusupov, A   128

Z

zugzwang center   125

Adams-Kramnik, 1998   167
Adams-Lputian, 1997   188
Akesson-Heidenfeld, 1997   43
Akopian-Volzhin, 1996   181
Alekhine & Landau - NN, 1934   59
Anand-Granda Zuniga, 1998   174
Anand-Kamsky, 1995   89
Anand-Kasparov, 1998   208
Anand-Kramnik, 1999   191
Anand-Nunn, 1990   205
Andersson-Belyavsky, 1997   42
Arnason-Pribyl (I), 1990   43
Atalik-Belyavsky, 1998   121
Atalik-Naiditsch, 1998   203
Averbakh-Spassky, 1955   124
Balashov-Filippov, 1998   40
Benjamin-Shaked, 1998   159
Bogolyubov-Meister, 1912   43
Bogolyubov-Spielmann, 1919   39
Bronstein-Euwe, 1953   17
Capablanca-Lasker (Ed.), 1915   70
Chiburdanidze-Polugayevsky, 1992   157
Christiansen-Karpov, 1993   12
Conquest-Rozentalis, 1996/1997   35
Dadiani-Durbov, 1896   43
Dautov-Hickl, 1996   115
de Firmian-Granda Zuniga, 1996   217
Depasquale-Kavian, 1992   129
Dolmatov-Azmaiparashvili, 1995   137
Dolmatov-Romanishin, 1992   202
Dückstein-Sigurjonsson, 1970   34
Dzhindzhikashvili-Gurevich (D), 1992   25
Evans-Suttles, 1972   84
Fedorov-Khurditse, 1998   188
Fischer-Polugayevsky, 1970   54
Gelfand-Illescas, 1996   220

Games

Gelfand-Kramnik, 1994   44
Glek-Belitsev, 1998   89
Gligoric-Donner, 1970   208
Goldin-Yakovich, 1991   154
Goloshchapov-Movsesian, 1995   168
Groszpeter-Suba, 1979   204
Gulko-Miladinovic, 1995   203
Gulko-Shcherbakov, 1992   179
Gulko-Vaganian, 1996   93
Gurevich (I)-Rogers, 1992   130
Gurevich (M)-Kengis, 1995   193
Hamlisch-NN, 1899   43
Hodgson-Arkell, 1996   114
Ibragimov-Zhelnin, 1998   43
Illescas-Speelman, 1992   153
Ivanchuk-Hjartarson, 1995   9
Ivanchuk-Karpov, 1997   56
Ivanov (I)-Gausel, 1994   83
Jakovic-Rashkovsky, 1997   113
Jamieson-Tal, 1974   58
Kamsky-Karpov, 1996   190
Kamsky-Lautier, 1993   41
Kamsky-Short, 1994   29, 192
Karpov-Illescas, 1993   123
Karpov-Piket, 1995   181
Karpov-Timman, 1993   176
Karpov-Torre, 1973   119
Kasparov-Polgar (J), 1997   201
Kasparov-Karpov, 1987   82, 140

Kasparov-Korchnoi, 1983   131
Kasparov-Korchnoi, 1995   166
Kasparov-Lautier, 1995   17
Kasparov-Short, 1993   26
Kasparov-Speelman, 1989   160
Kasparov-Timman, 1998   16
Kavalek-Suttles, 1974   84
Keres-Wade, 1954   39
Kharlov-Yarats, 1997   187
Kholmov-Kiriakov, 1996   118
Kholmov-Sherbakov, 1997   14
Komarov-Razuvaev, 1996/1997   35
Korchnoi-Liardet, 1997   43
Korchnoi-Short, 1995   133
Kovacevic-Bisguier, 1989   157
Kramnik-Leko, 1998   216
Kramnik-Serper, 1993   224
Krasenkov-Hickl, 1996   195
Krasenkov-Psakhis, 1997   83
Lautier-Belyavsky, 1997   213
Lautier-Hall, 1998   115
Lautier-Leko, 1997   214
Lautier-Ponomariov, 1999   18
Lautier-Short, 1999/2000   198
Leko-Strikovic, 1996   91
Littlewood-Zeidler, 1995   12
Lugovoi-Aseev, 1996   175
Luzgin-Ioffe, 1962   43
Malaniuk-Piket, 1993   32
Miles-Almasi, 1996   33
Miles-Christiansen, 1987   51
Mozetic-Shirov, 1993   218
Neshewat-Garrison, 1994   188
Nesterov-Yandemirov, 1991   135
Ninov-Meister (Ja.), 1994-95   152
Nisipeanu-Kempinski, 1996   28

Olafsson (H)-Naumkin, 1988   140
Onischuk-Miles, 1996   95
Ovechkin-Kruppa, 1999   197
Piket-Dreev, 1996   163
Piket-Glek, 1997   20
Plaskett-Sadler, 1998/9   199
Podgaets-Vaganian, 1971   73
Psakhis-Ekstrom, 1998   206
Qin Kanying-Wang Pin, 1992   219
Relange-Sadler, 1997/1998   60
Romanovsky-Goglidze, 1935   125
Rudensky-Hodgson, 1991   9
Rukavina-Larsen, 1973   106
Sakaev-Sveshnikov, 1993   96
Seirawan-Ivanchuk, 1997   13
Seirawan-Karpov, 1994   98
Shabalov-Browne, 1997   48
Shaked-Kasparov, 1997   86
Shaked-Kramnik, 1997   88
Shcherbakov-Khenkin, 1988   32
Shirov-Adams, 1997   226
Shirov-Polgar (J), 1994   92
Shirov-Zviagintsev, 1995   221
Short-Gulko, 1995   177
Shtern-Benjamin, 1988   155
Slipak-Spangenberg, 1996   45
Slobodian-Kaminsky, 1995   186
Sokolov (I)-Oll, 1996   128
Sokolov (I)-Kasparov, 1999   17
Spassky-Polgar (J), 1993   169
Speelman-Short, 1980   142
Ståhlberg-Bohatyrchuk, 1935   104
Sumiacher-Polugayevsky, 1971   54
Summerscale-Adams, 1997   30
Sutovsky-A. Mikhalevsky, 1998   183
Svidler-Taimanov, 1995   222

Sydor-Tal, 1974   63
Szabo-Keres, 1953   212
Tal-Ivkov, 1974   27
Tal-Shtreicher, 1950   43
Tarrasch-Marco, 1892   27
Timman-Karpov, 1993   91, 200
Topalov-Kasparov, 1996   19
Toshkov-Kosten, 1987   189
Van Wely-Timman, 1998   197
Vanderwaeren-Glek, 1995   162
Vera-Gulko, 1993   94
Vuckovic-Kosic (D), 1999   178
Vyzhmanavin-Ruban, 1989   141
Vyzhmanavin-Tseshkovsky, 1991   223
Wilder-Kogan, 1987   194
Ye Rongguang-van Wely, 1996   14
Yermolinsky-Gurevich (D), 2000   181
Yermolinsky-Kaidanov, 1993   24
Yudasin-Kasparov, 1995   46
Yusupov-Hertneck, 1994   217
Yusupov-Karpov, 1989   90
Yusupov-Rozentalis, 1998   196
Yusupov-Timman, 1989   132
Zapata-Anand, 1988   51

Colophon

Typeset in Berthold Baskerville with chess diagrams from our C.R. Horowitz font.

Original cover design: Rob Long
Caricature art: Rob Long
Editing and keyboarding: Bob Long
Proofing: Bob Long, Nate Long, Andy Soltis

Catalog

All Thinkers' Press chess books may be found online at www.thinkerspress.com or www.chessco.com. A printed catalog of more than 1500 chess books, software, and equipment titles may be obtained by calling:

1-800-397-7117

Chessco has been in the retail business since 1971. Thinkers' Press since 1973.